D1597108

ENGLISH PORCELAIN FIGURES
OF THE
EIGHTEENTH CENTURY

A. *The Muse Clio. Mark, an anchor in gold.*
Modeller, Joseph Willems. Chelsea; about 1760. Height, 12 in.
Victoria and Albert Museum. (See p. 75)

ENGLISH PORCELAIN FIGURES
OF THE
EIGHTEENTH CENTURY

by

ARTHUR LANE

Keeper of the Department of Ceramics
in the Victoria and Albert Museum

FABER AND FABER

24 Russell Square

London

First published in mcmlxi
by Faber and Faber Limited
24 Russell Square London W.C.1
Printed in Great Britain by
R. MacLehose and Company Limited
The University Press Glasgow

CONTENTS

CONTENTS

ILLUSTRATIONS

COLOUR PLATES

MONOCHROME PLATES

at the end of the book

ILLUSTRATIONS

ACKNOWLEDGEMENTS

While collecting material for this book, I have learnt much from discussion with friends and colleagues. I am especially indebted to Mr. A. J. B. Kiddell, Dr. Bernard Watney and Mr. R. J. Charleston. My thanks are also due to the private collectors who have kindly allowed me to reproduce figures in their possession, especially Dr. and Mrs. Statham in this country and Mrs. S. J. Katz and Judge Irwin Untermyer in the United States.

The authorities of the Museums named in the plate-captions have given much help in study and in obtaining photographs, with the permission to publish them, and I should like particularly to thank Mrs. Kathryn Buhler of Boston, Miss Yvonne Hackenbroch of New York, Mr. Hugh Tait of the British Museum, and Mr. and Mrs. Winder of the National Trust.

I am also grateful to the antique dealers who have so kindly drawn my attention to important figures and enabled me to illustrate pieces that would otherwise have been missed—Mr. A. F. Green, Mr. Alexander Lewis, Mr. Bernard Perret, Mr. and Mrs. Frank Tilley, and Mr. Hans Weinberg.

1
INTRODUCTION

Some years ago the author undertook to attempt, in a single volume of the Faber Monographs, a general survey of the figures made in the eighteenth-century porcelain factories throughout Europe. It might just have been possible in this compass to compile an anthology of attractive illustrations; to evoke the restless euphoria of the Rococo style, which found in the fuss and glitter of porcelain its chosen instrument of surprise; and to show how potter, sculptor and painter collaborated to create the porcelain figure as a new art-form. But there would have been no space in which to draw any of those fine distinctions which form such a rewarding exercise for the collector and connoisseur. The quantity of surviving porcelain figures is enormous. Had they been made in any of the materials normally used by sculptors for work on this small scale—ivory, boxwood, bronze, wax, or terracotta—the task of classifying them, of recognizing the hands of different artists, would have defied human ability. One has only to observe the dilemma of the professional student of sculpture when confronted by an unsigned model in any of these media which cannot immediately be related to well-documented work on a larger scale. Fortunately, with porcelain figures, variations in the material itself, in its technical handling, and in its painted decoration all form contributory and revealing elements of 'style'. We can at least hope to recognize the work of different factories, if not always that of particular modellers.

In Germany alone there were about twenty factories making figures, and some of these were active for half a century or more. In England we are concerned with nine factories, and with about the same number in both France and Italy. The present book is therefore planned as the second in a series of three. The first, on German figures, and the third on French and Italian, have yet to appear.

It is perhaps no disadvantage to approach our subject, the English figures, with the same lack of preconceptions as the English public

1

of the mid-eighteenth century. They had long been familiar with the painted porcelain vessels of China and Japan brought back by the Dutch and British East India Companies since the beginning of the seventeenth century. There had been a vogue, started by Queen Mary II before her death in 1694, for arranging massive displays of oriental porcelain as a feature of interior decoration (the remains of Queen Mary's collection are still to be seen at Hampton Court and Windsor Castle, and they include a fair number of large seated figures of the goddess Kuan-yin, in the so-called *blanc de chine* porcelain from Fukien Province).[1] But this essentially Baroque conception of the 'Porcelain-Room' took no such firm hold in England as in Germany, where it survived far into the eighteenth century. Daniel Defoe in his *Tour thro' the Whole Island of Great Britain* (1724–7) writes somewhat disparagingly of the 'Custom or Humour, as I may call it, of furnishing Houses with China-Ware',[2] as if this custom introduced by Queen Mary was already a thing of the past. In the reigns of George I and George II the 'classical', or rather neo-Palladian, taste of Richard Boyle, third Earl of Burlington (*b.* 1694, *d.* 1753) prevailed in English architecture, which thus terminated its allegiance to the Baroque earlier than architecture in other countries of Europe. The soil was already prepared for the full 'Neo-Classical' style developed by Robert Adam after his return from Italy in 1758.

It was in interior decoration, furniture, silverwork, and porcelain, that the English sought a temporary escape from the severe Burlingtonian canons. Published designs for furniture by Matthias Lock, dating from 1740, are among the earliest evidence for the arrival in England of the French Rococo style.[3] At the same time, in the 1740's and 1750's, there was a renewed outbreak of *chinoiserie*, incongruously associated in England, but nowhere else, with what was believed to be the 'Saxon' or 'Gothic' style. The best people, the old Burlingtonians, no doubt shrank from decorating the mantelshelf with grotesque oriental images of bronze or porcelain; that was, however, done by the *avant garde*—among them the young couple in Hogarth's *Marriage à la Mode* (1743–5).[4] Those who could afford it used porcelain from China on the table. But hints from behind the scene,

[1] Arthur Lane, 'Queen Mary II's porcelain collection at Hampton Court,' *Transactions of the Oriental Ceramic Society*, vol. 25, 1949–50, pp. 21–31.
[2] G. D. H. Cole's edition, London, 1927, I, 166.
[3] Peter Ward-Jackson, *English Furniture Designs of the Eighteenth Century*, London (Victoria and Albert Museum), 1958, pp. 13 (where other early English Rococo pattern-books are referred to), 38–40, Figs. 48–69.
[4] *Marriage à la Mode II; Early in the Morning*, London, National Gallery. E. K. Waterhouse, *Painting in Britain: 1530–1790*, Pelican History of Art, London, 1953, Plate 102.

for example the specification of a patent taken out in 1744 by two aspirants to make porcelain in England,[1] suggest that not all the imported porcelain came from China. The Royal Saxon Porcelain Factory at Meissen near Dresden, founded by Augustus the Strong in 1710, had graduated to become an important alternative source of supply. Its wares were of true hard-paste porcelain, technically the equal of the Chinese, and in design even more attractive to European taste.

The year 1745 is a landmark for the manufacture of porcelain in Europe, for it was then that the Vincennes factory, later transferred to Sèvres, first obtained a Royal privilege from the King of France. Experiments had been going on, with many setbacks, since 1738. The Vincennes material was not a true porcelain, but an artificial 'soft paste', composed essentially of glassy matter mixed with white clay. 'Soft-paste' porcelain had been made in a small way in France since a patent for it was taken out in 1673 by Louis Poterat, a faience-manufacturer of Rouen. The Saint-Cloud factory traced its origin from before 1678, Chantilly from 1725, and Mennecy from 1734. During the 1730's and 40's these early French factories had added to their productions a limited number of grotesque figures, directly inspired by those in oriental *blanc de chine* or Japanese porcelain. But the nascent Vincennes factory made no mention of figures, or statuettes, in its petition of 1745; it aspired to make '*porcelaine façon de Saxe, c'est à dire peinte et dorée, à figure humaine*'—presumably vessels *painted* with figures in the Meissen manner. It is of interest that the same petition refers to '*un nouvel établissement qui vient de se former en Angleterre d'une manufacture de porcelaine qui parait plus belle que celle de Saxe*'.[2]

The first English factory so flatteringly described can only have been Chelsea. Apparently founded in 1745, it made during its first four years tea and coffee services and the like, mostly unpainted, and strongly influenced in design by contemporary silverwork. It was only after a change of management in 1749 that Chelsea seriously began to make painted ornamental wares and figures. 'Curious Dresden and Chelsea figures' were advertised in a London sale-notice of December 1750.[3] The Bow factory, founded in London in 1748, began its large production of figures in 1750. The Derby and Longton Hall factories, in the

---

[1] Edward Heylyn and Thomas Frye, who claimed that their invention 'would... save large sums of money that were yearly paid to the Chinese and Saxons' (see p. 85 below).

[2] Comte X. de Chavagnac and M. de Grollier, *Histoire des manufactures françaises de porcelaine*, Paris, 1906, p. 124.

[3] *General Advertiser*, Dec. 4, 1750; quoted by J. E. Nightingale, *Contributions towards the History of Early English Porcelain from Contemporary Sources*, Salisbury, 1881, p. vii.

English Midlands, made figures from their beginnings about 1750. The mysterious 'girl-in-a-swing' factory seems to have made nothing but figures, and small 'toys' in figural form, during its short existence between about 1751 and 1754. Bristol (1748), taken over by Worcester (1751), was alone among the early English factories in confining its production almost entirely to tablewares and ornamental vessels.

England was well abreast of European fashion. For even in Germany itself the widespread manufacture of porcelain, and of porcelain figures, had been delayed until the decade beginning in 1750. The Meissen factory had jealously guarded the 'arcana', the secret formulae and processes discovered by Böttger, and with one important exception had maintained its monopoly of making hard-paste porcelain for forty years. The exception was the Vienna factory, founded as a private concern in 1718, with the help of deserters from Meissen. The other main German factories all sprang up in or after 1750, in the wake of one or two wandering 'arcanists' from Vienna—Höchst (1750), Berlin (1752), Fürstenberg (1753), Nymphenburg (1753), Frankenthal (1755), and Ludwigsburg (1758). Without exception they embarked on figure-production from the very start. Thanks to the example set by Kaendler and his assistants at Meissen, figures had become almost synonymous with porcelain itself.

If we were to judge by the evidence from France and England alone, we should say that the Meissen figures first gained wide renown in the years between 1745 and 1750. We can observe rumour reaching England in the form of a letter written on February 4, 1748 to Henry Fox, later Lord Holland, from his friend Sir Charles Hanbury Williams, the British Minister in Dresden:

'I believe I never told you that the King of Poland has given me a set of China for a table of thirty Covers, which would cost *here* fifteen Hundred Pounds. I wish anyone would give me so much for it in England. Could not Digby speak to the Prince about it? No one else will buy such a thing. Tis prodigious fine. I design to send a description of the Desert China to Lady Caroline, because tis what no Englishman that has not been in Dresden can have an Idea of.'[1]

Hanbury Williams goes on to describe a dinner with two hundred and six guests given by Count Brühl, the Saxon Chief Minister: 'when the Desert was brought on, I thought it the most wonderful thing I ever beheld. I fancyd myself either in a Garden or at an Opera. But I could not imagine that I was at Dinner. In the middle of the Table was the Fountain of the Piazza Navona at Rome, at least eight foot high, which ran all the while with Rose-water, and tis said

[1] The Earl of Ilchester, 'A notable service of Meissen porcelain,' *Burlington Magazine* LV, 1929, pp. 188–90.

that piece alone cost six thousand Dollars.[1] I verily believe that Count Brühl has above thirty thousand Pounds worth of China in his house.' Hanbury Williams sent his own porcelain home, to be looked after by Henry Fox, in 1748; the list of pieces included 166 'Figures to adorn the middle of the Desert'. It is of interest to note that in 1751 arrangements were made to borrow pieces from this Meissen service to serve as models at the Chelsea porcelain factory. In a frivolous essay published in *The World* for February 8, 1753, Horace Walpole wrote: 'Jellies, biscuits, sugar-plumbs and creams have long given way to harlequins, gondoliers, Turks, Chinese and shepherdesses of Saxon china.'[2] In Germany, indeed, the porcelain figures were often designed and planned in whole series, with miniature temples and garden lay-outs, to take the place as ornaments on the dinner table formerly occupied by figures made in wax or confectionery. The English factories did not go to such lengths, though in the Chelsea sale-catalogue of 1755 several sets of up to eleven figures are described as 'for a Desart', and certain large circular groups were clearly designed as table-centres. But with few exceptions the figures were made in complementary pairs, or in sets of four or five (the Four Seasons, Four Continents, etc.). Many had branches with sockets for candles, and these, like the 'arbour groups', would only look well from the front. They would be stood about as decorations on the furniture, or shown in cabinets. In the third edition of Thomas Chippendale's *The Gentleman and Cabinet-Maker's Director*, published in 1762, we may note a considerable increase in the number of designs for 'china tables . . . china cases, china shelves . . . stands for porcelain jars' since the first edition in 1754. It is also perhaps relevant that 'china cabinets' do not appear as such among the fine engravings of architecture and furniture by Robert and James Adam, which came out in parts between 1773 and their publication as bound volumes in 1778 and 1779. One suspects that a Neo-Classical 'china cabinet' such as that designed by John Linnell about 1775[3] would be more likely to contain 'Etruscan' urns of Wedgwood's new black basalt and jasper ware than porcelain of any kind.

The vogue for porcelain figures in England was indeed brief, lasting at its height for less than fifteen years. It could be seen as a tribute to the fame of Meissen, whose imported figures were so often

[1] This porcelain fountain is probably identical with the one in part preserved in the Victoria and Albert Museum (no. 246–1870). It reproduces not the fountain in Rome, but that at Dresden raised between 1741 and 1744 by the architect Longuelune and the sculptor Lorenzo Mattielli.

[2] The passage is quoted in full by R. J. Charleston, 'A background to the earliest English porcelain figures,' *Antiques Review*, 1957, pp. 23–8.

[3] Ward-Jackson, *op. cit.*, Fig. 240.

closely imitated here in the decade after 1750. In 1757 the Derby factory even advertised its own figures as productions of the 'second Dresden'. But porcelain was a luxury, with figures as its most expensive form, and economic conditions in England were very different from those prevailing in the greater and lesser states of Germany. There the new porcelain factories were financed by autocratic princes as a matter of competitive prestige. In England the early factories were all private undertakings with limited capital, not always efficiently run, and with the exception of Chelsea they had to make ends meet by selling a high proportion of cheap useful wares to a middle-class public. Worcester made hardly any figures at all, and this prudent policy undoubtedly helped it to survive into the nineteenth century. Of the factories that plunged more heavily for figures, Longton Hall had to close in 1760; Chelsea became moribund after 1763, and in the same year Bow suffered a severe setback in the bankruptcy of its chief partner. Meissen itself was overrun by the troops of Frederick the Great of Prussia, England's ally in the Seven Years War (1756–63), and its immediate drop in exports was followed by a loss of prestige from which it never fully recovered. The European leadership of fashion in porcelain passed to Sèvres.

The French had shown less persistence and ingenuity than the English in overcoming the technical difficulties of making glazed and painted figures in soft-paste porcelain. In the numerous figures made at Vincennes and Sèvres from 1752 onwards, glaze and colour were both sacrificed in the interests of the admittedly excellent modelling. Whatever its merits, unglazed 'biscuit' is not porcelain in the full sense of the word; it repudiates its ceramic nature and attempts to imitate marble. Simultaneously with the spreading of a fashion for biscuit figures to other European factories after 1770, the porcelain figure as an independent art-form fell into discredit, along with the Rococo style in which it had flourished. In England, biscuit figures in the succeeding Louis Seize and Neo-Classical styles were produced in great numbers at Derby, a factory astute enough to continue also making the glazed and coloured figures that still appealed to a provincial public. It seems likely that the idea of using biscuit reached Derby in 1770 through contacts with the Tournay factory, which had previously had associations with Chelsea. A curiosity, more interesting for technical than artistic reasons, was the belated foundation in 1768 of the first English factory making hard-paste porcelain (at Plymouth, transferred in 1770 to Bristol). Ambitious coloured figures were attempted in both places, but apparently with little support from the public. Indeed England was already giving birth to new classes of ceramics that were to threaten the future not merely of porcelain figures, but of porcelain itself. Josiah Wedgwood's cream-coloured earthenware, elegant, practical and cheap, captured the markets for useful wares and inspired imitations throughout Europe. Wedgwood made very few figures in the round. But on his ornamental 'black basalt' and 'jasper' vases, perfected in the 1770's, there was figure-decoration of a new kind, moulded in the lowest possible relief. These vases became the approved embodiment in ceramics of the Neo-Classical style.

The eighteenth-century cult of porcelain, and of porcelain figures, was a European phenomenon, and it is relevant to ask in what ways the English contribution had a distinct character of its own. Here it may be said at once that neither in variety of invention nor in brilliance of modelling can the English figures compare with the best of those made in the great German factories. The general artistic *milieu* in England, with its bias in favour of classical restraint, offered less inspiring support than in countries where the Baroque and ensuing Rococo styles were more thoroughly at home. The English factories could not enlist first-class sculptors to model for them. The soft-paste material used was far less stable than the German hard paste, and therefore less suitable for representing figures or draperies in extended positions or swift movement. Moreover the paste, with its often rather thick glaze, did not readily pick up sharp detail either from the moulds or from hand-retouching by the 'repairers'. The English figures consequently lack the German devilry and élan; their mood is more sedate. But this is in keeping with the special nature of the glassy soft-paste material, which has at its best a sensuous appeal, a mellow richness, different in kind from the cold brilliance and glitter of the German hard paste. The English figures have a closer affinity with those made in soft paste at the early French factories, with which at times they might easily be confused. The earliest Derby figures are outstanding for the beauty of their rich material. Here, as at Bow, the enamel painting has at first a smeared and haphazard effect, and the Bow figures throughout show a naive, almost amateurish quality, in both painting and modelling, that gives them a charming freshness hard to parallel elsewhere. Far the most accomplished of the English figures were those made at Chelsea during the 'red anchor' period. Their modelling is competent, if unadventurous, and the slight painting is so tactfully applied as to enhance to the full the wonder of the material. By contrast, the later 'gold anchor' Chelsea figures hold a unique position through the breath-taking opulence of their heavy colour and gilding, and the profusion of their leafy 'bocages'. This pompous variant of the Rococo style is peculiar to England.

It may be said in no spirit of disparagement that the study of English porcelain in modern times has been principally carried on by amateurs. Professional *Kunstforschung* normally needs a solid diet of documentary fact, and in Germany, among the local state archives, records of the eighteenth-century porcelain factories have often survived intact. Dr. F. H. Hofmann's three-volume work on the Nymphenburg factory is a monument of scholarship, and if some other German factories still await such thorough attention, their productions have been fully illustrated in a series of fine albums and catalogues. The compilation of these has been helped by the fact that most German figures bear the distinguishing mark of the factory where they were made.

In England, on the other hand, the early factories have left no records; the very existence of Longton Hall was long forgotten; and what we know even of Chelsea has been pieced together from entries in rate-books and church registers, advertisements in the press, and catalogues of the intermittent auction-sales sponsored by the factory.[1] Chelsea alone normally marked its figures. There was much plagiarism; one factory copied the models of another, and all copied or adapted the models of Meissen. The classification of the English figures has therefore proceeded by conjuring all possible evidence from the surviving porcelains themselves, comparing the style and technique of one piece against another, and so building up groups and likely chronological sequences. No less revealing than idiosyncrasies of modelling are the distinctions in paste, glaze and painted decoration, which can only be appreciated by taking into account the useful and ornamental vessels made in the same factories as the figures. There are still differences of expert opinion, and 'problem pieces' whose attribution remains a matter for intelligent surmise.

It is understandable that in view of more recent discoveries, many of the existing books are untrustworthy. Until 1925 Derby figures were universally accepted as Chelsea. In writing monographs on their favourite factory, collectors have been misled by partisanship or pet theories into claiming for it pieces that properly belong elsewhere. The only previous book in which figures are segregated for study from other productions of the various factories is William King's *English Porcelain Figures of the Eighteenth Century* (London, 1925), and there

---

[1] It is exasperating to reflect that Jewitt was still able to collect many useful documents and draw on them for his *Ceramic Art of Great Britain* (1878), and that these documents have disappeared since his time—perhaps through the zeal of his executors in destroying what they believed to be waste paper. A few papers which they overlooked, relating to the Derby factory, were discovered by Mr. A. J. B. Kiddell in the drawer of a cabinet sent for sale at Messrs. Sotheby's; these are now in the Victoria and Albert Museum Library (some here quoted in Appendix II).

the excellent illustrations are accompanied by only a very brief text. There are no albums in which the full range of figure models of a particular factory are illustrated, and the student must still refer to a great variety of magazine articles and catalogues which are normally to be found only in a good art-library such as that at the Victoria and Albert Museum. One purpose of the present work is to supply useful references. The author must admit one shortcoming in advance; through concern for the human figures he has neglected the numerous figures of animals and birds. And the history of each factory, apart from its bearing on the figures, is given in the briefest possible summary. Further detail should be sought in more general works. Of these, W. B. Honey's *Old English Porcelain* (London, 1948) is still far the most reliable. Bernard Watney's *Longton Hall Porcelain* (London, 1956) is a valuable addition. Otherwise the results of more recent research are to be found scattered in periodicals, notably the *Transactions of the English Ceramic Circle*.

English porcelain figures may be studied in many larger and smaller public collections. In London, the most extensive are those in the Victoria and Albert Museum (including the Lady Charlotte Schreiber Collection) and the British Museum. There are also good examples in the London Museum and at Fenton House, Hampstead (bequeathed to the National Trust by Lady Binning). The Fitzwilliam Museum, Cambridge, has the magnificent collections given or lent by the late Lord Fisher, and the Cecil Higgins Museum, Bedford, is particularly rich in Chelsea figures. Lord Bearsted's fine collection at Upton House, near Banbury (National Trust) may be visited in the summer, as may the late Lady Ludlow's collection at Luton Hoo, Bedfordshire. In the United States of America, the Museum of Fine Arts, Boston, has most of the former Alfred Hutton collection, rich in Chelsea figures. There are also good figures in the Metropolitan Museum, New York, and in the Rhode Island School of Design at Providence.

2

TECHNIQUE: PASTE, MODELLING, MOULDING, REPAIRING, FIRING, AND PAINTED DECORATION

The paste

England shared from an early date in the general European curiosity about the technical nature of oriental porcelain. In 1671, and again in 1684, John Dwight of Fulham took out patents for making 'a transparent earthenware, commonly known by the names of porcelaine or china'. Dwight's researches did not lead to the discovery of anything that could properly be called porcelain; but his whitish salt-glazed stoneware was superior in quality to that currently made in Germany, and the use to which he put it is psychologically relevant in any study of porcelain figures. Between 1671 and 1678 he produced, and showed before the Royal Society, a number of stoneware figures and heads, the last as large as life.[1] In thus seeking to give his new 'porcelaine' the added significance of sculptural form, Dwight anticipated Augustus the Strong of Saxony, whose ambitions were ultimately responsible for the whole class of porcelain figures developed at Meissen in the following century.

In England, Dwight had no immediate successors in seriously attempting to make porcelain. But in France, as we have already observed,[2] artificial or 'soft-paste' porcelain was made perhaps as early as 1673, the date of Louis Poterat's patent, and certainly from about 1690 onwards, in a few factories which deviously learnt the technical methods from each other. An Englishman, Dr. Martin Lister, visited the Saint-Cloud factory in 1698, and in his account published in the following year remarked: 'I did not expect to have found it in this perfection, but imagined this might have arrived at the *Gomron Ware*; which is, indeed, little else but a total Vitrification. . . . Mons.

[1] A life-size bust of Prince Rupert is in the British Museum; smaller figures there and in the Victoria and Albert Museum include a half-length effigy of his young daughter Lydia inscribed with the date of her death in 1673.
[2] P. 3.

10

Morin in conversation told me that they kept their Sand as a secret to themselves . . . also he said they used Salt of Kelp in the composition, and made a thing not unlike Frit for Glass to be wrought up with white clay.'[1] This suggests that scientifically-minded Englishmen were already aware of the principles of soft-paste porcelain, as exemplified in the Persian so-called 'Gombroon' wares which had been imported by both British and Dutch East India Companies during the second half of the seventeenth century.[2] Lister's remark about the expensiveness of the Saint-Cloud ware may well have discouraged his fellow country-men, for the time being, from experimenting on French lines.

No Englishman at the time could have divined the nature of the hard-paste porcelain made at Meissen after 1710. But in 1712 and 1722 the Jesuit missionary Père d'Entrecolles wrote his two letters giving a detailed eye-witness account of the Chinese manufacture then carried on at Ching-tê-chên, stressing the importance of the *kaolin* (china clay) and *petuntse* (china stone). These were published in full in 1717 and 1724,[3] and abstracted in Du Halde's *Déscription . . . de l'empire de Chine* (Paris, 1735), of which popular work three English editions appeared between 1738 and 1741. These works were known to the Plymouth chemist William Cookworthy, who discovered the kaolin deposits in Cornwall in 1748, and at some later date the 'growan stone' (corresponding to the Chinese *petuntse*) which enabled him in 1768 to found at Plymouth the first English factory making true hard-paste porcelain. Cookworthy had also met, in 1745, a person who must have been the potter André Duché, who since 1738 had attempted to make hard-paste porcelain at Savannah in the American colony of Georgia.[4] Writing to a friend in 1745, Cookworthy spoke of 'the person who has discovered the Chinese earth. . . . It was found on the back of Virginia, where he was in quest of mines; and having read Du Halde, he discovered both the petuntse and the kaolin. It is this latter earth which he says is essential to the manufacture'. Duché arrived in England in May 1743 and it was doubtless his influence that inspired Edward Heylyn and Thomas Frye to take out a patent in 1744 for making porcelain with a kaolinic clay, called 'unaker', from 'the Chirokee nation in America'.[5] Twenty tons of the Chirokee clay

[1] M. Lister, *A Journey to Paris in the Year 1698*, London, 1699, pp. 138–40.

[2] A Lane, *Later Islamic Pottery*, London, 1960, pp. 75, 76.

[3] *Lettres édifiantes et curieuses, écrites des missions étrangères par quelques missionaires de la Compagnie de Jésus*, vols. 12 and 16; reprinted in S. W. Bushell, *Description of Chinese Pottery and Porcelain*, Oxford, 1910.

[4] R. P. Hommel, 'First porcelain-making in America', *The Chronicle of the Early American Industries Association*, vol. 1, nos. 8–11, 1934–5. H. Tait in Exhibition Catalogue; *Bow Porcelain 1744–1776*, British Museum, 1959, pp. 8, 9.

[5] The patent is quoted in full by Ll. Jewitt, *The Ceramic Art of Great Britain*, vol. I, London, 1878, p. 112.

11

were actually imported in 1743–4. But the process specified by Heylyn and Frye suggested that this clay was to be combined with a potash-glass frit instead of a fusible stone corresponding to the Chinese *petuntse*, so that if they had hoped to make hard-paste porcelain with it they inevitably failed. Frye alone took out a second patent in 1748, specifying in deliberately vague terms a glass frit containing calcined bones, to be mixed with white pipeclay whose origin was not named; this formula was thenceforward successfully used at the Bow factory.[1] Until Cookworthy's patent of 1768 there was no further public mention of any special clay corresponding to kaolin. But the various English manufacturers who began operations around 1750 were clearly under no illusion that their 'soft-paste' porcelains were more than substitutes for the real thing.

It has been too readily assumed that because 'soft-paste' porcelain had been made previously in France, the English factories must have learnt their technique direct from French sources.[2] No such assumption has been made about the excellent soft-paste porcelain of Capodimonte, the Royal Factory founded at Naples in 1743. If the manufacture of hard-paste porcelain depends absolutely on 'secret' knowledge of the rare mineral kaolin, and of a special kiln-procedure, soft paste can be made in many ways from readily accessible materials. The *Journal Book* of the Royal Society, on February 10, 1743, recorded the showing before the Society by a visitor, Thomas Briand or Bryand, of 'several Specimens of a sort of fine white Ware made here by himself from native materials of our own Country, which appeared to be in all respects as good as any of the finest Porcelane or China ware'.[3] There is nothing to indicate that Briand came recently from France or had contact with the French porcelain factories, though his French-sounding name might point to ultimate Huguenot origin. He has been conjecturally associated with the foundation of the Chelsea factory in 1745, and less plausibly with that of Derby about 1750. Briand certainly experimented in England. And the variety of formulae used by the English makers would in itself suggest that these were arrived at by individual experiment. The basic principle was to make first a glass 'frit' from sand or ground flint, melted together with potash or calcined lead as a flux (the lead was often incorporated in the

[1] Hugh Tait (in *Apollo* LXXII, p. 111) assumes that the Bow factory continued to import and use 'unaker' from 1748 onwards, and that this enabled it to make porcelain more cheaply than other English manufacturers. This seems improbable; any such practice would surely have aroused comment at the time and encouraged others to do the same.

[2] E.g. Chavagnac and Grollier, *Histoire des manufactures françaises de la porcelaine*, Paris, 1906, p. xvii: 'Vers 1742, l'Angleterre s'appropriant nos formules avait créé des fabriques à Bow, à Worcester . . .'

[3] Quoted by Dr. H. Bellamy Gardner, *E.P.C. Trans.*, no. II, 1929, pp. 23, 24.

form of broken 'flint' glass, itself made with a flux of lead). The frit was ground into powder and then, for use, mixed into a paste with the plastic element—white pipeclay or some other white clay, with lime (calcium) added as a purifier. At Chelsea a glassy paste of this general character was deliberately modified four times within fifteen years, on aesthetic or practical grounds. Too large a proportion of the glassy element (silica) in relation to the plastic clay (alumina) made the paste unstable and apt to collapse in firing; too much alumina reduced its luminosity and translucence. The mysterious 'girl-in-a-swing' factory used an even glassier paste than Chelsea, with an exceptionally high content of lead. Longton Hall too used a very glassy paste, and had evident difficulty in making it respond to modelling and keep its shape.

A peculiarly English invention was introduced at the Bow factory following Thomas Frye's second patent of 1748; the incorporation into a frit porcelain of the white powder from calcined ox-bones, in proportions varying up to 45 per cent. Besides helping the whiteness, the bone-ash greatly increased the stability of the paste, and was thus particularly welcome in making figures. It was adopted as an ingredient at Chelsea at the beginning of the 'gold anchor' period, about 1758–9, probably on the suggestion of workmen who had returned to the factory after a spell of temporary employment at Bow. At Derby, which had hitherto made a glassy porcelain, bone-ash was introduced after the amalgamation with Chelsea in 1770. At Lowestoft, founded in 1757, bone-ash was used from the start. It eventually became a standard ingredient, together with kaolin, in the 'bone china' made in England from the end of the eighteenth century till the present day.

A third distinct class of soft-paste porcelain was introduced at the first Bristol factory in 1748–9 and made thereafter at Worcester from 1751. It included up to 45 per cent of soapstone (steatite, a silicate of magnesia) from Cornwall as the plastic ingredient. This gave a harder body than that of the other English soft pastes, and in table-wares facilitated a neat and delicate precision of shape. There seems no good reason to suppose that the steatitic paste was unsuitable for figure-modelling; if Worcester alone of the major English factories almost entirely abstained from making figures, that was due to the deliberate policy of the practical-minded directors. It is significant that a few late Longton Hall figures show under chemical analysis a considerable proportion of magnesia; as if soapstone, perhaps from mines at Brassington in Derbyshire, had been introduced in an endeavour to overcome the poor plasticity of the normal Longton paste.[1]

[1] Bernard Watney, *Longton Hall Porcelain*, London, 1957, p. 18.

13

ENGLISH PORCELAIN FIGURES

Scientific tests of the paste have contributed much towards the proper classification of the usually unmarked English porcelains.[1] Unfortunately, chemical analysis is laborious and costly, and involves removing a small piece from the object. Spectrographic analysis, though less precise, is usually sufficient for practical purposes. The 'drop test' method for determining the presence or absence of phosphoric acid (due to incorporated bone-ash) by means of hydrofluoric acid, can be applied by a careful amateur, and is especially useful for distinguishing whether or not an early piece was made at Bow.[2] The drawback is that hitherto not enough pieces have been analysed, under similar conditions, to provide a sufficiently wide basis for accurate comparison. The analyses of single pieces have been repeated in one book after another, as if the pieces originally analysed were typical. In the early years the English factories were all to some extent experimental, and might vary their paste from week to week either deliberately, or because certain raw materials were at the moment in short supply, or because the materials were less easily freed from impurities than at a later stage in industrial technology. In recent years physical tests by ultra-violet rays have come into fashion, but at present these seem to be valid only for certain groups of porcelain, and the phenomena tend to vary subjectively according to the eye of the particular beholder.[3] A sceptic might say that the same variations could be detected by a sensitive eye without the accessory clutter of the ultra-violet lamp. The lamp is nevertheless extremely useful for its promptness in showing up modern restorations which might otherwise escape immediate detection. Generally speaking, scientific analysis is invaluable as a check on opinions arrived at by a more subjective route, and in particular doubtful cases it may cast the deciding vote. But it cannot be a substitute for human intelligence, and for the sensibility that can observe and interpret the many nuances that go to make up an artistic style.

[1] Comparative analyses carried out by Mr. Herbert Eccles, F.C.S., on forty-four pieces in the Museum were published by Herbert Eccles and Bernard Rackham, *Analysed Specimens of English Porcelain*, London, Victoria and Albert Museum, 1922. (Reproduced individually, often without acknowledgment, in many subsequent books and articles.) See also Donald A. MacAlister, 'The material of the English frit porcelains', in *Burlington Magazine*, LI, 1927, pp. 138–42, 177–81; LIII, 1928, pp. 140–1; and Arthur Hurst, 'Ceramic construction', *E.C.C. Trans.*, vol. 1, no. 4, 1937, pp. 28–42. Frank Tilley, *Teapots and Tea*, Newport, Mon., 1957, has a valuable section on analyses, including some figures; but most of his tests were made on highly untypical pieces whose attribution was uncertain.

[2] The spot-test method described by Dr. H. J. Plenderleith, *Burlington Magazine*, LI, 1927, pp. 142–3; also by George Savage, *18th-Century English Porcelain*, London, 1952, pp. 50–3.

[3] Discussion of ultra-violet testing in F. Tilley, *op. cit.*, p. 95, and by G. Savage, *op. cit.*, pp. 56 ff.

TECHNIQUE

Modelling

The eighteenth-century porcelain figures were made in plaster moulds taken from a master model, which was normally prepared in modeller's clay or wax (though moulds were sometimes laboriously taken from existing porcelain figures made at another factory, or from bronze figures). To facilitate making the various sections of the moulds, the master-model would be cut into pieces, and these subsequently discarded when they had fulfilled their purpose. Thus, neither in England nor elsewhere do any unquestioned original master-models for porcelain appear to have survived.[1] But there is some documentary evidence from Derby of models, together with the moulds, being sent to the factory from a distance by modellers working independently elsewhere.[2] It is possible that such a model would be the original 'master', whose pieces had been stuck together after the moulds had been made. But it is perhaps more likely that the 'model' referred to was a first pull, in terracotta, wax, or plaster, taken from the moulds and touched up by the artist who had designed it. It was suggested in an accompanying letter that the 'model' should be carefully preserved at the Derby factory and used for reference by the 'repairers' when they assembled copies of the figure in porcelain-paste. In 1772 Richard Champion, proprietor of the Bristol factory, wrote a long letter to an unnamed modeller giving exact specifications for two sets of figure-models representing the *Elements* and *Seasons*.[3] It is almost certain that his correspondent was Pierre Stephan, who was at that moment working under contract at the Derby factory. During the same period, about 1772–90, Josiah Wedgwood similarly ordered models from artists living elsewhere, to be sent to his earthenware factory at Etruria in Staffordshire. The English analogy may reflect a similar practice in other countries; for example, it is believed that Conrad Link continued to supply models to the Frankenthal factory after leaving in 1766 to work as a sculptor in Mannheim.

One point emerges clearly from a comparative study of the English porcelain figures. Once a figure-design had been invented, it might be subsequently revised by making a new model and a new set of moulds. Thus, there are successive versions of some of the early Bow figures;[4] and at Derby it became customary to issue the same figure-models in two or even three different sizes. Such revision could no doubt be

[1] The point will be further discussed by the author in *German Porcelain Figures*.
[2] See p. 109 and Appendix II.
[3] See p. 126.   [4] See pp. 89, 90.

15

entrusted to a skilled 'repairer'. It was in the creation of new models that the services of a professional modeller were especially needed.

Owing to the loss of records, there is a disappointing dearth of information about the modellers on the staff of the early English factories. Joseph Willems, a native of Brussels, appears to have worked as chief modeller at Chelsea from about 1749 until 1763, when he advertised his readiness to give lessons in sculpture.[1] No doubt the decline of the factory caused him to seek other work, and in 1766 he accepted an invitation to return to his native country and join the Tournay factory as a modeller. A pair of painted terracotta figures bearing Willems' signature and the date 1749 were probably not expressly designed as models for porcelain, though in style they resemble his later work at Chelsea. Many terracotta figures remained in Willems' possession at the time of his death, perhaps sketches for models previously executed in porcelain.[2] At Bow, the talented modeller of the early Muses and other related figures has not been identified. In November 1753 the factory advertised in Birmingham for new painters, and there is a touch of bathos in the postscript—'N.B. At the same House, a Person is wanted who can model small Figures in Clay neatly.'[3] The impressed mark 'T' or 'To' found on many Bow figures is believed to be that of a 'repairer' rather than of a designer-modeller. The subsequent appearance of this mark on ornamental vessels and figures made at Worcester and Bristol suggests that this man moved on, and even tried his hand at original modelling; he was probably identical with 'Mr. Tebo' who in 1774–5 made a brief and unsuccessful appearance as a modeller for Wedgwood at Etruria.[4] The gifted modeller of the earliest Derby figures and groups remains anonymous, but we have a fair amount of information about the Derby modellers from 1770 onwards.[5]

Moulding

Owing to the poor plasticity of the paste, which would not hold its shape until it had dried, a figure could not be modelled in porcelain direct. It had to be shaped in the negative plaster of Paris moulds taken from the original clay or wax master model. And according to the complexity of its undercut or projecting parts, it would be moulded

---

[1] See p. 64. [2] See p. 64 and Appendix I.

[3] *Aris's Birmingham Gazette*, Nov. 5, 1753; quoted by Nightingale, *Contributions*, p. xlv.

[4] See pp. 87, 121, 125–6. Also B. Rackham, 'Contributions to the study of English porcelain II: The modeller "Tebo",' *Burlington Magazine*, XXV, 1914, pp. 109, 110. (The assumption there made that Tebo was the modeller of the Bristol Seasons etc. requires qualification.)

[5] See pp. 105–111.

TECHNIQUE

in separate pieces—head, trunk, and limbs—which would be stuck together when dry. In the Continental factories of the eighteenth century the regular practice was to lay out the hollow sections of the moulds and press the dough-like paste into each by hand. The two or three sections making up a head, for example, would then be fitted together with the damp paste inside, and kept in place in a keyed plaster box fitting round them. Being porous, the plaster moulds quickly absorbed the moisture from the porcelain-paste, which shrank as it dried, enabling the shaped piece to be easily removed from the moulds in its 'leather hard' condition. This procedure is still followed today in the Manufacture Nationale at Sèvres. About twenty to twenty-five figures could be taken from a single set of moulds before they wore out. This number would meet the normal needs of a small factory with a limited market, and it might not be considered necessary to keep spare sets of moulds in reserve. A figure made by pressing the paste into the sections of the mould would be more or less hollow inside. If the base were left open, finger-marks or tool-marks would be visible on the rough inner surface, and it would be seen that the 'walls' of the figure were irregular in thickness. These phenomena are very noticeable in the unglazed interior of certain early Bow figures;[1] they can also be seen, though less conspicuously, in the glazed interior of the hard-paste figures made at Plymouth and Bristol, whose bases are habitually left open. The rare Worcester figures were, like those of Bow, made by the 'hand pressing' process.

In most modern factories where porcelain figures are still made, for example the Nymphenburg factory near Munich,[2] the moulding is done in a different way. The sections of the mould are fitted together first, and through a hole leading into the hollow thus formed the porcelain-paste is poured as a liquid slip, with a small admixture of soda. The porous moulds absorb the moisture, and the liquid paste begins to form a dry crust where it is in contact with the plaster. When this crust is thick enough, the superfluous liquid paste in the middle is poured off. A figure made in this way will be hollow, with thinnish walls of remarkably even thickness, and free from any tool-marks or finger-marks on the smooth interior—except along the horizontal line where two separately moulded sections have been joined. The 'pouring' method gives a cleaner cast than that of pressing the paste into the moulds by hand, but it has the disadvantage that the moulds wear out more quickly and thus need replacement.

[1] See pp. 21, n. 2, 86.
[2] I have to thank Dr. Fritz Bäuml, Director of the Nymphenburg factory, for valuable information about methods there in use, and also for illuminating suggestions about eighteenth-century methods.

17

It has been widely believed that the 'pouring' method of making figures—or 'slip-casting' as it is known in England—is of comparatively recent introduction. Alexandre Brongniart, the famous Director of the Sèvres factory, wrote in his *Traité des arts céramiques* (Paris, 1844, vol. I, p. 154) that the idea of shaping ceramic pastes by pouring (*coulage*) was then 'assez ancienne, elle remonte à plus de 60 ans'; according to him, it had apparently been introduced at the Tournay porcelain factory about 1784. It was later used for vessels of hard paste porcelain by M. Locré at the Rue Fontaine-au-Roi factory in Paris, and between 1814 and 1831 was brought to perfection at Sèvres (though apparently not for figures).

But 'slip-casting' had in fact been practised in Staffordshire by the makers of salt-glazed stoneware from as early as 1740 onwards.[1] It was this method that enabled them to make their teapots and other hollow wares with relief-decoration so thin and fine. They provided for frequent renewal of the plaster moulds by moulding, from the first set, a stoneware block with the patterns in positive.[2] From this 'master' new plaster moulds in negative could be taken as required.

Examination of the relief-decorated porcelain vessels made at the Chelsea factory during the 'triangle' period (about 1745–9) shows that the majority must have been formed by slip-casting; and the same is true of all the Chelsea figures made from the 'triangle' period onwards. There is reason to believe that the process was introduced by potters from Staffordshire employed at the factory. The mysterious factory that made the 'girl-in-a-swing' figures was probably founded with the help of Staffordshire workmen who seceded from the main Chelsea factory after 1749.[3] This factory too used the slip-casting process, not only for figures, but also for the miniature scent-bottles and other trinkets that soon won the European reputation which they have enjoyed ever since, under the name of 'Chelsea toys'. It is indeed difficult to see how these tiny, hollow objects could have been made in any other way. The 'girl-in-a-swing' factory failed after a few years, and was re-absorbed in the main Chelsea factory, which continued to make 'toys'. In 1764, and again in 1769, the Chelsea factory, in financial difficulties, advertised for sale 'all the materials, the valuable

[1] Simeon Shaw, *History of the Staffordshire Potteries*, Hanley, 1829, describes the slip-casting process on p. 146. On pp. 150, 163, 164 he says that plaster of Paris moulds were introduced to Staffordshire about 1750 by Ralph Daniel, who had learnt of them during a visit to a French porcelain factory. His date is at least ten years too late; and though the early French porcelain factories doubtless used plaster moulds, the evidence of their actual productions shows that they were unaware of the slip-casting process.

[2] C. F. S. Luxmore, '*Saltglaze*', *with the notes of a collector*, Exeter, 1924, pp. 23 ff. and Plates 44–76.

[3] See pp. 82–3.

and extensive variety of fine models in wax, in brass, and in lead; all the plaster moulds and others. . . .'[1] In 1924 much of this former Chelsea equipment was discovered in store at Messrs. Copeland's factory at Stoke-on-Trent, having been purchased in 1849 from the old Derby factory, which itself absorbed Chelsea in 1770.[2] The 'wax models', of which two are now in the Victoria and Albert Museum,[3] are not themselves originals, but hollow castings made from the first set of moulds prepared from the original clay 'master model'. They served in preparing additional sets of moulds when needed, in the same way as the stoneware 'master' blocks used by the Staffordshire makers of salt-glaze. Lead castings were used as 'masters' in the same way for smaller objects such as the 'toys'. The 'brass models' referred to in the Chelsea advertisment were negative stamps for pressing out small applied details such as flowers and leaves.

The Longton Hall figures appear to have been slip-cast, which is not surprising in view of the location of this factory on the outskirts of the Staffordshire potteries. A Staffordshire influence may also be suspected at the other Midland factory, Derby, which adopted slip-casting from its beginning about 1750. (Unless, as is possible, the process was introduced at Derby by someone who had worked previously at the Chelsea factory.) In 1771 Captain Joseph Roche, R.N., described a visit to the Worcester china factory where, he wrote, 'They make very fine figures or ornamental china, it being done much better and also cheaper at Derby; here [i.e. Worcester] they are obliged to mould it, but there [i.e. Derby] it is cast, which is ten times as expedicious.'[4] The few figures made at Worcester about 1769–71 appear to be the work of the 'repairer' Tebo, who evidently brought with him the hand-pressing technique he had seen practised during his previous employment at the Bow factory. Tebo evidently moved on to Bristol in 1772; but even before his arrival figures had been made there and at Plymouth (after 1768) by pressing the paste into the moulds. A technical trick of doubtful artistic propriety was the rendering of delicate lace-work on the dresses of figures by attaching, before

[1] Both notices, whose wording is closely similar, are quoted by Jewitt, *The Ceramic Art of Great Britain*, I, London, 1878, p. 175.

[2] Frank Stoner, 'Chelsea moulds: an important discovery,' *Connoisseur*, LXIX, May 1924, pp. 3–10. Some of these sold at Sotheby's, Nov. 8, 1960, Lots 118–121.

[3] No. C.315–1951, given by Mr. Alexander Lewis; the head and trunk of a peasant in Teniers style, actually the fiddler in the Maypole group (see p. 68). The number thirty-four is incised on the stump of one leg. The second wax, No. C.57–1960 (also given by Mr. Lewis), is the head and trunk of the raised anchor dwarf (see p. 63).

[4] Extract from diary for Oct. 21, 1771, quoted by H. R. Marshall, *Coloured Worcester Porcelain of the First Period 1751–83*, Newport, Mon., 1954, p. 61.

firing, pieces of actual lace which had been dipped in a mixture of porcelain-paste and water. The thread burnt away in the kiln, leaving the porcelain reproduction in place. The practice was introduced at Meissen about 1765,[1] and occasionally followed at Derby after 1771, when the Catalogue of the first Chelsea-Derby sale mentions items 'most curiously ornamented with lace'.[2]

'Repairing'

No lists of staff at the early English factories survive, but we may reasonably assume that as in the Continental factories the work of making figures was subdivided among specialists. After the moulders had performed their task, the leather-hard heads, bodies, and limbs were removed from the moulds and assembled into complete figures by the 'repairers'. Besides smoothing out the joins and the seam-marks left along the line where the sections of the mould had fitted together, these men touched up details in the faces and dresses, using sharp wooden or metal tools. They also used brass dies for pressing out separately in porcelain-paste the various small objects to be held by the figures, and the leaves and flowers for attachment to the bases and to the conventional tree-trunks which gave necessary support to the figures during firing. Over-elaborate 'frill vases' and shell-shaped salt-cellars on rock bases appear in closely similar form at Bow, Worcester, and Bristol, and are likely to be displays of virtuosity by the wandering 'repairer' Tebo. 'Arbour groups' of figures framed in Rococo scrolls or foliage were made in many German factories during the 1750's and 1760's, but none of these attain the excessive profusion of the flowery 'bocages' found in the English groups made at Chelsea during the 'gold anchor' period (1). In the myriads of singly applied leaves and flowers the 'repairer's' talent here runs riot. A 'repairer' without special training as a modeller might yet try his hand at creating new figure-models; and an artist of this kind, with a penchant for minia-ture work, seems to have been responsible for the 'girl-in-a-swing' figures and the related toys.

The bases on which the figures stand may be mentioned here; for though these were no doubt designed and moulded as parts of the complete model, they required additional attention at the 'repairing' stage. When figures were made by the slip-casting process, the

---

[1] See K. Berling, *Festive Publication . . . Meissen*, Dresden, 1911, p. 62.

[2] A pair of Derby figures with lace, dating from about 1830, is illustrated in B. Rackham, *Catalogue of the Herbert Allen Collection*, no. 127.

---

(1) *Plate* 29.

assembled moulds were often inverted (so that the head of the figure would be downwards) and the slip poured in through a fair-sized circular hole in what would be the underside of the base. The slip formed a crust all over the inside of the moulds, including the upper-most surface around the pouring-hole. The base of the finished figure would thus be closed beneath, except for the fair-sized circular hole opening into the hollow and smooth interior. Such bases occur in Chelsea 'triangle' and 'raised anchor' figures, in those of the 'girl-in-a-swing' class, and in some early Derby figures or groups.[1] The bases of a few early Bow figures and groups are left open beneath, permit-ting a clear view inside of the marks left by tools and fingers when the paste was pressed into the moulds.[2] Most later bases are closed under-neath, whether the figures were made by slip-casting or pressing. The 'repairer' himself may have applied a slab of paste to close the opening. Through it he usually pierced a small hole to let out the gases from the hollow interior while the figure was fired. In early Derby figures this hole is characteristically splayed outwards—the so-called 'screw-hole'. Peculiar to English figures are the holes pierced by the repairer at a point low down at the back of a figure or group, normally in the supporting tree-trunk; these holes, square at Bow and circular at Derby, were to receive the ends of metal branches which would fan out round the figure and carry porcelain flowers or sockets for candles. Only a few figures survive with these accessories intact. No doubt the repairer was often allowed or encouraged to vary the bases. Thus figure-models which first appeared on low rustic or pad bases were later re-combined with raised Rococo pedestals.

Firing

The English soft-paste figures received their main 'biscuit' firing at a temperature of about 1100 to 1150 degrees Centigrade, before the application of the glaze, which required a second firing at the lower temperature of about 1050 to 1100 degrees. They were enclosed in fireclay saggars, but there is no evidence that fireclay stilts or supports were needed for the projecting parts, as they were with figures made in the less stable soft pastes of the French factories. Among the figures that survive, a marked tendency to crack or wilt is confined to those made at Chelsea in its early 'triangle' period; to those of the 'girl-in-a-swing' group; and of course those made in the exceptionally hard

---

[1] Illustrations of the undersides in Y. Hackenbroch, *Chelsea and other English Porcelain . . . in the Irwin Untermyer Collection*, London, 1957, Plates 144–6.

[2] Y. Hackenbroch, *op. cit.*, Plate 145, Fig. 241 (Kitty Clive), and note on Fig. 240 (Scaramouche and Isabella group).

c

paste of Plymouth and Bristol, with its firing-temperature of almost 1500 degrees Centigrade.

Painted decoration

By the middle of the eighteenth century the brilliantly-painted Meissen figures had set the example that all wished to follow. If so many of the earliest figures made in the English and French factories were left in the white, that was not due to choice. There was at first a dearth of painters to meet the new need, and an appropriate technique and style for painting on porcelain had to be learnt.[1] Many of the figures now surviving 'in the white' were originally painted in un-fired, and therefore easily abraded, oil colours and gilding.[2] This was done not in the factories, but by independent decorators employed at piece-work rates by the china retailers. Chance has preserved the London note-books of one such decorator, William Duesbury (who in 1756 became part-proprietor of the Derby factory).[3] The period covered by the Duesbury note-books is 1751–3. The origin of the numerous figures that passed through his hands is seldom given, but Bow, Chelsea and Derby are named. He charged from 1s. 3d. to 5s. for painting a figure, according to size, and in a few cases specified 'inhamild' decoration at about three times the price. So far attempts to identify Duesbury's hand on surviving enamel-painted porcelain have failed. The painter whose distinctive flowers are seen on figures and 'toys' of the 'girl-in-a-swing' series, made about 1752–4, may have worked independently before or after joining that short-lived factory, for similar decoration appears on Chinese porcelain and on a Meissen figure.[4] Decoration in a much later style has been added to one pair of 'girl-in-a-swing' figures, perhaps by one of the painters working in the decorating establishment run by James Giles of Kentish Town and Cockspur Street, London, between about 1760 and 1776.[5] It is also possible that after 1763 the Bow factory itself sub-contracted with Giles for the decoration of figures and vessels.

The English porcelain factories probably recruited their first painters from the jewellers' workshops, where enamel-painting was already practised on a metal ground. In 1753 the Bow factory advertised for

[1] In 1750 Caillat, a painter at the Vincennes factory, was arrested and imprisoned at the moment when he had formed a plan to escape to England with the secret of the recipes he had been working on. (Chavagnac and Grollier, *op. cit.*, p. 133.)

[2] Contemporary unfired painting and gilding remains on a large Chelsea bust of George II, dating from about 1752, in the British Museum.

[3] Mrs. Donald MacAlister, *William Duesbury's London Account Book*, London, 1931.

[4] See p. 80.

[5] W. B. Honey, 'The work of James Giles,' *E.C.C. Trans.*, vol. I, no. 5, 1937, pp. 17–19.

painters in Birmingham, a leading centre for fine metalwork.[1] At Chelsea during the 'raised anchor' period (about 1749–52), and at Bow and Derby in the years immediately after 1750, the painting on figures had a very amateurish appearance; the colours were harsh and smeary in their application, especially on the faces. We may note similar defects in the contemporary figures made at Mennecy in France, which often resemble those of Bow in their colour schemes. The soft glaze tended to absorb the colours laid over it, giving an uneven, blotchy effect very different from the finely graded washes of colour seen in the flesh-tones on the Meissen figures. With the hard-paste porcelain, colours lay on the surface of the hard glaze without melting into it. Most of the glazed figures made in soft paste at Vincennes were left in the white. The attempts to paint them were considered particularly unfortunate—with reason, to judge from the few coloured Vincennes figures that survive, of which the large group *La Source* in the Louvre is the best known.[2] The problem was evaded at Vincennes and Sèvres by making figures from 1752 onwards in unglazed biscuit-porcelain. The English factories were more persistent and successful, particularly Chelsea, where figures made in the 'red anchor' period between 1752 and 1757 have the most exquisitely sensitive complexions. The sensuous bloom of the white material was enhanced by the slight floral sprigs pencilled on the dresses, and by plain washes of pale colour with an occasional accent in black or red. A few Bow and Derby figures show equal taste and restraint. But at Bow a liking for piquant clashes of gaudy colour, especially crimson and opaque pale blue, developed towards the end of the 1750's. And at Chelsea itself the 'gold anchor' figures made after 1758 are overloaded with sumptuous colour and much gold; a manner faithfully imitated at Derby. Little if any gilding appears on Chelsea figures before 1756, when it is often mentioned in the sale-catalogue of that year. Slight touches of gold are found on a few Derby figures made before 1756, but extensive gilding only began at Derby in the 1760's. At Bow, a rough granular gilding was applied over darker enamel colours on early figures of the 'Muses' type. Later Bow gilding is of relatively poor quality. The Longton Hall colours remained harsh throughout the 1750's, and a local idiosyncrasy was the use of a strong deep underglaze blue for some areas of the dress. A duller underglaze blue was more sparingly used on Bow figures made after 1763.

[1] *Aris's Birmingham Gazette*, Nov. 5, 1753; quoted by Nightingale, *Contributions*, p. XLV. The advertisement called first on 'Painters in the Blue and White Potting Way, and Enamellers on China-Ware', continuing 'Likewise Painters brought up in the Snuff-Box Way, Japanning, Fan-painting, &c. may have opportunities of Trial'.

[2] P. Verlet, S. Grandjean, M. Brunet, *Sèvres*, 1953, Plate 22.

In the German factories, especially at Höchst, Frankenthal and Ludwigsburg, the painted figures made after 1770 are often plastered all over with deep and muddy colour, leaving little of the white porcelain exposed; the flesh tones also become unpleasantly dark. This trend was avoided in the contemporary Chelsea-Derby figures (1770–1784), which show a revulsion against the overloaded decoration of the 'gold anchor' figures of the 1760's. Washes of pale colour, and slight flower-sprigs in colour or gold, allowed much of the white ground to appear. Nevertheless the opaque pale pink of the Chelsea-Derby flesh-tones is tiresome and characteristic of the age.

The unglazed biscuit-porcelain used for many Chelsea-Derby figures lacks the waxen surface and sense of mass of the best Sèvres biscuit figures. But towards the end of the eighteenth century the Derby biscuit was deliberately given a surface sheen which more satisfactorily suggests the appearance of marble.

3

THE PORCELAIN FIGURES
IN RELATION TO SCULPTURE

The European porcelain figure ultimately owed its existence as an art-form to the vision of Augustus the Strong, and to his appointment of a series of professional sculptors to work as modellers at the Meissen factory. He evidently hoped for large-scale sculpture in the prevailing Baroque style, but executed in porcelain. The chapel of his Japanese Palace was to have life-size statues of the Apostles; the galleries of the Palace were to have life-sized figures of animals and birds. We know how this grandiose scheme miscarried; how over the years between 1727 and 1741 the sculptors Kirchner and then Kaendler attempted to coax the great masses of porcelain through the kiln, with disastrous losses as the treacherous material cracked and collapsed in the firing.[1] The figures that survive from this heroic experiment appear to us today as fantastic curiosities.

Kaendler inherited his patron's vision after the death of Augustus the Strong in 1733. Work on his project for a colossal equestrian monument in porcelain to Augustus' successor was only abandoned on the outbreak of the Seven Years War in 1756. Meanwhile, in his spare time, Kaendler had carved in stone at least six sepulchral monuments with human figures. He had also successfully carried out in porcelain a series of large white religious groups and figures of saints in which the dramatic machinery of Baroque sculpture was fully employed. But to us now these too appear as curiosities. We prefer the other Kaendler, who worked with such true understanding from within the porcelain medium, and created a whole miniature world of coloured figures from the Italian Comedy, from the social comedy of manners at the Saxon court, and from the picturesque life of the common people. By the time that other porcelain factories began to spring up about the

[1] The most useful summary account, with bibliography, is given by W. B. Honey, *Dresden China*, London, 1954, pp. 84 ff.; H. Gröger, *Johann Joachim Kaendler, der Meister des Porzellans*, Dresden, 1956, adds further notes on Kaendler as a sculptor.

middle of the eighteenth century these had become the accepted themes.

Nevertheless, monumental sculptors were still engaged as modellers in many of the porcelain factories, especially in Germany. The Rococo style tended to break down formal distinctions between sculpture, painting and ornament, merging them all into a decorative ensemble. In a palace such as the Residenz at Würzburg, or in the garden-pavilions at Nymphenburg, the wall-painting, stucco-work, and free-standing figures are interdependent and inseparable. The ornamental statues carved in sandstone by Ferdinand Dietz, for the gardens at Seehof near Bamberg and Veitshöchheim near Würzburg, differ neither in subject-matter nor in spirit from the miniature figures made in the porcelain factories; indeed they were described as being 'painted in the porcelain manner'.[1] There is no evidence that Bustelli, the brilliant chief-modeller at the Nymphenburg porcelain factory, had ever worked in any other medium; yet the style of his figures comes so close to that of the painted wood sculpture carved by Ignaz Günther for the Bavarian churches that he has been improbably claimed as Günther's pupil. The Ludwigsburg porcelain factory might even claim to be the seed-ground of a new style in monumental sculpture; for it was here that Wilhelm Beyer first created, for porcelain, the models that he later executed on a large scale in marble, as statues for the gardens of Schönbrunn near Vienna. In France too the history of sculpture is closely interwoven with that of porcelain; at the instance of Madame De Pompadour, the sculptor Falconet spent the years 1757–66 as chief-modeller at the Sèvres factory, where his figures in biscuit-porcelain mark the transition from Rococo to the more serenely sentimental style known as Louis Seize. It was with relief that he escaped to Russia, to create there his equestrian bronze monument to the Tsar Peter the Great.

In Germany, the porcelain figure developed under court patronage as a by-product from the thriving local schools of late Baroque sculpture. In England the early porcelain factories, all private ventures, were in no such position to attract the personal co-operation of able sculptors. Moreover the sculptural background itself was far less rich, and for various reasons had assumed a form against which the porcelain figure could only appear as an irrelevant intruder. As early as the second quarter of the seventeenth century, in Rome itself, the Baroque movement in art had split into two factions. On the one hand was the extremist Bernini, who in Italy gained the day. On the other were the artists who cultivated the reason and restraint which they claimed to recognize in the art of classical antiquity. Among

[1] 'Auf Porzellanart Gemalt'. See Heinrich Kreisel, *Der Rokokogarten zu Veitshöchheim*, Munich, 1956.

them was the painter Nicolas Poussin, whose example had such a potent influence on the French Academy and the artists working for Louis XIV at Versailles. France developed its own national brand of 'classical' Baroque through the seventeenth century, and not until the eighteenth century did French sculpture admit a significant trend towards the dramatic manner of Bernini. Elsewhere in Northern Europe a vigorous 'classical' school of sculpture had developed at Antwerp. It traced its origin to François Duquesnoy, 'Il Fiammingo', who was born at Brussels in 1597 and went early to Rome, where he studied antiquity and became an intimate friend of Poussin.[1] Apart from his statue of St. Susanna and the great figure of St. Andrew under the dome of St. Peter's, Fiammingo left few complete works at his premature death in 1643. But his reputation was enormous— he had been invited by Louis XIII to become Professor of Sculpture at the projected French Academy; and his brother, who inherited his designs, established the 'classical' tradition of sculpture in Antwerp. It was this Antwerp school that formed Rysbrack and Scheemakers, who became leading sculptors in England during the second quarter of the eighteenth century. Fiammingo's memory had been kept green by the numerous small models in terracotta, bronze or wax ascribed to him on often doubtful grounds, but especially treasured by later sculptors. Most of them represented naked *putti*, a speciality of Fiammingo. No less than fifty such models were in the collection formed by the French court sculptor Girardon in a gallery at the Louvre at the end of the seventeenth century,[2] and others in England were in the possession of the sculptors Rysbrack,[3] Scheemakers,[4] and Roubiliac.[5] Reproductions of the Fiammingo *putti* were among the earliest figures made at the Chelsea porcelain factory between 1745 and 1750 (1).[6] And in 1755 the Vincennes factory in France produced a whole set of forty '*Figurines par La Rue pour le Service du Roi. D'après Francois Flamant*' (Fiammingo).[7]

[1] An excellent appreciation of Fiammingo's work is given by R. Wittkower, *Art and Architecture in Italy 1600–1750*, London (Pelican), 1958, pp. 177–80.

[2] Mariette Fransolet, *François du Quesnoy sculpteur d'Urbain VIII, 1597–1643*, Brussels, 1942, p. 186.

[3] M. I. Webb, *Michael Rysbrack Sculptor*, London, 1954, pp. 186, 189.

[4] Fransolet, *op. cit.*, p. 188, quoting the sale-catalogue of their possessions sold by Scheemakers and his partner Laurent Delvaux on the eve of their departure for Italy in 1726.

[5] Katharine A. Esdaile, *The Life and Works of Louis François Roubiliac*, London, 1928, pp. 80, 220.

[6] See p. 59.

[7] E. Bourgeois, *Le biscuit de Sèvres au XVIII⁰ siècle*, Paris, 1909, vol. II, p. 6; and Bourgeois and Lechevallier-Chevignard, *Le biscuit de Sèvres*, Paris, 1913, no. 238.

(1) *Plate 2.*

In England the Baroque had been forestalled by Inigo Jones, who between 1616 and 1635 erected the Royal buildings for which he is still most gratefully remembered—the Queen's House at Greenwich and the Banqueting House in Whitehall. Taking as his model the Italian academic architect Andrea Palladio (*b.* 1518, *d.* 1580), himself a student of Vitruvius, he introduced the then architecturally barbarous English to the form of modern Mediterranean architecture which they have ever since preferred. Sir Christopher Wren himself never ventured further than France, and his buildings may be regarded primarily as feats of structural engineering overlaid with correct classical elements derived from Palladio. Only in the work of Wren's successors Sir John Vanbrugh, Nicholas Hawksmoor and Thomas Archer, between about 1690 and 1720, did English architecture make a brief sortie in the direction of Roman Baroque. Wren's St. Paul's was exceptional in offering opportunities for sculpture on a grand scale, in the skyline statues and pediment of the west front; these were carved without distinction by Francis Bird, whose imagination had not been fired by his experience as a working sculptor in Rome. The other Protestant churches rebuilt after the Great Fire of London offered no scope for devotional sculpture. Indeed sculptors working in England depended for their bread and butter mainly on the ostentatious sepulchral monuments erected in churches throughout the land—monuments in which portraits of the deceased, often in Roman dress, were attended by conventional cherubs and allegorical Virtues. The sculptors were commonly provided with preliminary designs by architects, such as James Gibbs and William Kent, the protégé and collaborator of Lord Burlington. It was Lord Burlington who from about 1715 led the reaction against even the modified Baroque of Wren, and inaugurated the 'Rule of Taste' that dominated English architecture and ancillary arts for the next forty years.

Needless to say the Italian sculptor whom Lord Burlington imported about 1714, and maintained in quarters at Burlington House till 1734, was of the classical persuasion—Signor Guelfi, the author of the standing monument to Secretary Craggs (1725) in the south-west tower chapel of Westminster Abbey, and of many monuments elsewhere. A far more important sculptor was Michael Rysbrack (1694–1770), who arrived in England from Antwerp in 1720 and worked in London for the rest of his life. Rysbrack soon gained the approval and patronage of the Burlington circle, and his dignified monument to Sir Isaac Newton (1731), against the choir-screen of Westminster Abbey, is among the very best of its kind. Newton is shown half reclining in Roman dress against a pile of books, with attendant cherubs in the Fiammingo manner, and a globe supporting an

28

allegorical figure of Astronomy on a high pyramid behind. Rysbrack's pre-eminence was later challenged by his fellow-countryman Peter Scheemakers of Antwerp (1691–1781), who first arrived in England in 1717, and gained a wide reputation for his standing monument to Shakespeare in Poets Corner at Westminster Abbey (1741). The Shakespeare (so often reproduced in English pottery and porcelain, especially at the Derby factory (1)), is a spiritless and mediocre work, which yet shows Scheemakers following the same classical tradition as Rysbrack; indeed Scheemakers, unlike his more gifted rival, made the pilgrimage to Rome and returned about 1730 with numerous studies and copies which he had made there after the famous sculptures of antiquity.

The third of the leading sculptors who came to work in England, Louis François Roubiliac (*b.* about 1702, *d.* 1762), had a very different background. Born at Lyons of Huguenot parentage, he went first to work at Dresden under Balthasar Permoser, that venerable master of the extreme Baroque who influenced Kaendler, and through him the development of the Meissen porcelain figures. Returning to France, Roubiliac then worked under the court sculptor Nicolas Coustou. He arrived in England after 1731, and first attracted attention by his informally seated statue of Handel, erected in Vauxhall Gardens in 1738.[1] A brief visit to Rome in 1752 confirmed his admiration for the genius of Bernini, and his sepulchral monuments in Westminster Abbey and elsewhere mark a sensational departure from 'classical' decorum. In the monument to General Hargrave (about 1757) the resurrected corpse in its winding-sheet breaks out from the shattered and toppling obelisk of the tomb, while Time as a winged old man downs the skeleton that represents Death. In the monument to Lady Elizabeth Nightingale (1761) the distraught husband attempts to ward off the spear aimed at his dying wife by the draped skeleton emerging from the dungeon below. Horace Walpole found this 'more theatric than sepulchral', and Roubiliac has had scathing critics from Sir Joshua Reynolds onwards. His monuments are the English counterparts of the '*grandes machines*' contrived in France by such contemporary sculptors as René-Michel Slodtz and the brothers Adam, and this belated flourish of the Baroque was most enthusiastically received by a generation which had perhaps grown restive under the long rule of Lord Burlington's correct Palladianism, and had not yet succumbed to the even chillier wave of Greek neo-classicism that was to arrive with Robert Adam in the 1760's and 1770's. It was in this

[1] Now at Messrs. Novello's in Wardour Street.

(1) *Plate* 65.

same interlude that the early English porcelain factories flourished. There is, indeed, a tradition, which may go no further back than 1885,[1] that Roubiliac was actually employed as a modeller at the Chelsea porcelain factory; and a recent standard work on sculpture states this as if it were a fact.[2] The only documented fact is that in 1744, before the Chelsea factory opened, its later manager and proprietor Nicholas Sprimont stood godfather to Roubiliac's daughter Sophie.[3] It is not surprising that these two immigrant members of the Huguenot community in London knew each other. But in her standard work on Roubiliac[4] the late Mrs. Esdaile admitted the improbability that a busy and distinguished sculptor would take such employment: and the various attempts to identify Roubiliac's hand in surviving Chelsea figure-models are singularly unconvincing. Roubiliac's rather dry and nervous style is distinguished by its extreme naturalism and linear vivacity, in both the figures and draperies. It is quite distinct from the more ponderous, generalized, and easy-going style of the modeller Joseph Willems, to whom the majority of Chelsea figures may without hesitation be attributed.[5] A small group of *Britannia mourning for Frederick Prince of Wales* (I), in connection with which Roubiliac's name has been invoked, was in fact not made at Sprimont's Chelsea factory; it belongs to the 'girl-in-a-swing' series.[6] The large Chelsea bust of George II has been attributed by Mrs. Esdaile to Rysbrack,[7] and by Bernard Rackham, tentatively, to Roubiliac.[8] It bears no resemblance to the authenticated portrait busts of George II by either of these artists. The Chelsea bust of George III as Prince of Wales (2) comes closer to Roubiliac's style,[9] but the model is not among those he left at his death. A curious twist has recently been given to the

---

[1] W. King, *Chelsea Porcelain*, p. 57, suggests that it was first put about by Sir Arthur Church in that year. Mrs. Esdaile, on the other hand, writes that 'the tradition has always existed in the family' (*Life*, etc., p. 76).

[2] 'A year or so later [i.e. after 1748] Roubiliac was employed for a short period at the Chelsea china factory,' R. Gunnis, *Dictionary of English Sculptors*, London, 1953.

[3] Katharine A. Esdaile, *The Life and Works of Louis François Roubiliac*, London, 1928, p. 75.

[4] Esdaile, *Life*, etc., pp. 75–82.

[5] See p. 63. The red-anchor set of *Five Senses* mentioned by Mrs. Esdaile shows Willems at his most characteristic.

[6] See p. 77.

[7] *Op. cit.*, p. 81, n. 1. The attribution is ignored by Mrs. M. I. Webb, *Michael Rysbrack Sculptor*, London, 1954.

[8] *Catalogue of the Schreiber Collection*, I, p. 32 and no. 126.

[9] Esdaile, *op. cit.*, Plate XX; compare the busts of Sir Edward Walpole and Princess Amelia, Plates V, XXVIII.

(I) *Plate* 32; (2) *Plate* 9.

Roubiliac story by Mr. T. H. Clarke, who has published a primitive-looking coloured porcelain figure of a reclining pug-dog, and identified it as being derived from a terracotta portrait of Hogarth's dog 'Trump' modelled by Roubiliac.[1] Unfortunately for the presumed connection between Roubiliac and the Chelsea factory, the paste of this porcelain dog has since been chemically analysed and shown to be quite different from any Chelsea paste, containing a fair proportion of soapstone.[2] It might have been made at Longton Hall; in which case we must assume that Roubiliac allowed casts of his terracotta to be sold to the public. Four plaster dogs were included in the Catalogue of his models sold after his death.

It is convenient at this point to recall that the eighteenth-century sculptors eked out a living by selling plaster-cast reproductions of their work. In some cases they also sold the small terracotta models which had served as preliminary studies for larger statues. The porcelain factories may thus have been able to acquire sculptors' models which they had not specially commissioned. The English public had a special interest in portrait sculpture, and not only of living celebrities. Between 1730 and 1737 Queen Caroline erected two buildings in which such portraits played a prominent part: the Grotto or Hermitage at Richmond, containing busts of English men of learning—

With Honour, thus by Carolina plac'd
How are these venerable Bustoes grac'd—

as a sycophant wrote at the time; and her Library in St. James's Park with busts of poets and philosophers. About the same time Lord Cobham built in his gardens at Stowe a Temple of British Worthies, with busts, among others, of King Alfred, the Black Prince, and Queen Elizabeth. For Lord Burlington's villa at Chiswick, Rysbrack carved two fine garden-statues representing Palladio and Inigo Jones; and in a bill made out to Henry Hoare of Stourhead in 1727 are 'two Figures of Inigo Jones and Palladio in Plaster—£1.10.0.'.[3] In 1743, as George Vertue tells us, Rysbrack made three terracotta statuettes, about 2 feet high, of Rubens, Vandyke, and 'Fiamingo Quenoy'; these were

[1] *E.C.C. Transactions*, vol. 4, Part 5, 1959, Plate 27; the portrait of Trump also discussed by Mrs. Esdaile, *op. cit.*, Plate IX and pp. 50–1, 178. The terracotta was sold after the death of Hogarth's widow in 1789 and published as an engraving in Samuel Ireland's *Graphic Illustrations of Hogarth*, 1799, but has since disappeared.

[2] Frank Tilley, *Teapots and Tea*, Newport, Mon., 1957, p. 122 and Colour Plate 1.

[3] M. I. Webb, *Michael Rysbrack Sculptor*, p. 103; the Chiswick statues *ibidem*, Figs. 38, 39. A full-size cast of the Inigo Jones still stands on the staircase of no. 4 St. James's Square (now occupied by the Arts Council), where it was seen by Horace Walpole in 1761.

cast in plaster and sold at seven guineas the set.[1] Rysbrack was later
under-sold by Scheemakers, who in 1747 offered for only five guineas
his set of five casts from terracottas after ancient statues in Rome—
the 'Hercules, Flora, Venus, Faunus, Zingara Egyptian woman'.
It is quite possible that one of these casts was used at the Bow porcelain factory for the figure after the Farnese Flora made there in the
late 1750's (1);[2] and not impossible that Rysbrack, who had never
been to Rome or seen the original, used one of Scheemakers' casts
when in 1758–9 he modelled a small terracotta Farnese Flora as a
sketch for the large marble Flora which he carved for Sir Richard
Hoare of Stourhead in 1760–1.[3] The Rysbrack terracotta differs in
certain details from the Bow figure, for which it is unlikely itself to
have served as a pattern.

A whole class of small sculptures dating from about the middle of the
eighteenth century represented famous English poets. They are, or
were, some 18 inches or 2 feet high, with the figure holding a book
or scroll and standing beside an architectural pedestal. The type no
doubt became popular after the success in 1741 of Scheemakers'
monument to Shakespeare in Westminster Abbey. The Victoria and
Albert Museum has a quite different *Shakespeare* and an *Alexander
Pope* by unidentified sculptors, and a *Matthew Prior* which may be by
Roubiliac, all three in lead and about 18 inches high (nos. A.3,
4–1955; A.30–1931). Other models which have failed to survive were
probably circulated in the form of plaster-casts, for there exist adaptations from them in porcelain and other ceramic materials. The
Scheemakers' *Shakespeare*[4] was reproduced in miniature porcelain
scent-bottles and seals by the 'girl-in-a-swing modeller' between 1751
and 1754,[5] and in a number of Derby porcelain figures whose 'first
edition', considerably modified to suit the Rococo fashion, appeared
about 1758 (2). Later Derby adaptations of this first version have

[1] M. I. Webb, *op. cit.*, p. 110. Bronze versions of Rubens and Vandyck are in the
Victoria and Albert Museum, A.24 and 123–1955.

[2] See p. 93 for further discussion. A plaster Flora at the Soane Museum, 20½
inches high, may be one of Scheemakers' casts. The Bow Flora is only 18½ inches
high. The Rysbrack terracotta, 22½ inches.

[3] Rysbrack later sold the terracotta model to Sir Edward Littleton of Teddesley
Hall, Staffs. Mrs. Webb, *op. cit.*, Appendix I, reproduces in full Rysbrack's long
and interesting correspondence with this patron; in his letter of Dec. 16, 1758,
he refers to a plaster cast of the Flora which was evidently not his own work.

[4] Mrs. Esdaile quotes an instance where Scheemakers sent to his friend the
painter Smibert a cast from his own terracotta model of the *Shakespeare*; *E.C.C.
Trans.*, I, no. I, 1933, p. 10.

[5] Bryant, *Chelsea Porcelain Toys*, Plate 27, no. I; Plate 36, no. II.

(1) *Plate* 52; (2) *Plate* 65.

Neo-Classical bases. Larger Shakespeares with square bases, about 18 inches high, were produced in Staffordshire salt-glazed ware about 1780 and in white Staffordshire earthenware by Enoch Wood about ten years later;[1] these follow the Scheemakers' casts directly and are not derived at second hand through the Derby versions. The first Derby Shakespeare had as companion a *Milton* (1) standing beside a cylindrical pedestal on which the Expulsion is represented in low relief. This Milton also reappears with Shakespeare in Enoch Wood's Staffordshire earthenware.[2] The Milton monument in Westminster Abbey is a bust, and was carved by Rysbrack in 1737. But Mrs. Esdaile has plausibly suggested that the Derby-Staffordshire Miltons derive, like the Shakespeares, from casts of a Scheemakers model, for in 1756 a 'terracotta model of a figure of Milton' was included as Lot 23 in a sale of the models then in the sculptor's studio.[3] We should, however, be on our guard, for there existed another Milton prototype quite distinct from the one reproduced at Derby. It was followed in a rare porcelain figure made at Chelsea about 1749–50,[4] and again in cream-coloured earthenware made in Germany at Dirmstein (between 1774 and 1788) and Flörsheim (between 1790 and 1793).[5] The pedestal beside which the poet stands is rectangular, not cylindrical; there are differences in the drapery; the figure is slighter, and the attitude and expression more severe. We may mention one other white porcelain figure, probably made at Longton Hall, possibly after a lost model by Scheemakers (2). It shows a dramatic poet holding a scroll and leaning against a pedestal on which are masks in relief, and almost certainly represents *Dryden*, whose bust was carved by Scheemakers for the Westminster Abbey monument in 1731.[6] A figure of *Chaucer* is known in Staffordshire earthenware of the Enoch Wood type,[7] but has not been recorded in porcelain.

Given the predilections of a democratic public, it is not surprising

[1] *Schreiber Catalogue*, II, 95 (salt-glaze); 311 (Enoch Wood).
[2] Victoria and Albert Museum, no. 54–1874.
[3] *E.C.C. Trans.*, I, no. I, 1933, p. 10.
[4] See p. 59.
[5] Baron Ludwig Döry, 'Keramische Dichterfiguren in England und Deutschland,' *Keramos* (Deutsche Keramische Gesellschaft no. 10, 1960, pp. 51–63. The author of this interesting article fails to recognize that the Milton existed as early as the 1750's in two distinct prototypes.
[6] The Dryden porcelain figure closely resembles in pose a drawing by Scheemakers for the monument to young Turner (*d.* 1739), in the Mausoleum at Kirkleatham Church, Yorks; he also leans on a pedestal and holds a scroll (Soane Museum, no. 21 in Album, 'A Series of Drawings and Sketches by Scheemakers, Roubiliac, Nollekens, etc.').
[7] Victoria and Albert Museum, no. 89–1874.

(1) *Plate* 64; (2) *Plate* 79.

that many more portraits of contemporary popular heroes were made in the English porcelain factories than in those on the Continent. From Bow came figures of *General Wolfe*, the *Marquess of Granby*, and *Frederick the Great*, the military leaders in the Seven Years War, as well as character portraits of *Kitty Clive*, *Woodward*, *Quin*, and *Garrick*, the well-known actors. Derby created an extensive portrait-gallery including the politicians *Chatham*, *Wilkes* and *Conway*; the Judge *Lord Camden*; and the historian *Mrs. Macaulay*. But the majority of these were derived from engravings; and if they often suggest sculptured originals, that merely shows the influence on official portrait-painting of the conventions established in the sepulchral monuments.

Apart from portraiture, the English sculptors received many commissions for ornamental fireplaces in the rich town and country houses. But this work, involving caryatid figures and overmantel panels in low relief, had no possible connection with the porcelain figures. It may have been otherwise with the ornamental statuary made for gardens. As at Versailles, much of this was cast in lead.[1] We hear of figures made by Caius Gabriel Cibber in 1688 for the Duke of Devonshire at Chatsworth, including Apollo and Pallas; for Welcombe, in Warwickshire, Cibber made a genre figure of a blind bagpiper and his dog.[2] The sculptor John Nost (flourished 1686–1729) specialized in such work; between 1700 and 1706 he supplied to Thomas Coke of Melbourne Hall, 'two boys after Fiammingo, modelled a-purpose and cast in a hard metal,' and figures of Perseus, Andromeda, Mercury and Psyche, an Indian, and a blackamoor. Andries Carpentière (or Carpenter) began making lead statues in his yard at Hyde Park Corner before 1722, when he sent a price-list of classical and mythological subjects to Lord Carlisle; besides Narcissus, Flora, Adonis, Apollo, Winter and Autumn, four Signs of the Zodiac, and the Seasons, he offered a 'French paisant and paisanne', 4 feet 2 inches high. John Nost's business was taken over about 1739 by Sir Henry Cheere and his brother John, the first an able sculptor who passed on to become a public administrator. There are many surviving accounts of work done by John Cheere. Thus for the Duke of Atholl at Blair he made in 1742–3 a Farnese Hercules, Flora, Ceres, and Father Time, all in lead; a Diana in stone, and Four Seasons in marble.[3] For Henry Hoare and the gardens at Stourhead he made in 1757 and later a river-god and a nymph, a Hercules, and numerous other lead

[1] Sixteen lead figures of the late 17th and early 18th century, formerly owned by Lady Charlotte Schreiber, were sold at Christies, 29 June 1961 (eight illustrated in catalogue).

[2] Now in the Victoria and Albert Museum, A.3–1930.

[3] Unpublished papers in possession of the present Duke of Atholl.

figures, these costing only from £25 to £40 each (Rysbrack charged £300 for the single marble statue of Hercules which he carved for Stourhead). Indeed, the yard at Hyde Park Corner became a cheap statue-factory, and attracted ribald comment: a writer in 1772 described 'figures in stone, lead and plaster you would swear was a country fair or market, made up of spruce squires, haymakers with rakes in their hands, shepherds and shepherdesses, bagpipers and pipers and fiddlers, Dutch skippers and English sailors enough to supply a first-class man-of-war'.[1] J. T. Smith recalled that, 'The figures were cast in lead as large as life and frequently painted with an intention to resemble nature. They consisted of Punch, Harlequin, Columbine and other pantomimical characters; mowers whetting their scythes, haymakers resting on their rakes, gamekeepers in the act of shooting and Roman soldiers with firelocks, but above all that of an African, kneeling with a sundial on his head found the most extensive sale.' The range of subjects invites immediate comparison with that of figures from the porcelain factories, and in its later phases the establishment at Hyde Park Corner may well have borrowed more ideas from porcelain than it ever gave. Little is known about the sources from which Carpenter and Cheere obtained their models; some no doubt were casts after the antique, and others casts after near-contemporary French sculpture (Girardon's *Rape of Proserpine* and *Winter* at Versailles were reproduced in lead for the gardens at Southill).[2] But there must also have been original work. Roubiliac himself worked for Carpenter at Hyde Park Corner on his first arrival in England, and Joseph Willems could easily have done the same, had not Sprimont persuaded him to join the Chelsea porcelain factory as modeller. Some of the statues themselves are still to be seen in the gardens of country houses, but the majority must have been melted down for the lead, or because fashion had changed; for example G. Lipscombe in his *Buckinghamshire* (1834) writes that in the gardens of Hartwell House there were formerly many statues, but they disappeared 'when an improved taste began to prevail'.

As an alternative to marble or lead, garden-statues were also made in artificial stone, an extra-hard kind of fired terracotta. The first patent for this was taken out in 1722 by the architect Thomas Ripley and his partner Richard Holt.[3] In 1730 Holt published a *Short Treatise of Artificial Stone*, with a dedication to Lord Burlington, in

---

[1] *Leaves in a Manuscript Diary*, London, 1772; quoted by R. Gunnis, *Dictionary of English Sculptors*, together with the passage from J. T. Smith's *Streets of London*.
[2] M. I. Webb, *Michael Rysbrack Sculptor*, p. 35.
[3] Mrs. K. A. Esdaile, 'Coade Stone,' in *The Architect and Building News*, CLXI, 1940, pp. 94–6, 112–14, and Gunnis, *Dictionary*.

which he wrote that the material was 'cast in the assign'd Moulds, as fast as the Lead-Men do their most fluid Metal', adding that as 'the Lead-Casters can afford to under-sell the Stone-Carvers, so much more can he under-sell the Leaden Figure-Makers'. From his workshop on Lambeth Embankment Holt supplied not only figures, busts, and vases, but all kinds of ornamental revetments for buildings. A sale of 'all this last year's produce of the Artificial Stone Manufactory' took place at Christie's in 1767, but the factory was in decline when taken over and vigorously revived about 1769 by Mrs. Eleanor Coade from Lyme Regis, who proved a most competent business-women. She promptly engaged as her manager the young sculptor John Bacon (*b.* 1740, *d.* 1799), the future R.A., and also obtained models from other promising sculptors of the day—John Flaxman, R.A. (*b.* 1755, *d.* 1826); John Charles Felix Rossi, R.A. (*b.* 1762, *d.* 1839); John De Vaere (*b.* 1755, *d.* about 1826); Joseph Panzetta (*fl.* 1789–1830), and possibly Thomas Banks, R.A. (*b.* 1735, *d.* 1805). Illustrated catalogues were issued in 1777, 1784 and 1799, prices ranging from thirty shillings for an 18-inch *Flora* to 105 guineas for a large *river-god* 9 feet high. Under Eleanor Coade (*d.* 1796) and her nephew and partner John Sealy (*d.* 1813) the factory enjoyed enormous success, its most considerable achievement being the west pediment at Greenwich Palace (1810–13), after a design by Benjamin West. Needless to say the later figure-models were mainly in the neo-classical fashion of the time.

The Coade factory had certain contacts with porcelain; John Bacon had served his apprenticeship between 1755 and 1762 with the jeweller Nicholas Crisp of Bowchurch Yard, Cheapside; and Crisp, with his partner Saunders, also ran a mysterious porcelain factory in Lambeth or Vauxhall.[1] The young Bacon evidently visited this factory, and according to a later story, was first inspired to become a sculptor by seeing the terracotta sculptors' models sent for baking at a pottery in the same building. (Still later accounts that he actually modelled figures for Crisp's porcelain factory are untrustworthy.) A memorandum quoted by Haslem shows that in 1769 Bacon was paid £75 7s. 2d. for models supplied to William Duesbury of the Derby porcelain factory;[2] but these may have been figures in Coade's Artificial Stone for the instruction of the Derby modellers, rather than designs actually to be carried out in porcelain. There is further evidence of some mysterious connection between artificial stone and porcelain. When Duesbury decided in 1783 to close the Chelsea

[1] See p. 94.
[2] J. Haslem, *The old Derby China Factory*, London, 1876, p. 43, from information supplied by Duesbury's grandson in 1862. See also p. 103 below.

factory which he had maintained for the last thirteen years as a subsidiary of his main Derby works, some very curious items were advertised in the Christie sale-catalogue;[1] '*A Quantity of Artificial Stone Figures* and Foxes, as large as the Life, with the moulds thereof'; large and small standing and sitting figures, a set of the 'Four Quarters', and 'the moulds of a large figure of Britannia, 5 feet high'. From the fact that it possessed the moulds for most of these it might seem that the Chelsea factory under Duesbury added a limited output of artificial stone garden-figures to its work in porcelain. In 1790 Joseph Lygo, agent of the Derby factory in London, wrote to the younger William Duesbury passing on information he had obtained from a key worker at Coade's—the fireman William Coffee, who had evidently just quarrelled with his employers and left.[2] Lygo was trying to persuade Coffee to go and work at Derby; and this Coffee eventually did, between 1794 and 1810.[3] In the course of his work as fireman, Coffee had evidently picked up enough knowledge to become a competent modeller for porcelain. He later made terracottas on his own in Derby.

Activities at the Derby factory from 1770 onwards are referred to in an exceptionally large number of surviving documents, and though these have not yet been thoroughly sifted, they throw considerable light on the relations between the factory and its modellers. It was difficult to persuade artists to go to Derby and bind themselves to work there for any length of time. Pierre Stephan signed on for three years in 1770; but in the same period he evidently sent models to the Bristol factory, in response to letters from its director Richard Champion; and after 1773 he left Derby to work as a freelance. But in that capacity he continued to send models both to Derby and to Josiah Wedgwood at Etruria. In London, the Derby ag: at Lygo, and the clockmaker and jeweller Benjamin Vulliamy, were constantly on the look-out for modelling talent. Particular models were obtained from sculptors and modellers who could also have supplied Wedgwood and Coade's Artificial Stone Factory; among them Rossi, John Deare, and Charles Peart. In 1790 Lygo and Vulliamy were fortunate to catch Jean Jacques Spengler, a gifted Swiss who had just arrived in London; but they had endless trouble in keeping him. It is clear that in this

[1] A unique priced copy of the *Catalogue of all the Remaining Finished and Unfinished Stock of the Chelsea Porcelain Manufactory*, Dec. 11–13, 1783, which belonged to Mr. Christie himself and is now in the possession of Mr. Alexander Lewis, is published by F. Severne MacKenna, *Chelsea Porcelain: the Red Anchor Wares*, Leigh-on-Sea, 1951. The artificial stone figure and moulds were mostly bought in by Duesbury's London agent Lygo. The moulds of the large Britannia were still at Chelsea awaiting destruction or disposal in February 1784 (Jewitt I, p. 184).
[2] Two relevant letters from Lygo are published by Jewitt, II, p. 140.
[3] See p. 111.

late phase, when biscuit figures in the neo-classical style were the fashion, it was no longer thought necessary for the modeller to work continuously at the factory in day-to-day contact with the 'repairers' and painters. In a sense porcelain had drawn closer to sculpture, but at the expense of its independence as a distinct branch of art.

One further group of sculptors remains for consideration, if they can be called a group; the workers in miniature, in bronze, ivory, and silver. The small bronze figure had been created during the Italian Renaissance for the delight of the sophisticated collector and connoisseur. It reached England in the seventeenth century, under that great collector Charles I: an inventory of sculptures in the Cabinet Room at Whitehall lists 'a little St George on horseback with a dragon by being of brass', and 'a little running horse Cupid sitting on and another Cupid running by which was made by ffrancisco the one-eyed Italian'.[1] Francesco Fanelli of Florence (d. 1665) arrived in England some time after 1610, and left for France about 1642;[1] John Evelyn, on a visit to Hampton Court in 1662, observed the 'rich and noble fountaine, with syrens, statues, &c cast in copper by Fanelli'.[2] Vertue gives a list of nine small bronzes, mostly of equestrian subjects, in the collection of Lord Oxford (who had acquired them from the Duke of Newcastle at Welbeck), and goes on to say that such pieces were 'sold to persons that were Curious to sett on Tables cupboards shelves by way of ornament'.[3] A porcelain group made at the Longton Hall factory about 1755 is directly copied from one of these Fanelli bronzes, showing a Cupid galloping on horseback (I).[4] Another late Renaissance bronze imitated in porcelain was the figure of a seated boy playing the bagpipes, from the workshop of Giovanni da Bologna.[5] This reappears as the handle surmounting a covered pot-pourri vase made at Bow about 1760,[6] and also as a separate figure. After the Restoration we hear no more about small bronze figures being made

---

[1] J. Pope-Hennessy, 'Some bronzes by Francesco Fanelli,' *Burlington Magazine*, XCV, 1953, p. 157.

[2] *Diary*, June 9, 1662.

[3] *Walpole Society*, vol. XXIV (Vertue Note Books IV), 1936, p. 110.

[4] See p. 116. There is actually a pair of Longton groups, galloping in reverse directions (examples in the British and Victoria and Albert Museums); but both are probably based on a single Fanelli group (Pope-Hennessy, *loc. cit.*, Fig. 15, bronze in the Victoria and Albert Museum, A.37–1952). Other Longton groups appear to derive from Renaissance bronze originals that have not yet been identified (p. 116).

[5] An example in the Victoria and Albert Museum, no. A.59–1956.

[6] Victoria and Albert Museum, *Schreiber Coll. Cat.* I, 68, with the 'repairer's' mark 'To' impressed.

(I) *Plate* 81B.

in England, probably because here, as elsewhere in Europe, they were regarded as falling into the category of decorative art, and thus lost the publicity attendant on major sculpture.

In Germany during the second half of the seventeenth century ivory superseded bronze as the favourite medium for small 'cabinet pieces'; if bronze had suited the hard, athletic clarity of the Renaissance figures, ivory was more apt for rendering the opulent sensuousness of human flesh that appealed to the age of the Baroque. Ivory-carvers such as Ignaz Elhafen (d. after 1710) took their cue from Rubens.[1] The great sculptor Balthasar Permoser (b. 1651, d. 1732)[2] also carved many excellent small figures in ivory which anticipate in style and subject-matter the porcelain figures made half a century later; indeed Permoser's ivory Seasons were literally copied at the Fürstenberg and Doccia porcelain factories. Porcelain in its turn succeeded ivory as the chosen material of an age. But little ivory-carving had been done in England. David Le Marchand (b. Dieppe 1674, d. London 1726), has left a number of signed portraits and a few allegorical groups, well represented in the Victoria and Albert Museum. Later in the eighteenth century, about 1760–1, England appears to have received a brief visit from the most gifted contemporary German ivory-carver—Johann Christoph Ludwig von Lücke (b. about 1703, d. 1780); he showed at the Exhibition of the Free Society of Artists in 1761 the excellent relief bust of 'His late Majesty (George II) cut in ivory from the life', which is now in the Victoria and Albert Museum.[3] Lücke had thrice attempted to give up ivory for more lucrative employment as a porcelain-modeller; at Meissen in 1728–9; Vienna in 1751–2; and Copenhagen in 1754–5. But he had found it impossible to adjust himself to the medium. There is no evidence that he or any other ivory-carver did any work for the English porcelain factories.

There appears to have been a much closer relationship between porcelain and contemporary figure-work in bronze. But unfortunately bronze figures of the later seventeenth and eighteenth centuries, whether made in France, the Low Countries or England, have hitherto not been systematically studied or collected, and we can only assume that there were more in circulation than appear to have survived today. Roubiliac owned quite a number, briefly mentioned

[1] For German ivories, C. Scherer, *Studien zur Elfenbeinplastik der Barockzeit*, Strasburg, 1897, and *Elfenbeinplastik seit der Renaissance*, Leipzig, 1903.

[2] E. Michalski, *Balthasar Permoser*, Frankfurt a.M., 1927, Figs. 12–18; Wilhelm Boeck, *Balthasar Permoser, der Bildhauer des deutschen Barocks*, Burg b.M., 1938.

[3] Victoria and Albert Museum, *Review of the Principal Acquisitions*, 1932, p. 9 and Plate 4D.

in the sale-catalogue after his death in 1762.[1] Others appear as mantel-shelf ornaments in the background of painted 'conversation-pieces'; for example, the *Dalton family* by John Zoffany, and the same artist's *Sir Lawrence Dundas with his grandson*, in which a miniature of Giovanni da Bologna's *Mercury* can be recognized.[2] But bronze figures, often gilt, were more characteristically attached as fixed ornaments to minor pieces of furniture such as clocks, candlesticks or inkstands. The *Minerva* crowning a famous clock made by Thomas Tompion for the Bedchamber of William III at Hampton Court was repeated in porcelain at Longton Hall about 1758, and at Bow a little later.[3] A very grand musical clock, of which part survives in Kensington Palace, was made by Charles Clay, who died in 1740; it was surmounted by a bronze group of Hercules and Atlas by Roubiliac; had bronze pedestal figures of the Four Monarchies, also by Roubiliac, and silver high reliefs of the Arts and Sciences by Rysbrack; historical paintings by Amigoni; and musical works playing tunes by Geminiani, Handel and Corelli.[4] In 1742 another grand piece, a silver cistern, was designed by George Vertue; two groups of mythological figures on the handles, and the seated dogs on which it rested, were modelled in wax by Rysbrack; and the whole executed in silver by the German silversmith Frederick Kandler. The cistern was made for a lottery and eventually passed into the Imperial Russian Treasury.[5] Other human figures in silver bearing Kandler's mark are known[6] and human figures are also incorporated in some of the highly ornate silver vessels made by Nicholas Sprimont between 1742 and 1747, before he devoted himself entirely to the Chelsea porcelain factory.[7] But there is no clear connection in style between the figures that appear on Sprimont's silver, for which he may have obtained designs from some sculptor, and the early Chelsea porcelain figures, the models for which were sought from a variety of random sources until in Joseph Willems the factory acquired a modeller of its own. No doubt the other English porcelain factories were at first glad to use as models whatever suitable bronzes chance brought their way. And as the bronzes themselves are

[1] K. A. Esdaile, *Life and Works of L. F. Roubiliac*, pp. 224, 229.

[2] Sacheverell Sitwell, *Conversation Pieces*, London, 1936, Figs. 29 and 47.

[3] R. W. Symonds, *Thomas Tompion, His Life and Work*, London, 1951, Fig. 33; B. Watney, *Longton Hall Porcelain*, Plate 78; F. Hurlbutt, *Bow Porcelain*, Plate 56B, with cypher of George III. (First observed by Dr. Watney.)

[4] E. Croft-Murray, 'The ingenious Mr Clay,' *Country Life*, CIV, 1948, pp. 1378–80.

[5] M. I. Webb, *Michael Rysbrack Sculptor*, pp. 138, 139.

[6] Pair of ewers of 1739, *Amtliche Berichte a.d. Königlichen Preussischen Kunstsammlungen*, XXIX, 1908, p. 287.

[7] Bellamy Gardner, 'Sprimont as silversmith,' *Antique Collector*, August, 1938.

usually unknown to us, we have to judge from style and subject which porcelain figures are likely to have had bronze originals. Reclining or seated animals made at Chelsea, Bow and (perhaps) Longton might well have been moulded or copied from bronze paper-weights;[1] in some cases they show gadrooned borders or detailed surface tooling on the bases. The early Bow and Chelsea sphinxes suggest, with their (for English porcelain) premature Rococo bases, a possible derivation from contemporary French ormolu.[2] Some groups with Neptune, Pluto, etc. made at Bow and Derby (I) show a Baroque elan and complication that on this small scale would be more appropriately rendered in bronze than porcelain.[3] A red-anchor Chelsea head of a child, once believed to be a portrait of Sophie Roubiliac,[4] has also been reported in bronze and marble. And the contemporary Chelsea group of two putti with a dolphin is also known, on a smaller scale, in French porcelain and in bronze.[5] A Bow figure of a pedlar, made in the 1750's (2) is found also in wooden and bronze versions which, on grounds of style, have been regarded as probably Flemish work of the Romantic period, early in the nineteenth century;[6] but this dating may have to be revised. It is possible that the existence of datable porcelain copies may help in classifying the eighteenth-century bronzes, whenever this is undertaken.

[1] See pp. 59, 89.
[2] Hugh Tait, 'Some consequences of the Bow Special Exhibition III,' *Apollo*, June 1960, Figs. III, V–XI.
[3] See pp. 91, 99.   [4] See p. 70.
[5] T. H. Clarke illustrates all three versions together in *E.C.C. Trans.*, vol. 4, 1959, plate 24.
[6] J. G. Mann, *Wallace Collection Catalogues: Sculpture*, London, 1931, no. S244; the similar figure formerly belonging to Dr. Hildburgh is now in the Victoria and Albert Museum.

(I) *Plates* 48, 60A; (2) *Plate* 49.

4

SUBJECTS AND SOURCES

To some extent this chapter overlaps the last, for among the sources drawn on in designing porcelain figures was the work of contemporary and earlier sculptors. But the English factories soon learnt, partly by their own experience and partly by example, that they could not treat porcelain figures as a straightforward exercise in miniature sculpture. The material had too insistent qualities and limitations of its own. Fine detail was swamped by the thick glaze, especially in the faces; subtleties of surface modelling were lost to view because the brilliant paste reflected too much light, eliminating the play of shadow; and the glitter from the glaze followed no rational pattern. These short-comings can be seen at their worst in the early 'snowman' figures of Longton Hall (1). But even the well-modelled Chelsea *Ceres* (2), which would have made a dignified garden statue, looks curiously insipid in porcelain, and the same could be said of other figures whose sculptural character has not been modified to suit the new medium (3). The English modellers at first sought their effects by plastic means alone, leaving their figures 'in the white', and to overcome the apparent unresponsiveness of the material, they exaggerated details of the modelling. The 'Muses modeller' at Bow gave his figures open mouths, outsized earrings, and strings of beads (4). He and his anony-mous contemporary at Derby (5) developed a rugged style which in so refined a material as porcelain looks almost uncouth.

The answer to this problem had of course been discovered years before at Meissen. It was to admit some slurring of detail in the modelling, and make good the points of emphasis later with added enamel colour. Modelling and painting were to play complementary and almost equally important parts. A Meissen figure left white looks blind and incomplete. But colour enhances even further the fantastic vivacity of porcelain as a material; and in accepting it for his smaller figures Kaendler had the genius to perceive that he must break com-pletely away from the world of monumental sculpture in stone and bronze. The material called for subject-matter to match its own in-

(1) *Plate* 78A; (2) *Plate* 1; (3) *Plates* 4, 79, 85;
(4) *Plates* 36–45; (5) *Plates* 56–61.

substantial and illusory appearance. It could add a third dimension to all those transient images that had hitherto been reserved for painting and the graphic arts; particularly images from real or imagined contemporary life.

Kaendler may even have implied a connection between the brittleness of porcelain and the frailties of human nature, for in his earliest small figures, the outrageous Harlequins and Italian Comedians, there is a derisive satirical humour whose traces persist in all his later work. This harsh vitality is of a part with the late Baroque style, with the caprice of the Saxon court, with Kaendler's own German origin. It can be seen in early figures made at the other German porcelain factories. But towards the middle of the eighteenth century, when the English factories began, fashion was turning to the more effeminate airs and graces of the Rococo, diffused through Europe from the court of Louis XV. There is little satirical content in the English porcelain figures (here Hogarth was forgotten); in fact no serious social or intellectual comment of any kind. The poet Milton, General Wolfe, the artisans and beggars, have all been promoted to the same make-believe world as the shepherds and shepherdesses and the fancy-dress Chinese. It is interesting here to observe that the Derby Milton (1) is a re-interpretation for porcelain of a sculptor's model closely similar to that more literally reproduced in a Longton Hall figure of Dryden (2), while the Bow General Wolfe (3) is the re-interpretation for porcelain of an engraving. In both cases the modeller was helped by his added Rococo accessories.

Engravings were a far more accessible source of inspiration than sculptor's models, and offered a much wider range of suitable subjects. There were illustrated books, such as the many editions since 1593 of Cesare Ripa's *Iconologia*—a guide to rendering, with their proper attributes, the gods of classical antiquity and allegorical or abstract personifications of every kind. Other long-lived families of books illustrated the dress of different districts or nations, the habits of the religious orders, the street-criers and artisans of various cities, and the internationally popular characters of the Italian Comedy. Each generation added its own version of the traditional themes. In the early eighteenth century new life was given to the Italian Comedy characters by Antoine Watteau and the school of engravers who diffused his work.[1] Watteau and Boucher after him created an elusively

[1] E. Dacier and A. Vuaflart, *Jean de Julienne et les graveurs de Watteau au XVIIIe siècle*, Paris, 1929–31. See especially nos. 30, 82, 83, 260, 271 for engravings followed in English porcelain figures.

(1) *Plate* 64; (2) *Plate* 79; (3) *Plate* 53.

erotic pastoral vision that became the core of the Rococo decorative style. And between 1737 and 1746 the Comte de Caylus engraved the sixty incomparable drawings by Edme Bouchardon entitled '*Études prises dans le bas peuple ou les Cris de Paris*'.[1]

The Meissen factory had bought engravings at the Meissen Fair of 1728, and continued to receive them on loan from Count Brühl's secretary and librarian Heinecken. In 1745 more were on order from England, and in the next two years a Paris merchant named Le Leu sent engravings to the value of 327 Taler. In 1753 the Paris agent of the factory sent a whole series of water-colour designs of *Cris de Paris* by his brother, the engraver C. G. Huet. There are records of similar purchases of engravings by other porcelain factories in Germany and Italy. Their subjects were drawn on both by the painters of porcelain vessels and by the figure-modellers. But the latter adapted their sources very freely and supplemented them by new inventions in the same spirit, as we can see in the figures of street-criers which Kaendler devised on the basis of Bouchardon's *Cris de Paris*.

Joseph Willems, the Chelsea modeller, had a wide selection of engravings in his possession when he died in 1766, as well as original drawings which included twenty-four in ink of the *Cris de Paris*.[2] But for the use of engravings by the English modellers we must rely mainly on circumstantial evidence. Between 1750 and 1752 Chelsea adapted a whole series of bird-models from the illustrated books of George Edwards,[3] and some fine figures of oriental ladies came from engravings by Ravenet after Boucher.[4] The English factories were probably far less systematic than Meissen in collecting and exploiting the engraved sources. Sometimes they seem only to have acquired one or two engravings from a set; the 'girl-in-a-swing' modeller used Jacopo Amigoni's engraving for his group of *Water*, but drew on his own imagination for the companion group of *Air*. In some cases we can compare and contrast English and Meissen figures independently adapted from the same French engravings; such are some early Bow groups of Chinese and Italian Comedy subjects after Watteau.[5] But usually the English modellers preferred to imitate Meissen figures when these were available. So great was the debt to Meissen that without definite proof it would be unsafe to say that any English figure of the middle and later 1750's was an original invention. It might derive from some now rare and unfamiliar Meissen model.

Of the earliest English figures, made between 1749 and about 1752,

[1] Set in the British Museum, Dept. of Prints and Drawings, bound *en face* with the original sanguine drawings for presentation by Bouchardon to his friend the collector Mariette.

[2] See Appendix I, p. 135.　　　　[3] See p. 61.
[4] See p. 62.　　　　[5] See pp. 87, 88.

relatively few show Meissen influence in style or subject-matter. The English modellers had to make their first steps alone, with such help as they could find from engravings or sculptural sources. We might infer that Meissen figures were still rather uncommon in this country; in May 1751 Sir Everard Fawkener actually wrote to Sir Charles Hanbury Williams, British Minister in Dresden, asking if he could buy locally examples of Meissen porcelain to serve as designs for the Chelsea factory.[1] It was instead arranged that the factory should borrow from Hanbury Williams' own collection, then stored at Holland House in London, and consisting of pieces made during the previous decade. The Chelsea 'red-anchor'-marked figures of about 1752–6 are in many cases adaptations of Meissen models, or in the Meissen manner, but not in the very latest fashion. It was about 1748 or 1749, notably in the series of 'craftsmen', that Kaendler and his assistants at Meissen first began regularly to set their figures on scrolled Rococo bases. At Chelsea such bases only begin to appear in a few of the models listed in the sale-catalogue of 1756; they are more characteristic of the 'gold-anchor' figures made after 1758. But we could deduce from the work of other English factories that by 1753 the importation of Meissen figures had sharply increased,[2] and that among them were some of the most recent Rococo design. Thus we find several stages of stylistic development telescoped in England into a very few years. At first even actors and peasant figures were made to stand on rectangular plinths, as if they were sculptured statues (1); then come simple pad bases, often with applied flowers and leaves, with the suggestion that the figures were disporting themselves in a flowery meadow, in the open air (2); and almost simultaneously there arrive the Rococo pedestals, which in England were at first grotesquely misunderstood. Two early Derby figures (3) were adapted from the *absinthe-seller* and a *peasant woman* in the Meissen 'Paris cries' series of 1753 already mentioned,[3] which must thus have become

---

[1] See p. 60.

[2] This is borne out by Horace Walpole's essay in *The World* for February 1753 (already quoted, p. 57); and by the unsigned and undated complaint drafted in or just after 1753 by the 'Undertaker' of the Chelsea factory (Nicholas Sprimont), in which he calls for stricter enforcement of customs duties on imported Meissen porcelain (text from the MS. in the British Museum quoted by Jewitt, vol. I, pp. 171–2).

[3] See p. 44. Sixteen of the Meissen set illustrated, Emma Budge Sale Cat., Hamburg, Sept. 27–9, 1937, no. 828; also G. von Klemperer Sale Cat., Dresden, 1928, nos. 634–46. The night-watchman and other figures were later illustrated in Chelsea gold anchor.

---

(1) *Plates* 5, 6, 31B, 36, 37, 40; (2) *Plates* 14, 15, 17, 22B, 23B, 42; (3) *Plate* 61B, C.

available for imitation in England almost within the year. And the early Bow *Liberty* and *Matrimony* (1) are again after practically brand-new Meissen Rococo models. But generally speaking the Rococo-style bases only become normal in the English factories during the later 1750's. The most immediately beneficial result of studying the Meissen figures was the tidying-up of the modelling, as may be seen by comparing the smaller Bow figures of the mid-1750's with the earlier and rougher efforts of the 'Muses modeller' (2).

As was the practice elsewhere, the English figures and groups were almost invariably designed in complementary pairs or sets, unless they were sufficiently large and imposing to stand on their own. But in the Chelsea sale-catalogues not more than about five figures were offered in one lot, and the sets were never so extensive as at Meissen, where a single set of street criers or artisans might include twenty or more figures. Thus it appears that Chelsea only reproduced five of the twenty-odd figures in the Meissen *monkey orchestra* (3).

A brief survey of the commonest subjects may begin with the *classical gods and goddesses*, of which the Chelsea red-anchor series is by far the best (4). Joseph Willems was here working independently of Meissen, perhaps after engravings that have not been identified. Sets of smaller gods were produced in the first few years at Bow and Derby, and in the 1760's Derby issued a number of large Rococo figures which compare unfavourably with those of Chelsea. The *Nine Muses* are represented in early Bow figures (5) and in the fine Chelsea gold-anchor series (6); at Derby only two of the Muses were attempted, large reclining figures after French engravings by Daullé (7). The *Four Elements* could be represented by Jupiter with the eagle, Neptune with a dolphin, Cybele with a lion and cornucopia (Earth), and Apollo or Vulcan with a brazier (Fire); this is a series which appears at Bow and in gold-anchor Chelsea. There are isolated large figures of *Minerva* (Bow, (8)); of *Flora* with cupids (Chelsea), and of course the very large Bow *Flora* so incongruously moulded from a cast after the antique Flora Farnese (9). In very few cases are the classical gods or heroes composed into groups, but we have from Chelsea *Perseus and Andromeda, Leda and the Swan*, and the *Rape of the Sabines* (red anchor); and *Mercury and Argus, Mars and Venus* and *Hercules and Omphale* (gold anchor). Another version of the last-mentioned subject, dating from the early 1750's, was adapted from a French engraving after Le Moyne by the 'girl-in-a-

---

(1) *Plates* 44, 45; (2) *Plates* 49–51; (3) *Plate* 22A;
(4) *Plates,* 10, 11; (5) *Plate* 39; (6) *Colour Plate* A;
(7) *Plate* 68; (8) *Colour Plate* C; (9) *Plate* 52.

swing' modeller (1), who also made candlestick-groups of *Ganymede and the eagle* (2) and the *Rape of Europa*. Derby offered two cheerfully ludicrous rapes, in which the large Leda and Europa almost overwhelm their puny ravishers (3). The classical gods generally received more dignified treatment from the Baroque artists than from their eighteenth-century successors, and Joseph Willems at Chelsea evidently regretted the passing of the grand style. His gold-anchor group of Spenser's *Una and the lion*[1] is unique both for subject and size.

It is not easy to draw a sharp line between the classical pantheon and the allegorical personifications that were so often rendered in the same manner. Thus *Britannia*, in the fine large Derby version, is a standing figure virtually indistinguishable from Minerva, except that she has the Union Jack on her shield instead of a Gorgon's head. Figures in pseudo-classical dress often do service in the sets whose allegorical meaning was merely a pretext for grouping them together. They are perhaps easier to recognize than the same personifications in modern dress, where a peasant-girl sniffing a flower might be Spring, the Sense of Smell—or merely a 'gardener's companion'. Each of the English factories produced several such sets—the *Five Senses*, the *Four Elements*, the *Four Continents* (or 'Four Quarters of the World'), the *Four Seasons*, the *Seven Liberal Arts* and so on. Conspicuously fine are the large seated 'classical' *Senses* in red-anchor Chelsea (4), with their appropriate symbols—eagle for *Sight*, pot-pourri-vase and dog for *Smell*, tortoise under bare foot and sharp-clawed parrot on hand for *Touch*, musical instrument for *Hearing*, fruit for *Taste*. An early Derby set exceptionally represented the Senses by Chinese figures in five groups (5). The large standing 'classical' *Continents* of Longton Hall (6) were later reproduced, evidently from the same moulds, at Plymouth; and the 'classical' children as *Continents* made in red-anchor Chelsea (7) were imitated at the time, and for years afterwards, in several sizes, at Derby. An early Derby series of nude putti as *Seasons* (8) are shown in exactly the same attitudes as the adult Bow Seasons in contemporary dress (9). In another early Derby series there are eight figures, each Season being represented by a pair of peasants. Bristol had two sets of Seasons, one composed of 'classical' adults with signs of the Zodiac on their belts, the other of contemporary children (10). The *Liberal Arts* is in England a rare subject, only represented at

[1] See p. 74.

_____

(1) *Plate* 34; (2) *Plate* 30A; (3) *Plate* 66; (4) *Plate* 12;
(5) *Plate* 58, *Colour Plate D*; (6) *Plate* 83; (7) *Plates* 22B, 23B;
(8) *Plates* 56A, 57A; (9) *Plate* 50B; (10) *Plates* 90, 92, 93.

Chelsea by some charming nude children standing on pedestals.[1] And as for the *Virtues*, they had by the eighteenth century gone quite out of fashion, appearing like robust ghosts from the past. The large early Bow group of *Charity* (1) looks very Baroque (she might equally well be *Fécondité*, from some seventeenth-century print), and the huge *Roman Charity* group by Willems of Chelsea (2) was in fact based on an engraving after Rubens. The aberrant instance of filial piety recalled in this 'very large and curious group' apparently failed to appeal to contemporary taste, for two examples were left on the hands of the factory, to be disposed of in its final sales of 1769 and 1770.[2] Willems once again missed the mark in a huge revived Baroque group of two stark naked standing females, unexpectedly identified as *Liberality and Modesty* from their source, an engraving after Guido Reni published by Sir Robert Strange in 1755. The genteel mode of Louis Seize appeared punctually in 1771, when the first sale-catalogue of the combined Derby and Chelsea factories offered a 'curious group of *Minerva crowning Constancy, and Hercules killing the Hydra*'; the figures were shown as nude children, as were '*Prudence* and *Discretion* with antique urns, on pedestals'. There followed in 1778 Chelsea-Derby biscuit groups of *Bacchants adoring Pan*, *Virgins awaking Cupid* (3), and *Virgins distressing Cupid*, taking their ladylike sentiment from engravings after Angelica Kauffmann.

Cupids, or nude children, were more happily treated in the 1750's, when some of the earliest Chelsea figures were moulded from early bronzes or terracottas purporting to be by the seventeenth-century sculptor François Duquesnoy, 'Il Fiammingo' (4). A fine large Chelsea red-anchor group of two putti struggling with a dolphin is Baroque in feeling, and may also derive from an earlier bronze.[3] But the most attractive models were the Chelsea red-anchor sets of 'Cupids for a desart', or of 'Love in disguise' (5), and the miniature scent-bottles by the 'girl-in-a-swing' modeller, with their amorous mottoes (6).

Subjects in contemporary dress take as their starting-point the splendid series of 'crinoline figures' created by Kaendler at Meissen in the late 1730's and 1740's—ladies grouped or paired with their cavaliers, and wearing extravagantly wide flaring skirts. This late

[1] Victoria and Albert Museum, *Schreiber Coll. Cat.*, I, no. 135.

[2] Nightingale, *Contributions*, pp. xxvii, xxviii, Appendix pp. 4, 76; they sold for £6 16s. 6d. and £8 15s. respectively.

[3] See p. 67.

---

(1) *Plate* 42; (2) *Plate* 28; (3) *Plate* 71; (4) *Plate* 2B, C; (5) *Plate* 23A; (6) *Plate* 35.

Baroque fashion hardly survived to reach English porcelain, though there are Bow reproductions of one Meissen pair, the 'baseless' cavalier kissing his hand and supported by his trailing robe, and his lady with a fan. Ladies and gentlemen in hunting attire are again less commonly found in English than in German figures, and none are associated with the national sport of fox-hunting. It seems that the English preferred to see figures of the gentry in fancy dress, or as definite portraits. Far more numerous are the English figures of street-criers, artisans and peasants. Kaendler's large Meissen series, itself inspired by the Bouchardon *Cris de Paris* engravings, was imitated in a number of Chelsea red-anchor models and a few from Derby and Bow. But Chelsea added some original models of its own, such as the 'Italian beggars' (1), the carpenter, and the fisherman's wife (2); and it is worth noting that Willems left at his death a series of twenty-four ink drawings of *Cris de Paris* which may have been his own inventions.[1] Especially fine are his large red-anchor models of a seated fruit-seller and companion (3). Bow produced a fine large original model in the Thames waterman wearing the badge of the Admiralty barge (4). A few Chelsea gold-anchor models with Rococo bases were copied from the smaller and later Meissen series of Paris Cries made in 1753, mentioned above.[2]

A closely similar series produced at Meissen in 1753 showed 'Cries of London', some of the subjects being taken from the seventy-four engravings by Pierce Tempest after Marcellus Laroon, published in London in 1711. It is rather surprising that the English porcelain-modellers apparently made no use of this well-known English book. Figures of peasants had a great vogue at Chelsea. Some were imitated from Meissen originals—a *seated beggar* playing a hurdy-gurdy (raised anchor mark), from Kaendler's set of 1741, and the red-anchor groups of *Tyrolean dancers* and *Dutch dancers* from Eberlein's models, first issued in 1735 and later remodelled with Rococo bases. There is also a Bow version of the *Tyrolean dancers*. At the Chelsea factory this class was referred to as 'Teniers figures', and Willems evidently produced a number of new models on the basis of the engravings after Teniers that had such a wide popularity in the eighteenth century. Most impressive of these models is the large red-anchor 'Maypole group' (5), with a lady and gentlemen and four peasants dancing round a mound on which stand two other figures, one a fiddler. The

[1] See p. 135.   [2] P. 44.

(1) *Plate* 16; (2) *Plate* 17; (3) *Plates* 14, 15; (4) *Plate* 41A; (5) *Plate* 20.

fiddler is also known as a separate figure. The well-known Chelsea *nurse* was first issued in the raised anchor period about 1750, and remained a popular item in the sale-catalogues of 1755 and 1756; it was exceptional in being adapted from an early seventeenth-century figure in colour-glazed earthenware, made at Avon near Fontaine-bleau by a follower of Bernard Palissy. The charming small Chelsea 'family groups' of about 1757–60 (I) may in some cases have been adapted from Meissen originals. *Sailors* with their lasses appear in two different pairs at Bow (2) and yet again at Derby;[1] these are pecu-liarly English. *Gardeners* with their companions of course formed a stock theme at all dates. Among the most striking of the English peasant figures are the large Bristol *goatherd* and *milkmaid*, prob-ably designed about 1775 by Pierre Stephan (3).

It would be a mistake to imagine that the figures mentioned in the last paragraph showed a realistic interest in the contemporary social scene. They were intended to be picturesque, and the peasants and countrymen belonged to a convention already established in the seventeenth century. Another convention was that of the erotic pastoral, the youthful shepherds and shepherdesses in fine clothes attended by their lambs and lap dogs. These derive from the engravings after Watteau and Boucher and other French Rococo artists. But it seems likely that the English porcelain-modellers drew less often on the engravings themselves than on the Meissen figures which these had already inspired. At Meissen the pastoral subjects began their vogue about 1750, and were usually associated with Rococo scroll bases. The early Bow group of lovers with a bird-cage (4) was evidently derived direct from an engraving after Lancret, but other Bow figures of shepherds and shepherdesses are obvious adaptations from Meissen (5). At Chelsea, in the gold-anchor period, the same subjects were staged with a lavishness of decoration that goes far beyond that of their sources (6). A simple-minded erotic symbolism lies behind the play with musical instruments and the bird and the open bird-cage ('Liberty and Matrimony'). The pastoral convention began to lose its Rococo finery after 1770, and towards the end of the eighteenth century the shepherds and shepherdesses are more realistically clad in the bourgeois fashion of the time. The Derby biscuit subjects, 'The dead bird', 'The Russian shepherds' and so on, share the sentimental romanticism we encounter in James Thomson's *Seasons* (7).

[1] W. King, 'Early Derby porcelain figures,' *Old Furniture*, I, 1927, p. 43, Figs. 9, 10.

(I) *Plate* 24; (2) *Plates* 40, 55; (3) *Plates* 94, 95; (4) *Plate* 38; (5) *Plates* 44–47; (6) *Plates* 26, 27; (7) *Plates* 74–77.

The inherent frivolity of the porcelain medium would seem ill-suited to religious subjects, though such were often attempted by factories in the Catholic countries. A Chelsea red-anchor group of the *Virgin and Child* standing on the globe (1) is a unique model in English porcelain, and undoubtedly owes its origin to the Baroque leanings of the modeller Joseph Willems. The group seems to have been a popular one. Willems was also responsible for the ambitious Chelsea gold-anchor group of the *Virgin and an angel mourning over the dead Christ*,[1] which recalls in spirit the paintings of Van Dyck, though its possible engraved source has not been traced. These serious compositions have nothing in common with the numerous figures of *monks* and *nuns* made at Chelsea, Bow and Longton Hall in the 1750's (2). Here the intention is purely picturesque, the subjects deriving from the numerous illustrated guides to the habits of the various religious orders current in the seventeenth and eighteenth centuries.[2] Meissen originals may no doubt be found for most of these figures, but in one case at least Willems at Chelsea used an obscure seventeenth-century book.[3] There are some charming Chelsea miniature scent-bottles in the form of monks and nuns (3), and equally engaging groups in 'Chelsea-Derby' porcelain (4).

With its Far Eastern antecedents, porcelain was naturally biased in the direction of oriental and exotic themes, and we shall have to refer to the direct mouldings from Chinese *blanc-de-chine* figures which were made at Chelsea, Bristol and Longton Hall in the early days of those factories.[4] The purely bizarre aspect of Chinese subjects was much exploited at Meissen in the 1720's and 1730's. But in the hands of Watteau and Boucher, Chinoiserie was assimilated into the decorative elegance of the Rococo style, and thus inspired some excellent early figures and groups made at Chelsea, Bow and Derby (5). At Meissen, Turks, blackamoors (always described as 'Indians') and other exotically dressed figures were drawn from illustrated books such as de Ferriol's *Recueil de cent estampes représentant différentes*

[1] King, *Chelsea Porcelain*, Plate 64, 15 inches high. To be compared with a similar but less satisfactory group in biscuit-porcelain which Willems may have modelled for the Tournay factory in 1766. See p. 74.

[2] For example, *Briefve Histoire de l'Institution des Ordres Religieux*, illustrations by Odoardo Fialetti, Paris, 1658 and later editions; *Courte et solide Histoire de la Fondation des Ordres Religieux*, engravings by Adrien Schoonebeck, Amsterdam, 1688; the same with new engravings, Augsburg, Daniel Steudner, 1692–3; Filippo Bonanni, *Ordinum Religiosorum in Ecclesia Militanti Catalogus*, Rome, 1706–10 and later editions.

[3] See p. 69.　　　　[4] See pp. 60, 115, 120.

(1) *Plate* 13; (2) *Plates* 19B, 51; (3) *Plate* 35H; (4) *Plate* 70B; (5) *Plates* 7, 21, 58.

Nations du Levant etc. (Paris 1714, engravings by G. Scotin and others). The exotic figures made at all the English factories during the 1750's are for the most part direct imitations of Meissen models. But Willems at Chelsea modelled some of his earliest figures of Levantine women from a rare set of engravings after Boucher by Simon-François Ravenet, probably engraved in France before Ravenet's arrival in England about 1747 (1). The oriental subjects retired from fashion in the porcelain figures of the 1760's, though the English generally retained a lively interest in the dress of other countries and ages, as is shown by the illustrated albums published after 1757 by Thomas Jefferys.[1] With its early taste for the grotesque, the Meissen factory produced in the 1720's a whole series of comic dwarfs. They were based on engravings in *Il Calotto resuscitato*, a book published by Wilhelmus Koning at Antwerp in 1716.[2] Dwarfs from the same source were made later in other Continental factories, especially Vienna and Höchst. *Il Calotto resuscitato* seems not to have been available in England. But a Chelsea red-anchor male dwarf in a high hat was taken from one of Callot's own engravings,[3] and a female companion dwarf made a little later, in the red-anchor period, seems to be an original Chelsea design. The male Chelsea dwarf was reissued by the Derby factory after 1770, with a new male companion, also taken from Callot, and this pair, described in the 1784 Derby sale-catalogue as 'grotesque Punches', enjoyed a long popularity in a number of succeeding versions. They are now generally known as the 'Mansion House dwarfs'.[4]

The fantastic dresses and attitudes of Harlequin and his companions in the Italian Comedy provided Kaendler at Meissen with some of his finest subjects, and he was able to add many new inventions to those he found already in engravings after Watteau and

---

[1] *A Collection of the Dress of Different Nations, Ancient and Modern, particularly Old English Dresses after the Designs of Holbein, Vandyke, Hollar and others. . . . London, published by Thomas Jefferys, Geographer to the Prince of Wales,* I and II (1757); III and IV (1772). This handsome anthology from all the best earlier illustrated books seems, unaccountably, not to have been used in the porcelain factories.

[2] *Il Calotto resuscitato; oder Neu eingerichtes Zwerchen Cabinett.* The engravings with captions in doggerel verse are signed by various artists and have nothing to do with Callot's own work, being in contemporary Baroque style.

[3] The set of twenty, entitled *Varie figure gobbi,* is dated 1616 on the title-page. It is reproduced by J. Lieure, *Jacques Callot,* Paris, 1925, Part 2, vol. II; no. 417 is the Chelsea dwarf, no. 415 its later Derby male companion. For the Chelsea figures, see p. 63 below.

[4] See p. 107.

(1) *Plate* 5.

others. This phase at Meissen covered the late 1730's and 1740's. Willems at Chelsea borrowed his fine raised-anchor Dr. Baloardo from an engraving after Watteau, and adapted the companion Isabella (1) from an unexpected source, a sixteenth-century Venetian book on costume.[1] Bow may have used the Watteau and Boucher engravings for some early Comedy groups, but generally speaking the numerous Comedy figures made at all the English factories are reproductions of the smaller and less important Meissen models, to which they added no new inventions. The Italian Comedy figures went right out of fashion in the 1760's. But Chelsea then produced a fine set of eight 'Ranelagh dancers' in fantastic dresses (2), and also a large pair of masqueraders. The English factories showed a more characteristic interest in the 'straight' drama and in the roles taken by certain popular actors and actresses. Engravings of such subjects were readily available. Thus Kitty Clive and Henry Woodward, as the 'Fine Lady' and 'Fine Gentleman' in Garrick's farce *Lethe* (3), were among the earliest Bow figures, in a series which also included a Falstaff and an unidentified actor, perhaps Garrick himself, in eighteenth-century dress. Derby during the 1760's produced a different Falstaff after an engraving showing James Quin in the part, and a Garrick as Tancred in Thomson's *Tancred and Sigismunda*. A contemporary Derby female figure (4) has been regarded as a companion to the last, and described as 'Mrs. Cibber in the character of a Vivandière'; but both assumptions appear unfounded, for she is probably not an actress at all, but a street-crier. The Chelsea-Derby sale-catalogue of 1773 includes a figure of Garrick as Richard III which remained popular well into the nineteenth century, and appears to have been reproduced, from the original Derby moulds, in 'Parian ware' made by Copelands of Stoke-on-Trent after 1849.[2] Contemporary performers on a lower level were also represented in porcelain of the 1760's; Price the trick horseman, shown kneeling or standing on the backs of two horses in a pair of small bocage groups from Bow (he was performing in Dobney's tea-garden at Islington in the 1760's); similar groups from Bow with pairs of boxers; John Coan, the 'English Dwarf', and David Gabarisco, the 'Prussian Dwarf', bocage-groups listed in the Chelsea 1761 sale-catalogue.

Subjects from Aesop's Fables enjoyed a long popularity in England

[1] See p. 62.

[2] These figures are more fully discussed in the chapters on the respective factories. I am much indebted for information about them to Mr. Raymond Mander and Mr. Joe Mitchenson.

(1) *Plate* 6; (2) *Plate* 25; (3) *Plates* 36, 37; (4) *Plate* 69A.

after the success of the first edition with illustrations by Francis Barlow (1666). Aesop himself, as a hunch-backed negro, was taken from the frontispiece of the 1687 edition to become a large Chelsea figure, probably dating from about 1752–3. A print in the *Weekly Apollo* for 1752 inspired a group of the Fox and the Stork, by the 'girl-in-a-swing' modeller. And in the 1760's Chelsea produced a number of bocage groups with the name of the subject written in capitals on the scrolled pedestals—'The Vain Jack Daw', the 'Dog with the Clog', 'Maid killing the Cock', and so on. It will be recalled that Fable subjects were also much used in the painted decoration of early Chelsea table-wares.

Reference has been made in the previous chapter to the special interest of the English public in portrait sculpture, and the appropriation by the porcelain factories of sculptors' models for portraits. The Chelsea factory about 1750–2 produced its large busts of George II and of George III as Prince of Wales (1) and the smaller head of the Duke of Cumberland, but this experiment was not repeated. Sculptors' models in the manner of sepulchral monuments were used for the standing figures of Milton, Shakespeare, and Dryden (2), but other portraits, though in the same convention, seem mostly to be based on engravings. They often have as their background the historic events of the day. The death of Frederick, Prince of Wales, in 1751 is commemorated in the Chelsea and 'girl-in-a-swing' groups of *Britannia mourning* (3), and a rare Chelsea group represents George III and Queen Charlotte at the time of their marriage in 1761.[1] The Seven Years War produced its heroes; Frederick the Great standing, in a rare Bow figure; John Manners Marquess of Granby, who lost his wig as he led the charge of the Blues at the Battle of Minden in 1759; General James Wolfe, the victor of Quebec in the same year (4); and Ferdinand Duke of Brunswick, the commander at Minden, shown on horseback in a Longton Hall group (5). William Pitt, whose policies lay behind the success of the Seven Years War, was ennobled as Earl of Chatham and Lord Privy Seal in 1766, and in 1770 led an attack on the arbitrary policy of George III's government towards the American colonies. This is referred to in the Chelsea-Derby figure of about that date, in which Chatham receives the homage of a kneeling American Indian woman.[2] Another popular opposition hero was John

[1] *Untermyer Cat.*, Fig. 57.
[2] Victoria and Albert Museum, *Schreiber Coll. Cat.*, I, no. 306 (probably dated too early, about 1767).

(1) *Plate* 9; (2) *Plates* 64, 65, 79; (3) *Plates* 8, 32; (4) *Plate* 53; (5) *Plate* 80B.

Wilkes, whose stormy career was precipitated by his alleged libels on George III in the *North Briton* in 1763. Wilkes was supported by General Henry Seymour Conway and by Charles Pratt (created Baron Camden and Lord Chancellor, 1766). All three men were represented in porcelain figures made at the Derby factory, probably about 1770, that of Camden being based on an engraving by Ravenet after Sir Joshua Reynolds (1).[1] But the factory also paid homage to George III in a set of three figures of the King and his family on pedestals, based on Earlom's engraving after the family portrait at Windsor painted by Zoffany in 1770; the figures appear in the sale-catalogue of 1773 (2). When war broke out again, with the American colonies aided by France, Derby commemorated General Howe, Admiral Rodney and other leaders in a series of biscuit-porcelain figures. Literature was honoured somewhat surprisingly in a Derby figure of the historian, Mrs. Catharine Macaulay, leaning against a pedestal (after a statue of 1777 by J. F. Moore); and a pair of rather insignificant Chelsea-Derby busts represented Pope and Jean-Jacques Rousseau.[2] Rousseau and Voltaire, however, are better known in the black basalt figures by Wedgwood.

[1] Wilkes and Conway, *Schreiber Coll. Cat.*, I, nos. 362, 362a.
[2] *Schreiber Coll. Cat.*, I, nos. 360, 361.

(1) *Plate 72*; (2) *Plate 73*.

5

CHELSEA (LONDON)

On the evidence of some inscribed and dated cream-jugs moulded with two recumbent goats and a bee, this most accomplished of English factories was probably founded in 1745. Figures of the highest quality were made between about 1750 and 1763. The factory was sold in 1769, after a period of decline, and thereafter carried on as a subsidiary of the Derby factory. Figures of this 'Chelsea-Derby' period (1770–84) are more appropriately discussed under the heading DERBY.[1]

The founder appears to have been the silversmith Nicholas Sprimont (*b.* Liège 1716; entered at Goldsmiths' Hall 1742, *d.* 1771), in partnership with Charles Gouyn, a French jeweller and china-dealer established in London between 1737 and his death in 1781. Gouyn withdrew in 1749, when Sprimont found a more influential and active supporter in Sir Everard Fawkener (*b.* 1684, *d.* 1778), secretary to the Duke of Cumberland (a son of King George II). He was thus able to reorganize the factory, and after Fawkener's death continued as sole proprietor till 1769, when he sold it to James Cox and retired. The work owed much of its excellence to Sprimont's own taste and application, and production fluctuated during his periods of ill-health, dwindling especially after 1763. In 1770 William Duesbury and John Heath acquired the Chelsea works from Cox and intro-

---

[1] More has been written about Chelsea than any other English factory; many valuable but scattered articles by Bellamy Gardner, William King and others are in the *English Porcelain Circle* and *English Ceramic Circle Transactions*, the *Connoisseur*, and *Apollo*. References hereafter abbreviated are to W. King, *Chelsea Porcelain*, London, 1922, and *English Porcelain Figures of the Eighteenth Century*, London and Boston, 1925; F. Severne Mackenna, *Chelsea Porcelain, the Triangle and Raised Anchor Wares* (Leigh-on-Sea, 1948); *Chelsea Porcelain, the Red Anchor Wares* (Leigh-on-Sea, 1951); *Chelsea Porcelain, the Gold Anchor Wares* (Leigh-on-Sea, 1952). *The Cheyne Book of Chelsea China and Pottery*, ed. R. Blunt (London, 1924) is a valuable exhibition catalogue with copious, but very small illustrations. Illustrations also in B. Rackham, *Catalogue of Porcelain Earthenware, etc. collected by Charles Schreiber Esq. M.P. and the Lady Charlotte Elizabeth Schreiber* (Victoria and Albert Museum, 1928); Yvonne Hackenbroch, *Chelsea and other English Porcelain in the Collection of Irwin Untermyer*, Cambridge, Mass., 1957; and G. Savage, *18th-Century English Porcelain*, London, 1952.

duced the traditions of their own factory at Derby. They finally closed the works in 1784 and removed the moulds to Derby.

The independent work at Chelsea falls into four not very sharply defined periods, each with its characteristic paste and mark. Under the Sprimont-Gouyn partnership, from 1745–9, the mark, if any, was an incised triangle, or at the end of the period the rare trident inter-secting a crown in under-glaze blue. Between about 1749 and 1752 the mark was a 'raised anchor' stamped in relief on a small oval applied pad; the anchor itself was sometimes picked out in red, especi-ally on late pieces. From about 1752–6 a small anchor in red enamel (occasionally also in brown or purple) was inconspicuously painted directly on to the surface, appearing on the back or upper part of the base of figures. The use of a painted gold anchor overlapped and eventually superseded that of the red anchor from about 1758 on-wards.

The triangle-marked porcelain made before 1749 is milk-white in colour and very glassy in texture, being a 'frit' composition akin to that used at Saint Cloud and other French factories. The presence of a French 'arcanist' at Chelsea has been suspected but not confirmed. In an unsigned and undated draft appeal for stricter duties on imported 'Dresden' china, written after 1753, Sprimont described himself as a professional silversmith who had begun to make china 'from a casual acquaintance with a chymist who had some knowledge this way'.[1] It has been suggested, again without confirmation, that this 'chymist' may have been one Thomas Bryand or Briand, who in 1742–3 showed before the Royal Society some samples, made from English materials, of what appeared to be soft-paste porcelain. Apart from their material, and perhaps some of the rare painted decoration, the vessels made at Chelsea during the 'triangle period' show no influence from French porcelain.[2] Their shapes, with elaborately-moulded overlapping leaves and floral decoration in relief, were such as might be found in contemporary silverwork; in fact, they reflected the interests of Sprimont himself. As a silversmith Sprimont had developed a highly personal style and great technical virtuosity, and this was quickly recognized by the more discriminating art-patrons of the time—among them Frederick Prince of Wales, whose plate is still preserved in the Royal Collections. A silver-gilt centrepiece at Windsor, 27 inches high, bears the date-letter for 1741 and the mark of the maker Paul

[1] Lansdowne MSS., no. 892, quoted in full by Ll. Jewitt, *The Ceramic Art of Great Britain*, I, p. 171.
[2] T. H. Clarke, 'French influences at Chelsea,' *E.C.C. Trans.*, vol. 4, part 5, 1959, 45 ff. makes the most of correspondences with Vincennes porcelain, but these might also be explained by common dependence on Meissen.

Crespin, but has been attributed to Sprimont on grounds of style;[1] it is a complex fantasy of marine ornament, with a nude figure of Neptune seated on the cover, and dolphins and two mermaids supporting from below. A set of four shell-shaped sauce-boats, with Sprimont's mark and date-letters for 1743 and 1744, have large and excellently modelled figures of Venus and Adonis seated on the rims as handles.[2] In the Victoria and Albert Museum is a signed but undated pen-and-wash design by Sprimont for a tureen, with heraldry of Thomas Coke, Earl of Leicester.[3] Six shell-shaped sauce-boats, with four oval stands and ladles, were made by Sprimont for Thomas Wentworth, Earl of Malton, just before and after the latter's creation as Marquess of Rockingham on April 19, 1746.[4] And a ponderous tureen supported by two goats, with the arms of John, second Earl of Ashburnham, bore Sprimont's mark and the date-letter for 1747.[5] In that year Sprimont became tenant of a house in Chelsea, but he did not finally vacate his house in Compton Street, Soho, till Christmas 1748.[6] From all this it appears that Sprimont continued to practise as a silversmith for at least three years after the founding of the Chelsea porcelain factory, to which, when he made it his full-time concern, he was able to bring first-class talent as a designer and executive craftsman.

Bearing in mind the figures that appear in his silverwork, we are tempted to look for Sprimont's own hand in the earliest English porcelain figures, made at Chelsea between 1745 and 1749. There are shell-shaped porcelain salts supported by crayfish, in the same manner as his silver-work, and a grotesque Chinaman (1) who appears both as a hollow incense-burner, and as a teapot, with the addition of a detachable hat and a spout in the form of a parrot or serpent. But there are very few actual figures, and these mostly seem to have been taken from pre-existing designs by other artists. Thus a nude *child*

---

[1] C. Oman, 'The Exhibition of Royal plate,' *Connoisseur*, CXXXIII, 1954, p. 151; Victoria and Albert Museum, *Cat. of an Exhibition of Royal Plate from Buckingham Palace and Windsor Castle*, 1954, no. 39, and do., *Picture Book*, Fig. 9. Sprimont could have worked under Crespin's aegis before entering his own mark at Goldsmiths' Hall on Jan. 25, 1742; he is known to have taken a house near Crespin in Compton Street, Soho, in 1743.

[2] Victoria and Albert Museum, *op. cit.*, no. 42; *Picture Book*, Fig. 11.

[3] No. E. 2606–1917.

[4] Christie, Sale Cat., June 9, 1948 (Earl Fitzwilliam), Lots 81–3.

[5] Christie, Sale Cat., March 24, 1914 (Ashburnham), Lot 109.

[6] For biographical documents of Sprimont, see O. Glendenning and Mrs. Donald MacAlister, 'Chelsea, the triangle period,' *E.C.C. Trans.*, vol. I, no. 3, 1935, pp. 20–35.

(1) *Plate* 2A.

asleep on a mattress, with the incised date 'June ye 26th 1746' (1);[1] a seated *child playing a reed pipe* (2);[2] and two other *children seated on rocks*,[3] were evidently moulded direct from the popular reproductions of models by the seventeenth-century Flemish sculptor François Duquesnoy ('Il Fiammingo').[4] A standing figure of *Milton*[5] suggests a sculptor's model for a monument, and it might have been taken from a plaster cast of a model known to have been made by Peter Scheemakers, the sculptor of the monument to Shakespeare in Westminster Abbey (1741). It is not from the same model of Milton which, together with the Shakespeare, is known in later porcelain versions made at the Derby factory.[6] On the other hand, a figure of a *Chinese fisherman* seated on rocks (3) looks more like a silversmith's design, and here there is a possibility that Sprimont himself was involved. A pair of triangle-marked *sphinxes* on rococo bases[7] and a figure of a reclining *greyhound*[8] were almost certainly cast direct from models in bronze or some other metal; the latter bears the rare crown and trident mark in underglaze blue which was used right at the end of the 'triangle' period. The same mark appears on a seated group of two *rustic lovers* (4), which has a variant in which the hands are differently arranged.[9] Here, and in a large unmarked standing figure of *Ceres* (5) there are possible links with later Chelsea figures; in fact these could be early work by Joseph Willems, who perhaps as early as 1749 joined the Chelsea factory as its regular modeller. All these early figures are left 'in the white', and all were cast hollow, with very thin walls, by pouring liquid slip into the plaster moulds.[10] The fine detail

[1] T. H. Clarke, *E.C.C. Trans.*, vol. 4, part 5, Plate 22, with a bronze version; W. Little, 'Three sleeping children,' *Connoisseur*, CXXIX, 1952, p. 35, for an ivory version dated 1641.
[2] F. Tilley, 'The clue of the oak-leaf,' *Antique Collector*, XXI, 1950, p. 13 for example with a tree and candle-sconce behind.
[3] Sotheby, Sale Cat., May 18, 1954, Lot 138, there described as of the raised-anchor period.
[4] See p. 27.
[5] 10 inches high. On the back of the pedestal, 'F' incised and a six-petalled flower in relief. Illustrated by Tapp, *Apollo*, XXXVII, 1943, February; and F. Tilley, *Teapots and Tea*, Newport, Mon., 1957, Plate LIX; and Sotheby Sale Cat., May 18, 1954, Lot 126. For the model and its reproduction in Germany, see p. 33 above.
[6] See pp. 33, 101.
[7] E. Allman Collection, illustrated by H. Tait in *Apollo*, June 1960, p. 184.
[8] A. Lane and R. J. Charleston, 'The girl-in-a-swing porcelain and Chelsea,' in *E.C.C. Trans.*, vol. 6, 1960, Fig. 23 (Mr. Stewart Acton's collection).
[9] Savage, Plate 10 (S. J. Katz collection, unmarked). See below, p. 80, for a smaller remodelled version made at the 'girl-in-a-swing' factory.
[10] See p. 18.

---

(1) *Plate* 2c; (2) *Plate* 2b; (3) *Plate* 3; (4) *Plate* 4; (5) *Plate* 1.

on the rockwork bases is treated in a way that would be appropriate in bronze or silver, but is too unemphatic to make its effect in porcelain with its obscuring coat of glaze. There is little sign of additional work by the hand of the 'repairer', after the paste had been formed in the moulds.

Raised-anchor period, ca. 1749–52. The 'raised anchor' mark was probably adopted by Sprimont about 1749–50 to distinguish pieces made in a new, less glassy and far more stable paste, which is a cool white in colour and looks rather dull and opaque. The reorientation of taste that accompanied this technical improvement may have been largely due to the initiative of Sir Everard Fawkener. Designs for vessels were no longer mainly inspired by silverwork, but by the painted porcelain of Meissen, and at last serious attention was given to figures. A London sale of 'curious Dresden and Chelsea figures' was advertised in December 1750. In May 1751 Fawkener wrote to Sir Charles Hanbury Williams, British plenipotentiary in Dresden, asking him to purchase and send examples of Meissen porcelain 'in order to furnish the undertakers (of the Chelsea factory) with good designs'.[1] Hanbury Williams arranged that his own large collection, then stored at Holland House, should be made available for this purpose, and a contemporary inventory shows that it included many Meissen figures. These must still have been quite rare in England—importation only became considerable after 1752, and relatively few of the Chelsea 'raised anchor' models were directly copied from Meissen originals. Such were the seated *beggar playing a saltbox*, a *Chinese boy* with a hat of leaves, and a large *Dottore* and small *Pantalone* from the Italian Comedy.[2] A seated *Kuan-yin* and a *boy with a gourd* standing on rocks were moulded from blanc-de-chine models, and the well-known *nurse* from an early seventeenth-century figure in colour-glazed earthenware made by Bernard Palissy's followers at Avon near Fontainebleau.[3] Three fine portrait busts, all unmarked and with one exception unpainted, were apparently based on sculptors' models which had come into Sprimont's hands. The head of the *Duke of Cumberland*,[4] $4\frac{1}{2}$ inches high, is treated in a manner appropriate to bronze, and as it is designed for a front view, it can

[1] Earl of Ilchester, 'A notable service of Meissen porcelain,' *Burlington Magazine*, LV, 1929, p. 188. See pp. 4, 5 above.

[2] King, *Chelsea Porcelain*, Plate 13, 2, height $7\frac{1}{4}$ inches (Dottore), and Plate 13 (beggar); Mackenna, *Chelsea (triangle)*, Fig. 74 (Chinese boy); *Untermyer Cat.*, Fig. 13 (Pantalone).

[3] Victoria and Albert Museum, *Schreiber Collection Cat.*, I, no. 122. This popular model still figured in the Chelsea sale of 1755.

[4] Bellamy Gardner, 'Origins of design in old Chelsea porcelain,' *Connoisseur*, CVI, 1940, p. 3; *Schreiber Cat.*, no. 127; coloured example in the Willett Collection, Brighton Museum.

hardly have been based on the profile medallion struck to commemorate the Duke's victory at Culloden in 1746, as Dr. Bellamy
Gardner has suggested. Roubiliac's name has been mentioned in
connection with the more sensitive bust of *George III as Prince of
Wales* (1) (post-dating his brother Frederick's death in 1751),[1] but
falls quite out of question for the very large bust of George II,[2] which
with its separately modelled pedestal measures $17\frac{1}{2}$ inches high. A
small *head of a young child*, once supposed to portray Roubiliac's
daughter Sophie, is more likely to have been copied from a French
bronze.[3] The death of Frederick, Prince of Wales, in 1751 is commemorated by a large white group of *Britannia mourning*; she sits
on a globe over a dejected lion and gazes at a blank shield on which the
features of the deceased may once have been rendered in unfired oil
paint.[4] It is possible that various sculptors at the time prepared models
in the hope of obtaining a commission to carve a monument, and that
one of these, or a cast of it, reached the Chelsea factory. But the
Britannia is closely related in style to other Chelsea figures such as the
Ceres (2) and the Levantine women (3), and probably by the same
modeller. A quite different model of the same subject, on a smaller
scale, appears among the porcelain figures of the 'girl-in-a-swing'
family, whose origin remains so uncertain (4).[5]

The 'raised anchor' models so far mentioned all appear to have
been copied from plastic originals made elsewhere. But the factory
now had its own modeller. Not, perhaps, an inventive genius, he
soon developed an extraordinary flair for re-creating engraved designs
as three-dimensional models for porcelain. A series of twenty or more
birds perched on tree-trunk bases were thus adapted from the illustrations of George Edwards' *Natural History of Uncommon Birds* (London, 1743–7).[6] Many 'raised anchor' figures were left 'in the white', or

[1] 11 inches high. King, *Chelsea Porcelain*, Plate 15; *Cheyne Book*, no. 212 (there
attributed by Mrs. Esdaile to Roubiliac). The model is also known in Staffordshire
colour-glazed earthenware.

[2] *Schreiber Cat.*, no. 126; *Untermyer Cat.*, Fig. 10. An example in the British
Museum has unfired oil painting and gilding. The late Mrs. K. A. Esdaile did not
accept the attribution of the model to Roubiliac; Rysbrack's name also has been
mentioned, but not by Mrs. Webb in her monograph. One porcelain example has
been attributed to the Plymouth factory, without justification. The paste of these
large busts is greyer than usual in Chelsea porcelain.

[3] Mackenna, *Chelsea (triangle)*, Fig. 83; *E.C.C. Trans.*, vol. 1, no. 3, 1935,
Plate VI.

[4] King, *English Porcelain Figures*, Fig. 1 (as Bow); later tested and found
non-phosphatic, *British Museum Quarterly*, II, no. 1, p. 31.

[5] See p. 77.

[6] Bellamy Gardner, 'The Chelsea birds,' *E.P.C. Trans.*, no. III, 1931, p. 55.

(1) *Plate* 9; (2) *Plate* 1; (3) *Plate* 5; (4) *Plate* 32.

handed over to independent outside decorators for painting in unfired oil-colours which have since worn off, leaving only slight traces behind; the surviving account-books of William Duesbury frequently refer to Chelsea figures so decorated by him between 1751 and 1753.[1] But the birds are excellently painted in rather strong, harsh, enamel colours that include a glossy brick red, a warm purple-brown, and a transparent turquoise. Queer straggling patches of moss, in clear turquoise laid over short strokes or vermiculations in black, are seen on the bases of these and other raised-anchor figures, and human faces are sometimes painted in an unpleasantly dark red.

Of far greater interest than the birds is a series of large standing human figures mostly on low square bases. First come two *ladies in Turkish dress* (1),[2] their somewhat limp and boneless character being due less to the modeller than to the engravings by Ravenet after Boucher from which they were adapted. The modeller has given a far more robust and personal interpretation to a third engraving from the same suite (*Fille de St. Jean de Patmos, Isle de l'Archipel*) in the figure formerly identified by English collectors as a 'gardener's companion'[3]—a heavily-built young woman leaning forward, with a flower-basket on a hummock under her right hand, and an irregular rustic base. Of two figures from the Italian Comedy, the masked *Dr. Baloardo*[4] strides forward enveloped in a black coat, with a letter tucked into his belt inscribed 'Memoire Disabella 1750' (presumably the date of the model). He is apparently adapted from a foreground figure in an engraving by C. N. Cochin after Watteau entitled *L'Amour au Théâtre Italien*.[5] On the other hand his companion, the majestic lady in sixteenth-century dress who passes for *Isabella* herself (2), is taken from a woodcut in an early Venetian book on costume

[1] *William Duesbury's London Account Book 1751–53* (E.P.C. Monograph, ed. Mrs. D. A. MacAlister), London, 1931. Some of the cursory descriptions, which apparently refer to Chelsea figures, suggest that certain supposedly red-anchor models may have been introduced earlier.

[2] Former Lady Ludlow Collection; reproduced by permission of Major-General Sir Harold Wernher, Bt. See A. Lane, 'Chelsea porcelain figures and the modeller Joseph Willems,' *Connoisseur*, CXLV, 1960, pp. 245–51, Figs. 1–4, with the engravings 'Femme du Levant' and 'Dame de Constantinople'.

[3] King, *English Porcelain Figures*, Fig. 17 (white); and Bellamy Gardner, *Connoisseur*, LXV, 1925, p. 150, who suggests that the figure was based on a model by Roubiliac. Mackenna, *Chelsea (triangle)*, Plate 85 illustrates a second coloured example. Illustrated with engraving, A. Lane, *Connoisseur, loc. cit.*, Figs. 5, 6.

[4] $11\frac{1}{4}$ inches high. Savage, Plate 10 (Katz Collection). The authenticity of other examples, including that in the Lady Ludlow Collection at Luton Hoo, has been rightly questioned.

[5] Dacier and Vuaflart, *Jean de Julienne et les graveurs de Watteau*, Fig. 271.

(1) *Plate* 5; (2) *Plate* 6.

where she is described as a 'Noble French Matron of Orleans'![1] The same book contains a woodcut from which was adapted, with the pose in reverse, a coloured Chelsea figure of a *peasant girl selling roses*.[2] Engravings by Balechou and Aveline after Boucher were used for the coloured group of a standing *Chinese Lady with two children*,[3] one of which is modelled separately from the main group, and for another splendid white group of a *Chinese Lady and child playing with a cat* (1).[4] A figure of a *dwarf wearing a high hat*[5] derives from an engraving by Callot, and was later provided with a female companion, during the 'red anchor' period. This whole range of rather large figures, mostly from 9 to 11 inches high, shows an increasingly confident breadth of handling, and a nobility of attitude that continued for the next thirteen years to be characteristic of the best work done at Chelsea. We find their immediate successors in the 'red anchor' period. It is a natural assumption that this prevailing factory-style was the creation of one particularly gifted master-modeller. Reasons have already been given for discarding the idea that it owed anything to the sculptor Roubiliac.[6]

The creator of the Chelsea 'factory style' was undoubtedly Joseph Willems (*b.* Brussels 1716; married at Tournay 1732).[7] The exact date of Willems' arrival in England is unknown, but a pair of painted terracotta figures in the Ashmolean Museum, Oxford, bear his incised

---

[1] Cesare Vecellio, *Degli Habiti Antichi e Moderni di tutto il Mondo: di nuovo accresciuti di molte figure*, Venezia, 1590, pp. 269, 270. Woodcut reproduced, A. Lane, *Connoisseur*, CXLV, *loc. cit.*, Figs. 7, 8. Bellamy Gardner, 'Chelsea figures from the Italian Comedy,' *Apollo*, XXXIX, 1939, p. 338 mistakenly seeks the source in the 'Recueil Fossard' (*Recueil de plusieurs fragments des premières Comédies Italiennes qui ont esté représentées en France sous le règne de Henry 3*, ed. A. Beijer, Paris, 1928). Another example of this rare figure in Boston, Mus. of Fine Arts, *English Porcelain Figures*, Figs. 19, 20.

[2] *Connoisseur*, CXLV, *loc. cit.*, Figs. 9, 10, with woodcut from Vecellio, pp. 191, 192, 'Donzelle contadine di Parma.' See also Bellamy Gardner, 'Chelsea porcelain rarities,' *Connoisseur*, CX, 1942, p. 126.

[3] King, *Chelsea Porcelain*, Plate 18, 8⅞ inches high; the engraving is entitled *Les délices de l'enfance*.

[4] A coloured example published by Bellamy Gardner, 'An early Chelsea group with the raised anchor,' *Apollo*, XXIX, 1939, pp. 32–3. The engraving is entitled *Le mérite de tout pais*.

[5] Victoria and Albert Museum, *Schreiber Coll. Cat.*, I, 131, with the female companion. For the source, see p. 52 above.

[6] See p. 30.

[7] W. H. Tapp, 'Joseph Willems, china modeller, died 1766,' in *Connoisseur*, CI, 1938, p. 176; documentary sources more reliably quoted in H. Soil de Moriamé, *Les porcelaines de Tournay*, Tournai, 1910, pp. 95, 96, and C. Deroubaix, *Les porcelaines de Tournai*, 1958, p. 77. (See Appendix I, p. 133 below.)

(1) *Plate 7.*

signature 'Willems' and the date 1749.[1] Their subjects, a dancing youth and girl in contemporary dress, are highly appropriate to porcelain, and Willems was probably engaged as modeller by his fellow-countryman Sprimont in that same year. The rate-books show 'Mr Williams or Mr Sprimont' as occupiers of a house in Chelsea between 1755 and 1758, and between 1760 and 1766 'Mr Williams' showed models at the annual exhibitions of the newly-formed Society of Artists of Great Britain. In Mortimer's Universal Director for 1763 appeared the notice: 'Willems, Joseph, Modeller, at the Brussels Coffee House, Chelsea; this artist teaches Drawing, Modelling, and has modelled for the Chelsea China Manufactory for many years.' The decline of the factory had then begun, and Willems needed to eke out his livelihood. Early in 1766 he accepted an invitation to join the porcelain-factory at Tournay, only to die there six months later. An inventory of his effects included twenty-seven terracotta models and a large collection of drawings and engravings, covering between them the whole range of figure-subjects treated at the Chelsea factory.[2] He had evidently carried with him to Tournay the full equipment of a chief-modeller of porcelain.

The signed terracotta figures of 1749 show a ponderous realism. Heavily built, with disproportionately short legs, they convey little of the intended sense of movement; the bodies lack the curve, the tilt of hips and shoulders, necessary to compensate for the displacement of weight on to one foot. The faces are broad, with full cheeks curving down to a pointed chin, arched brows, and eyes set wide apart. The lips are parted in a half-smile, and in profile there is a strong suggestion of double chin. The heavy folds of the dresses suggest some thick, blanket-like material. Some or all of these characteristics are typically found in the Chelsea porcelain figures made during the next fourteen years. A porcelain cane-handle in the form of a woman's head[3] comes near in style to the terracotta figures, and as this is made in the 'triangle' paste, with appropriate colouring, it suggests that Willems was already working at the factory in 1749–50.

Red-anchor period, ca. 1753–7. Chelsea figures with the painted red-anchor mark show that from about 1753 onwards the factory profited much by study of the Meissen figures made during the previous decade, but now for the first time commonly to be seen in England. They brought a revelation not only of how porcelain might be handled, but also of its full range of appropriate subjects. Many

---

[1] A. Lane, 'Chelsea porcelain figures and the modeller Joseph Willems,' *Connoisseur*, CXLV, 1960, pp. 245–51, Figs, 12–14.
[2] Quoted in Appendix I, pp. 135–6.
[3] *Connoisseur*, CXLV, 1960, p. 250, Fig. 18.

Meissen models were literally copied, and even original designs were couched in the same general idiom. But the boisterous, satirical quality of the German figures was at Chelsea replaced by a gentler mood; the modelling was less sharp, the movement more leisurely. To some extent this difference was inherent in the nature of the soft-paste material. The fine-grained white paste, less opaque-looking and cold in tone than during the raised-anchor period, was evenly and not too thickly covered by a clear glaze usually quite free from crazing. It has a softly luminous effect whose beauty, in the figures, is greatly enhanced by the sparing washes of pale colour—especially rose-pink, mauve, turquoise and straw-yellow. Slight floral sprigs on the dresses were pencilled in fastidiously sensitive outline, and stronger accents in black, red and yellow-green were confined to hats, shoes, and the leaves and flowers applied to the square or pad bases. Flesh tones were well suggested by faint graded washes of salmon-pink, used in a darker shade on the lips. There was at first very little gilding.

In March 1754 the factory advertised a fourteen-day auction-sale of its recent productions, and similar sales followed in 1755 and 1756. Catalogues of the last two have fortunately survived,[1] and are of great value in identifying and dating the models. More figures were offered in 1755 than in 1756, which had few new models to add. It thus appears that most of the known red-anchor groups and figures were created in 1755 and the immediately preceding years. But the 1755 Catalogue also included the *nurse* and many birds, raised-anchor models that had retained their popularity. A 'fine large figure representing winter'[2] and an unmarked *Aesop*,[3] shown as a hunchbacked negro after an engraving by Francis Barlow, could also be early models related to the raised-anchor *Isabella*. Curiously enough figures composing a set often appear as disconnected items in the Catalogues, and except for a shepherd with nine animals no more than about five small figures are offered together. We can fairly assume that red-anchor-marked figures not mentioned in either catalogue date either from 1753–4, or else from 1756–7. To this last category belong some small family groups with wide Rococo bases. In 1757 Sprimont

---

[1] The 1755 Catalogue (copy in the Victoria and Albert Museum Library) is published in full in W. King, *Chelsea Porcelain*, pp. 69–130. The 1756 Catalogue, first reprinted at Salisbury in a limited edition by R. W. Read in 1880, forms a convenient appendix in G. Savage, *18th-Century English Porcelain*. No copy of the 1754 Catalogue has been found.

[2] King, *Chelsea Porcelain*, Plate 16; unmarked, 12 inches high. The companion *Seasons* are not mentioned in the Catalogues and surviving examples await discovery. The *Ceres* and *Bacchus* (Mackenna, Figs. 112, 133) appear to belong to a later series of Seasons.

[3] *E.P.C. Trans.*, IV, 1932, p. 17, with engraving; Savage, Plate 15b. Not in the 1755–6 Catalogues.

announced that owing to his illness no sale would take place, and in 1758 Sir Everard Fawkener died. For about a year the factory was apparently closed, many of the workmen transferring to the Bow factory. But in 1759 annual sales were resumed under Sprimont's sole proprietorship. That year, or the end of 1758, may be regarded as the beginning of the 'gold anchor' period.

A brief survey of the red-anchor figures[1] may begin with the allegorical subjects. In a set of five very large seated male and female figures representing the *Senses*, the best are *Sight*, a man with an eagle, and *Smell*, a man with a perfume-vase and a dog (1).[2] These rank with the most impressive of all European porcelain-sculptures. The complex, twisted poses, offset by heavy diagonal folds of drapery, are broadly handled in the full Baroque manner, and the wide-browed faces are full of character. Willems was notably more success-ful with seated than with standing figures. The four *Seasons* appear in at least five different sets, of which the most vivacious and original shows the small single figures in contemporary peasant dress standing on low circular bases (2). The grouped pairs of *Seasons* as putti on low rock bases are borrowed from Meissen models,[3] as is a group of four putti with a tree.[4] Later *Seasons*, one set with single peasant children, the other with children in pairs, are mounted with candlesticks on wide heavily scrolled Rococo bases.[5] The *Continents* appear as children in pairs on two candlesticks, after Meissen models.[6] *Fame*, described in the 1756 Catalogue as 'a most beautiful lustre, richly embellished with flowers and a fine figure of a woman sounding a trumpet', must have been a very large figure which has apparently failed to survive. The *Arts* and *Sciences* are each represented by charming miniature sets of children.[7]

Subjects from classical mythology start with a series of nine *gods* and *goddesses* mentioned in the 1755 Catalogue (3), where Jupiter is

[1] See Lord Fisher, 'Nicholas Sprimont and his red anchor figures,' *Apollo*, XXXIX, 1944, pp. 122–31 for an excellent detailed survey of these models and their Meissen originals.

[2] *E.P.C. Trans.*, no. II, Plates 1, 2 (whole set); Savage, Plate 18a (*Hearing*); Boston Museum of Fine Arts, *English Porcelain Figures* (Picture Book), Figs. 29, 30 (*Sight* and *Touch*).

[3] Savage, Plate 30.

[4] Mackenna, Figs. 122, 123, with a later inferior version.

[5] Mackenna, Figs. 124–8.

[6] *Cheyne Book*, no. 253; Mackenna, Figs. 136, 137.

[7] V. &. A. Museum, *Schreiber Cat.*, no. 135 (Arts); *Cheyne Book*, no. 196, Mackenna, Fig. 117, E.C.C. *Exhibition Cat.*, 1948, no. 272. (Sciences seated on pedestals, after Meissen models.)

(1) *Plate* 12; (2) *Plate* 18; (3) *Plate* 10.

described as 'exceeding fine, high'.[1] They measure from 10 to 12 inches, and stand on small square bases. Closely similar but slightly larger figures of *Ceres* (1) and *Bacchus* are not catalogued, and may belong to a set of Seasons.[2] Although a parallel series of gods was modelled by Eberlein at Meissen between 1741 and 1747, the Chelsea figures are quite independent; in their slightly awkward stance, as well as in facial features, they show the hand of Willems. A very large group of *Flora and Cupids*,[3] first mentioned in the 1756 Catalogue, is closely related in style, as are a reclining *river god* and *goddess*,[4] a scantily-draped '*Leda on a dolphin*' (1755 Catalogue), and accompanying figures of *children* riding on a *sea-horse* and on a *seal*.[5] These last three models have no bases and probably belonged to a set of table-ornaments. A large and complex group of *Perseus and Andromeda*,[6] a '*Sabine rape*',[7] and a *Leda with the Swan*[8] are all mentioned in 1755. Figures of *Atalanta and her dog*[9] and *Meleager with the boar's head* sit beside large pot-pourri vases on Rococo bases which, at Chelsea, look precocious for their early date (1755 Catalogue). Small *Cupids* ('Love in disguise' 'Cupids for a desart' (2)) appear as single figures, some copied from Meissen, and also in groups of three or four shaped for attachment to the top of a clock-case.[10] A large group of two *Cupids struggling with a dolphin* appears to have been copied from a French bronze.[11] Finally, the 1755 Catalogue mentions a set of four small 'bustos of heathen gods and goddesses' on pedestal bases.[12]

The red-anchor figures in contemporary dress show above all, in

[1] Savage, Plates 22, 23a (Venus, Mercury, Diana, Apollo); Mackenna (*Chelsea Red Anchor*), Figs. 109, 111, 114 (Mars, Apollo, Saturn); Jupiter is in the British Museum (Eckstein Bequest); Juno and Minerva have apparently not been recognized and published; *Cheyne Book*, no. 220, is a goddess lacking attributes.

[2] Mackenna, *op. cit.*, Figs. 112, 113.

[3] Savage, Plate 27, height 17 inches, mound base with tree.

[4] Mackenna, *op. cit.*, Figs. 103, 104.

[5] Mackenna, *op. cit.*, Figs. 105–7; Dixon, Plate 18.

[6] King, *Chelsea Porcelain*, Plate 42, height 11½ inches. This model was again listed, twice, in the 1761 Catalogue.

[7] Mackenna, *op. cit.*, Fig. 110.

[8] V. & A. Museum, *Schreiber Cat.*, no. 134, adapted from Boucher.

[9] Mackenna, Fig. 91. Examples of both in the British Museum.

[10] *Cheyne Book*, nos. 110–15, 165, 166. These are also found with gold-anchor marks.

[11] *E.C.C. Trans.*, vol. 4, part 5, 1959, Plate 24. The presumed bronze itself was doubtless a reduced version of a fountain figure of the same general kind as those with children at Versailles; see Charles Seymour, Jr., 'Versailles fountains; two sculptures from the Théâtre d'Eau in America,' *Gazette des Beaux Arts*, XXII, 1942, pp. 41–52.

[12] Mackenna, Fig. 108.

(1) *Plate* 11; (2) *Plate* 23A.

their choice of subject-matter, the influence of the Meissen street-criers modelled by Kaendler and his associates in the 1740's. Some of these are closely copied—the *map-seller* and the standing *salt-box player*; but other models appear to be original Chelsea creations.[1] Such are the *carpenter* with his bag of tools, two admirable *beggars* (1), two different *fishermen*, and a *fisherman's wife* (2). As with the Meissen figures, the low square or pad bases have applied and painted leaves and flowers. In pose, and in the simplified modelling of the dresses, the soft-paste figures lack the quick vitality of their Meissen counterparts, but this is amply compensated for by the exquisite material and colouring. A young *gardener* and his companion seated beside fruit-baskets are among the most vigorous of all Chelsea models (3); to them are related a seated *'Spanish sportsman'* and his companion[2] and a *gardener* and companion seated with baskets as flower-holders between their knees (this last pair imitated from Meissen).[3] The spirited Meissen group of two *Dutch dancers* or *Tyrolean dancers* first modelled by Eberlein in 1735[4] was twice revised by Kaendler, and the last version, which has a Rococo base, was closely copied at Chelsea.[5] A second Chelsea group with a pad base, in which the *dancers* are indubitably *Dutch*, is far more loosely composed and ponderous in movement, recalling in style the terracotta models in Oxford signed and dated by Willems in 1749.[6] These figures all fall into the category of 'Teniers' subjects referred to in the 1755 Chelsea Catalogue, as does the famous all-round *Maypole group* of a lady, gentleman and peasants dancing round two others on a central mound (4). The fiddler from the middle of this group is also known as a separate figure, and a wax 'master model' of the head and body, found among the old Chelsea equipment at Messrs. Copelands, is now in the Victoria and Albert Museum.[7] In the same vein is a charming series

[1] Mackenna, Figs. 143–5, 147–50; King, *Chelsea Porcelain*, Plates 32, 33; *Porcelain Figures*, Figs. 27, 28; *Untermyer Cat.*, Figs. 41–4.

[2] Mackenna, Figs. 140, 141.

[3] Savage, Plate 25.

[4] According to E. Zimmermann, *Meissner Porzellan*, Leipzig, 1926, p. 152, Eberlein modelled in 1735 two groups showing 'Dutch' and 'Tyrolean' dancers respectively, but if so, only one seems to have survived, with its later versions. Honey is unable to resolve the point (*Dresden China*, p. 111 and note 184).

[5] *Schreiber Cat.*, I, no. 137; *Untermyer Cat.*, Fig. 38.

[6] *Untermyer Cat.*, Fig. 37; Mackenna, Fig. 139. It is just possible that this reproduces the missing Eberlein group.

[7] Fiddler in the Katz Collection. Wax model, Victoria and Albert Museum, C. 57–1960, given by Mr. Alexander Lewis. A Bow imitation of the fiddler is in the Statham Collection.

(1) *Plate* 16; (2) *Plate* 17; (3) *Plates* 14, 15; (4) *Plate* 20.

of small peasant *family groups* or single figures (1)[1] on wide, heavily scrolled and gilt bases sometimes supported on raised feet. These are not identifiable in the 1755 or 1756 Catalogues, and with their more pronounced Rococo style may be regarded as an intermediate class between the 'red anchor' and 'gold anchor' periods, made both before and after the temporary closing of the factory in 1757–8. They are found with either the red-anchor or gold-anchor marks—in one case marks in both colours appear on the same piece. At least one of the models can be traced to a Meissen original.[2]

The numerous small red-anchor figures from the *Italian Comedy* (2) owe their vivacity to the Meissen originals from which most of them were copied. They are often shown playing musical instruments. 'A set of five figures *representing monkies* playing on musick in different attitudes' mentioned in the 1756 Catalogue suggests that only five were imitated from the Meissen 'monkey orchestra', which itself numbers over twenty pieces (3). A series of seated or standing *monks* and *nuns* (4) has parallels at Meissen and Bow, and derives ultimately from the current illustrated accounts of the various religious orders. Thus a charming *nun* with a ruff can be traced to one of these books dating from the late seventeenth century.[3] It is perhaps more surprising that Chelsea, with its Huguenot associations, should have produced in the seated *Madonna and Child* (1755 and 1756 Catalogues) one of the most successful religious groups in European porcelain.[4] Oriental figures include *Turks*, inspired by Meissen; an *'Indian Prince and his Queen'* shown as negroes (1755 Catalogue); *Chinese* of various sizes, one being an actor as 'a Chinese mask';[5] and most important, the very large all-round group of *three seated*

---

[1] King, *Chelsea*, Plates 11, 40, 41 (fruit gatherers and milkmaids with children, red anchor); King, *Figures*, Figs. 32, 33 and *Cheyne Book*, nos. 148, 149 (family at table, family eating off barrel, gold anchor), 147 (boy and girl eating cherries off tub, red anchor); Boston Museum, *English Porcelain Figures*, Figs. 33 (man selling fish, red anchor), 34 (couple shelling peas, gold anchor); *Untermyer Cat.*, Fig. 50 (musical families, unmarked), 53 (vintners, red anchor).

[2] Boy and girl eating cherries off tub; Meissen example in the Wadsworth Athenaeum, Hartford, Conn., no. 17, 1531.

[3] Dixon, *English Porcelain of the Eighteenth Century*, Plate 22 (Cecil Higgins Museum, Bedford); Sotheby, Sale Cat., Nov. 8, 1960, Lot 147. The engraving of 'A noble Canoness of Cologne, St. Maria im Capitol', in Daniel Steudner, *Kurze und grundliche Historie von dem Anfang und Ursprung Gott-geweihten Orden aller Kloster Jungfrauen*, Augsburg, 1693, Plate XIV. (*Connoisseur*, CXLV, p. 250, Fig. 20.)

[4] King, *Chelsea Porcelain*, Plate 39. Still made in the gold-anchor period; see p. 72.

[5] Honey, *Old English Porcelain*, Plate IIc.

---

(1) *Plate* 24; (2) *Plate* 19A; (3) *Plate* 22A; (4) *Plate* 19B.

Chinese musicians and a boy ((1), 1756 Catalogue).[1] There is also a large urn with Chinese heads as handles, and with a seated Chinese at the base holding out a cup to the spout while a boy stokes the fire under the urn.[2]

The large raised-anchor portrait busts have only one successor in the red-anchor period—a delightful coloured *head of a laughing girl*.[3] It has been suggested that she is a portrait of the sculptor Roubiliac's daughter Sophie, but this cannot be seriously considered. Versions of the head are known in marble, terracotta, and bronze (in two sizes), probably all replicas of a popular work by an unidentified French sculptor, one example of which found its way to the Chelsea factory.

Gold-anchor period, ca. 1758–69. As already related, the factory was temporarily closed in 1757–8, after which it resumed full activity with Sprimont as sole proprietor. Sales were held in 1759, 1760, and 1761, then not till 1763, when the moulds and factory-premises were also offered, as Sprimont proposed to retire.[4] Nevertheless he remained in charge of a dwindling production till the sale of the factory to James Cox in 1769. The last sale of Chelsea porcelain took place in 1770.[5] The chief-modeller Willems left for Tournay early in 1766, and few if any new figure-models can have been made after that date.

From 1758 the paste was reinforced by including a high proportion of calcined bone-ash, and this encouraged the making of larger pieces with complicated projecting parts. A similar paste had long been used at the Bow factory, where some former Chelsea workmen had found temporary employment before rejoining Sprimont; but the formula need not necessarily have been transmitted by them, for it was now made public by Robert Dossie in his *Handmaid to the Arts* (London, 1758). With the new paste came a glassier and more thickly applied glaze, which was very subject to crazing and showed a green tinge where it collected in the hollows. Many items in the 1756 Catalogue had already been described as 'richly gilt', and profuse gilding now appeared on vessels and figures alike. The anchor mark came to be

[1] Another example, *Untermyer Cat.*, Fig. 39.

[2] Bedford, Cecil Higgins Museum, Dixon, Plate 25.

[3] Bellamy Gardner, 'Sophie Roubiliac in Chelsea porcelain,' *Connoisseur*, CII, 1938, p. 59; bronze there illustrated, p. 275. The porcelain head on loan to the Ashmolean Museum, Oxford, from Mr. Cyril Andrade. A terracotta version sold at Sotheby's, March 3, 1961. The porcelain head also illustrated by T. H. Clarke, *E.C.C. Trans.*, vol. 4, Plate 5, 1959, Plates 28d and e.

[4] Part of a copy of the 1761 Catalogue survives and is published by Mackenna, *Chelsea Porcelain, the Gold Anchor Wares*, 1952, pp. 77–95.

[5] Catalogue published by J. E. Nightingale, *Contributions Towards the History of Early English Porcelain*, Salisbury, 1881, pp. 1–14.

(1) *Plate* 21.

painted in gold by the gilders as they completed the decoration, but it still sometimes appeared in red.

In the gold-anchor period at Chelsea the main interest shifted from figures to large ornamental vases in a fantastic local variant of the Rococo style. The influence of Meissen, now engulfed in the Seven Years War, was replaced by that of the Sèvres porcelain vessels, with their rich coloured grounds. The figures differ from their red-anchor predecessors chiefly in being overloaded with sumptuous ornament. They characteristically stand on heavily scrolled bases with feet, and the supporting tree behind them breaks into a luxuriant *bocage* or bush with multiple leaves and flowers, to which sconces for candles are often added. Dresses are painted and lavishly gilt with heavy floral diapers and rosettes, which yet further distract the eye from the modelling. This is broadly handled and grand in effect, but seldom rewards closer inspection. The detail is far less thoroughly wrought than in the red-anchor period. With their small heads, long necks, and disproportionately short legs, the figures strike open-handed, theatrical attitudes empty of meaning. The oval faces show no emotion, only a vague amiability, with huge eyes and arched brows of exaggerated length. These, like the flesh tones, are painted in darker colours than before. If we discount the decoration, and consider the forms alone, we can see that they carry to a highly mannered conclusion a style already found in the larger figures of the red-anchor period—the style associated with the chief-modeller Joseph Willems. Light relief from that style had formerly been provided by the smaller figures made in the vivacious Meissen manner of the 1740's. In the gold-anchor period there were fewer direct imitations of Meissen, and the models chosen were those of the early 1750's, standing on Rococo bases.

A transitional class between the red- and gold-anchor styles has already been mentioned— the series of small peasant figures arranged singly, in pairs, or in *family groups* with children, on very wide scrolled bases.[1] One of these may be referred to in the 1761 Catalogue as 'A small Dutch groupe of gardeners'.[2] Also transitional in character are some small mythological groups with rockwork bases—a *Triumph of Galathea*[3] and *Mercury and Argus*;[4] and there is also a scroll-based *Mars and Venus*,[5] and a pair of groups in Lord Bearsted's Collection at Upton House showing *Hercules and Omphale* and

[1] See p. 69.
[2] An unpublished group answering this description is in the Museum of Fine Arts, Boston.
[3] *Untermyer Cat.*, Fig. 52.
[4] Victoria and Albert Museum.
[5] King, 'Some notes on gold anchor figures,' *Apollo*, XXXIX, 1944, p. 133, Fig. 3 (Lord Fisher's Collection).

Hercules Slaying the Hydra. The 1761 Catalogue further mentions a *Pyramus and Thisbe* and a *Death of Adonis*. The fine large children as *Continents* (1) are early gold-anchor models better known in later Derby imitations. Many red-anchor models, including the large seated *Five Senses* and *Leda and the Swan*, were re-issued with added bocages and scroll bases, and the *Madonna and Child* of 1755 appears again in the 1761 Catalogue 'upon a Pedestal of the fine mazarine blue enriched with gold'.[1]

It is unfortunate that no Catalogues of the 1759 and 1760 sales survive, and only a fragment covering the first four days of the sale in 1761. In the latter we can identify a group of '*pilgrims seated under a tree*'[2] and a '*gypsy telling a Lady's fortune under a tree*, upon a rich gilt ornament foot'.[3]

The *shepherd* and *shepherdess* theme constantly recurs, and is represented by some of the largest and most elaborate surviving gold-anchor models. Such are a standing pair, the *shepherd with dogs* and the *shepherdess with sheep*, adapted from a Meissen pair of the early 1750's (1);[4] and the two huge seated groups with bocages—the well-known *music-lesson* after Boucher,[5] and the less familiar *dancing-lesson* in the London Museum (2), where the shepherd and shepherdess are teaching two dogs. In the same vein are the splendid figures of a *harvester* and companion,[6] and paired groups of figures in fancy dress representing the *Seasons*.[7] The impressed mark 'R' of an unidentified 'repairer' is often seen on such pieces, and at one time inspired the wholly untenable idea that they were modelled by the sculptor Roubiliac. Bocage candlestick-groups of animals and birds in some cases illustrate Aesop's *Fables*, after the editions with Barlow's engravings, and have bases inscribed accordingly ('The Vain Jac-daw' and so on).[8] Apart from a pair of seated *Chinese* with flower-holders,[9] and a large pair of *actors in Turkish dress*,[10] oriental themes were no longer represented, and the Italian Comedy subjects had also passed

---

[1] Perhaps identical with the example from the Eckstein Bequest in the British Museum. [2] *Untermyer Cat.*, Fig. 58.
[3] A. Hayden, *Lady Ludlow Collection*, no. 205.
[4] For the Meissen originals, Berling, *Festive publication*, 1911, Plate 13, nos. 5 and 7.
[5] *Schreiber Cat.*, no. 197; *Untermyer Cat.*, Fig. 73. Two examples appeared in the Chelsea Sale-Catalogue for 1769 and again in 1770, when one was sold for only £8 15s. [6] *Schreiber Cat.*, no. 196; the companion at Fenton House, Hampstead.
[7] *Schreiber Cat.*, no. 198; *Untermyer Cat.*, Fig. 74.
[8] *Untermyer Cat.*, Fig. 76; *E.C.C. Trans.*, vol. 2, Plate XLVIII (Dog with the Clog, Woman killing the Cock).
[9] *Cheyne Book*, no. 233; *E.C.C. Trans.*, vol. 2, no. 8, Plate XLVIII.
[10] *Schreiber Cat.*, no. 201; Mackenna, *Chelsea (gold anchor)*, Fig. 108.

---

(1) *Plates* 22B, 23B; (2) *Plates* 26, 27; (3) *Plate* 29.

out of fashion. Instead, we have the set of eight slender *'Ranelagh'* *masqueraders* dancing or playing musical instruments (1), which achieve a swiftness of movement altogether exceptional in the gold-anchor period. Figures in somewhat similar dresses appear in a print by Bowles after Maurer representing the masquerade ball held at Ranelagh Gardens in May 1759. Equally topical are the inscribed figures, mentioned in the 1761 Catalogue, of the *English dwarf* John Coan and the *Prussian dwarf* David Gabarisco,[1] dressed respectively as a Beefeater and a Cossack; these were contemporary showmen. Only one unglazed example survives of a large group showing *King George III and Queen Charlotte*, perhaps taken from an engraving made at the time of their marriage in 1761.[2] The many smaller gold-anchor figures hardly call for individual mention, except perhaps for a *night-watchman* and companion[3] copied from the later Meissen series of 'Paris Cries' made in 1753.

We may pass to a series of works which represent the culmination of Joseph Willems' career as modeller at Chelsea. A series of *Apollo* and the *Nine Muses* (2)[4] on high scrolled detachable bases inscribed with their names, are closely related to the red-anchor gods of 1755, though more perfunctory and mannered in their modelling. Willems had always had aspirations for sheer size in his porcelain figures, and this was greatly encouraged by the more stable paste containing bone-ash that was adopted after 1758. A very large group of two scantily-draped female figures standing before a parapet represents *Liberality* and *Modesty*, literally copied from an engraving by Sir Robert Strange after Guido Reni published in 1755.[5] The stark effect of the sculptor's model has not been tempered in any way to suit the needs of the por-celain material, apart from the irrelevant applied leaves and flowers. The same sculptural quality is seen in a big group of the *Deposition from the Cross*, possibly based on an engraving after Van Dyck;[6]

---

[1] Mackenna, *op. cit.*, Fig. 95; A. Hayden, *The Lady Ludlow Collection*, nos. 198, 199.

[2] *Untermyer Cat.*, Fig. 57.

[3] *Untermyer Cat.*, Fig. 55; also in the Victoria and Albert Museum.

[4] Mackenna, *op. cit.*, Fig. 103 (whole set); King, *Porcelain Figures*, Fig. 38 (Clio), and *Chelsea Porcelain*, Plate 62 (Urania and Thalia). A whole set in Lord Bearsted's Collection at Upton House.

[5] Mackenna, *op. cit.*, Fig. 91 (coloured, unmarked, height $16\frac{1}{2}$ inches): Detroit Institute of Fine Arts, Exhibn. Cat. 1954, no. 168 (white, from the Rhode Island School of Design, Providence).

[6] Mackenna, *Chelsea (red anchor)*, Fig. 19, coloured but unmarked; King, *Chelsea Porcelain*, Plate 64, white, with mazarine blue and gilt pedestal attached, 15 inches high.

(1) *Plate 25*; (2) *Colour Plate A.*

this is known in coloured and in glazed white examples, the latter standing on a high base with 'mazarine blue' ground and gilding. A terracotta group representing this subject was in Willems' possession when he died at Tournay in 1766, and it can hardly be coincidence that a Tournay group in biscuit-porcelain repeats the Chelsea group with minor variations.[1] It was presumably modelled by Willems or under his supervision, in the last months of his life. Willems' taste for borrowing themes from the seventeenth-century Baroque is again manifest in the very large *Roman Charity* group (1),[2] or the aged Cimon in prison nurtured by his daughter Pero—this adapted from an engraving by William Panneels after Rubens' painting in the Prado. A terracotta model of this curious and rare subject was among those left by Willems when he died. A huge figure of *Una* (or Britannia) on a scrolled base stands no less than 26 inches high.[3] These outsize groups and figures appear grotesquely large for porcelain, and reflect the ambitions of Willems the sculptor, the contributor to the Society of Artists' Exhibitions of 1760–6. Yet if we consider in retrospect the earlier raised and red-anchor figures attributed to him, and especially the seated *Senses* and seated *gardeners*, we may gratefully recognize him as one of the most capable and distinguished of eighteenth-century modellers for porcelain.

As a postscript, it should be stated that a gold-anchor mark resembling that of Chelsea is commonly found on the figures and groups made by Samson of Paris from about 1870 onwards. These reproduce Derby as well as Chelsea models, and should be easy to recognize by their hard-paste material and thin, watery gilding.

The Chelsea 'toys'. Though few of them are purely decorative figures, we are bound to consider here the so-called 'Chelsea toys'—the tiny scent-bottles, bonbonnières, needle-cases, seals, etc. skilfully modelled in human and animal form. The view previously held, that these were a monopoly of Sprimont's Chelsea factory and its Chelsea-Derby successor, must be radically revised in view of recent study.[4] Reasons are given later in this book for believing that the initiative in developing the whole class of porcelain 'toys' was taken by the mysterious factory, probably also located in Chelsea, which made the *girl in a swing* and other related figures. This factory appears to have come to an end

[1] H. Soil de Moriamé, *Les porcelaines de Tournay*, Tournai, 1937, Plate 11.

[2] Other examples, King, *Chelsea Porcelain*, Plate 4, *Untermyer Cat.*, Fig. 75.

[3] King, *op. cit.*, Plate 63; Savage, Plate 33, both unmarked. An example with the red-anchor mark is known.

[4] A. Lane and R. J. Charleston, 'The "girl-in-a-swing" porcelain and Chelsea,' *E.C.C. Trans.*, vol. 6, no. 2, 1960. An excellently illustrated corpus of the material is G. E. Bryant, *The Chelsea Porcelain Toys*, London, 1925.

(1) *Plate* 28.

in the late autumn of 1754, when its existing stock of 'toys' was acquired by Sprimont and offered for public auction. The notice of the sale, beginning December 16, 1754, studiously avoided stating that the items were *made* at the Chelsea factory, and went on to say that 'Nothing of the above kind was in their former Sale, nor will any Thing of the same Sort as this be sold from the Manufactory until after next year'. It may be inferred that Sprimont had as yet no models for making 'toys' himself, and did not expect to have any ready until 1756.

This inference is borne out by examination of the existing 'toys' themselves. Those that look early must almost all be attributed on grounds of style, or analysis of material, to the 'girl-in-a-swing' factory. Very few have characteristics of Sprimont's factory in the 'red anchor' period. There are, it is true, a number of cane-handles and patch-boxes in the form of human heads, in the style of Willems, and one of these was made in the 'triangle' paste of about 1749–50. But the heads would fit figures of a fair size; they are not miniatures. Willems was not by temperament a miniaturist, and only became one when Chelsea took over the market for 'toys' created by the 'girl-in-a-swing' factory. We may see his first attempts in a series of rare scent-bottles in the form of monks and nuns standing before a tree, one or two of whose branches terminate in a stopper (1).[1] With their clear, pale colours, these are of 'red-anchor' character, and may be dated about 1756; they look as if they might be imitated from Meissen originals.

Sprimont's programme for making toys probably got under full way only after the break in production in 1757–8. The numerous new models have characteristics of the 'gold anchor' period—or rather, of the small 'family groups' which mark the transition from 'red anchor'. A series of lively miniature figures of gardeners and sportsmen, 2 to $2\frac{1}{4}$ inches high, is found with the anchor mark either in red or gold.[2] The miniature scent-bottles commonly show chubby children or cupids standing before, or grouped round, a central tree terminating in a stopper (2). One of them bears the date 1759, on a letter which a little boy is writing.[3] The bonbonnières show the children sprawling on a hummock. The modelling is very much in Willem's style, and the bases and tree-trunks are covered with the same profusion of small flowers and leaves in relief as the larger figures of this

[1] Bryant, Plate 7; Plate 8, no. 5. King, *Chelsea Porcelain*, Plate 44.
[2] Bryant, Plates 56, 57.
[3] Bryant, Plate 15, no. 1 (British Museum).

(1) *Plate* 35G; (2) *Plate* 35H, I.

time. Flower-sprays in tooled gilding are seen under the bases of the scent-bottles, and there is plenty of rich gilding on the étuis and pipe-stoppers which terminate in the head of a lady or actor, with the head elegantly inclined to one side.[1] It is interesting to note that a few of the gold-anchor scent-bottles are adaptations, remodelled by Willems in his own style, from subjects treated earlier by the 'girl-in-a-swing' modeller.[2]

Of the tiny seals in human or animal form, the earliest all seem to be the work of the 'girl-in-a-swing' modeller, but here too Sprimont's factory later produced its own models. There was evidently a revival of making seals at Chelsea in the Chelsea-Derby period; Jewitt quotes the weekly bills between 1770 and 1773 which show the painters Boarman, Wollams and Jinks steadily painting 'toys', including twenty-six different models of seals.[3] The old models probably continued in use at Derby, along with some new ones, till the end of the eighteenth century. Late seals have green bases with a line of gilt round the edge.

[1] Bryant, Plates 51, no. 4; 52, no. 6; 53; 55, nos. 2, 3; 58.
[2] E.g. compare Bryant, Plate 26, no 5 (standing lovers, 'girl-in-a-swing') with his Plate 21, no. 5 (Chelsea).
[3] *Ceramic Art of Great Britain*, vol. I, pp. 180–1.

6

'GIRL-IN-A-SWING' FACTORY
(CHELSEA, SECOND FACTORY?)

A primitive white figure of a *girl in a swing* slung between two trees
(1)[1] has lent her name to a very puzzling series of figures and groups
which at one time were believed to be experimental productions of
Sprimont's Chelsea factory. All are the work of a single modeller, and
must have been produced within a few years round 1751. Frederick
Prince of Wales, who died in that year and was not long lamented, is
portrayed in profile on a medallion held by a seated figure of *Britannia
mourning*, with the lion at her feet (2).[2] A fable-group of the *stork*
and *fox* is evidently based on an engraving published in the *Weekly
Apollo* in 1752.[3]

In a recent study,[4] twenty-nine different models of this family
have been listed; and of about eighty recorded examples, two thirds
are left 'in the white'. None have a factory-mark; two short incised
lines meeting at an angle are seen under the base of one or two
pieces, but apparently have no significance. The fine-grained paste is
cold white, sometimes verging on greyish or greenish, and looks very
solid; it is a glassy frit composition akin to the Chelsea 'triangle'
paste, but is shown by analysis to contain a much higher proportion of
lead—usually from 17 to 20 per cent or more, probably due to the
inclusion of quantities of broken flint-glass. It was obviously most
unstable, and many of the figures have wilted or cracked in firing.

---

[1] The trees once ended in candle-sockets, now broken off. The curious nozzles
sprouting from the trees have holes probably for the insertion of bronze stems
with porcelain flowers.
[2] Other examples of the group, e.g. *Untermyer Cat.*, Fig. 9, show a different
and less crudely modelled lion, probably moulded from a bronze.
[3] Bellamy Gardner, 'Primitive Chelsea porcelain,' *Connoisseur*, CIX, 1942,
p. 35, no. II (now in Boston Museum of Fine Arts, Picture Book *English Porcelain
Figures*, Fig. 2).
[4] A. Lane and R. J. Charleston, 'The girl-in-a-swing porcelain and Chelsea,'
E.C.C. Trans., vol. 6, 1960, part 2, where all the previous literature is discussed.

---

(1) *Plate* 30B; (2) *Plate* 32.

The glassy glaze is so thin and close-fitting that it hardly impairs the modelling. As at Chelsea, the figures were made by 'slip-casting';[1] some are left open below, while others may have one or two large circular holes through the closed base, revealing the smooth unglazed hollow inside.

The unknown modeller lacked the sculptor's gift of communicating articulate movement to his figures, which tend to droop sideways with a languid air; and his knowledge of anatomy was rudimentary. But in 'porcelain-sense', in instinctive understanding of the material, he surpassed all his English contemporaries. His figures have remarkable clarity of outline; the draperies are simplified, and interest is concentrated on the crisply defined facial features and such details as bows and ribbons on the neck, elbow, knees or shoes. The faces are especially characteristic, with their deep-set eyes and short upper lip, receding below to a small pointed chin. The mouths are sensitive and deeply incised, though rather weak in expression, and with real finesse a tear is shown in relief on the cheek of the mourning Britannia. The slender limbs taper to delicate but quite unrealistic hands and feet. Unlike those of figures made in other factories, the bases are free from the clutter of applied flowers and leaves. Instead, some of them have curious incised marks of the size and shape of a finger-nail paring. The leaves on the trees flanking the *girl in a swing* herself have veins and sharp serrated edges. On a few other figures they are replaced by oak-leaves resembling those on Chelsea 'triangle' or 'raised anchor' figures. In many cases the tree terminates in a socket for candle or taper, formed of overlapping leaves. With their combination of naiveté and crisply-wrought detail, the figures have a quite peculiar charm.

Apart from certain Chelsea affinities to be mentioned later, the 'girl-in-a-swing' figures are strangely isolated. They borrow nothing from the work of other English factories or from Meissen. But the modeller was *au fait* with the practice of adapting subjects from engravings. His largest group, showing *Hercules and Omphale* (I), is from Laurent Cars' engraving after a painting of 1724 by Charles Lemoyne. Another group, fitted as a candlestick, is adapted from *Water* in Jacopo Amigoni's engraved series of *Elements*;[2] on the right a young man stands holding a fish, on the left a young woman sits on the ground, with a basket of fish beside her. A pair to this group, also

[1] See pp. 17–18.
[2] Lund, Sweden, Kulturenmuseum. *E.C.C. Trans.*, vol. 6, no. 2, 1960, illustration with the engraving. Amigoni's engravings of *Water* and *Air* reproduced by A. Toppin, *E.C.C. Trans.*, vol. 2, no. 10, 1948, Plate XC.

(I) *Plate 34.*

in the Museum at Lund, represents *Air*—a youth seated with a falcon and dove, a girl standing with a basket. This group differs completely from Amigoni's engraving of 'Air' and may be the modeller's own invention. The *girl with a basket* and *boy with a fish* from these two groups also occur as separate figures standing on the bevelled hexagonal bases with alternate convex and concave lobes that are peculiar to the 'girl-in-a-swing' class.[1] Other mythological groups, probably from unidentified engravings, show *Ganymede on the eagle* (1) and *Europa on the bull*,[2] again fitted as candlesticks.

But most of the subjects are in the pastoral vein of current fashion. A fine group shows a *gentleman kneeling before a lady* with a bird's nest in his hat (2). There is a pair of smaller groups each showing a *youth seated on the ground and a girl seated on a bank*, fondling respectively a dove and a lamb.[3] Single figures include a *sleeping girl* paired with a *seated youth with one hand to his lips*, both mounted as candlesticks;[4] a small pair of *vintners*;[5] and a *dancing girl* paired with a *boy playing the hurdy-gurdy* (3). These last have square bases with chamfered edges; they are known with contemporary painting, and also with painting of heavy gilt floral rosettes that must have been added about ten years after the figures were made, probably by the independent decorator James Giles.[6] A standing figure of the *Mater Dolorosa* (4) is a rare instance of this subject in English porcelain, and may have been inspired by a Spanish bronze or ivory-carving. Animals include a pair of seated *hounds*[7] on simple pad bases, well modelled, but with curiously protruding eyeballs; similar hounds are found in later Bow porcelain, perhaps derived from a common bronze original. Pairs of *birds*[8] seated on tree-stumps appear in three different

---

[1] *Connoisseur*, CIX, p. 37, no. VIII (girl, coloured, now at Boston); VII (boy, incorrectly restored holding a spade); Sotheby, Sale Cat., May 1, 1756 (Goldblatt), Lot 42, pair, coloured (now Niarchos Collection).

[2] *Connoisseur*, CIX, p. 36, no. VI (both groups); Dixon, *English Porcelain*, Plates 4b, 5a.

[3] T. H. Clarke in *E.C.C. Trans.*, vol. 4, no. 5, 1959, Plate 23a, b (coloured pair, S. J. Katz Collection).

[4] *Connoisseur*, CIX, p. 39, no. XI, coloured; also *Untermyer Cat.*, Fig. 1.

[5] *Untermyer Cat.*, Fig. 2 (coloured); *Connoisseur*, CIX, p. 38, no. X.

[6] Girl with later colouring in the Victoria and Albert Museum, *E.C.C. Trans.*, vol. 1, No. II, 1934, Plate XVII; boy with late colouring, Sotheby, Sale Cat., Nov. 3, 1959 (Dyson Perrins), Lot 171.

[7] *Connoisseur*, CIX, p. 36, no. IV (now Boston Museum); pair to it in the Victoria and Albert Museum.

[8] *Connoisseur*, CIX, p. 37, no. VIII; Honey, *Old English Porcelain*, Plate 2A, c. Others illustrated with a Chelsea original by Lane and Charleston, *E.C.C. Trans.*, loc. cit.

---

(1) *Plate* 30A; (2) *Plate* 33; (3) *Plate* 31B; (4) *Plate* 31A.

sizes, often fitted as candlesticks or taper-holders; all are progressively simplified adaptations from one original pair made at Sprimont's Chelsea factory about 1749–50. Their feet are curiously rendered— one pressed tight against the breast, the other sprawling sideways over the branch.

These birds are important as a rare instance where the 'girl-in-a-swing' modeller imitated what must have been already obsolete models made at another factory—Chelsea. Another such case is a model of *rustic lovers*,[1] a smaller, re-modelled version of the Chelsea group with the crown and trident mark shown in Plate 4. It is tempting to think that the 'girl-in-a-swing' modeller may himself have worked previously at Chelsea, perhaps as a 'repairer', and that he may have obtained possession of a defective example of this rare experimental group to serve as the basis of his own version.

Roughly one third of the surviving 'girl-in-a-swing' figures have painted decoration, in such an individual style as to suggest that it was all done by one man. This would hardly have been the case if the figures had been distributed among several independent 'outside' decorators. But similar painting is found on a very few pieces of porcelain from other sources—Chelsea, Meissen and Chinese.[2] It is thus possible that the artist had worked independently before joining the 'girl-in-a-swing' factory as a regular employee. His decoration on the figures consists mainly of sprigs of flowers with small leaves scattered singly over the dresses and bases, conspicuous among them being a large crimson rose with a thick curved stem. Smaller tulip-like flowers are painted in iron-red with pale yellow highlights. Flowers and leaves are both outlined in purple. The hair of the figures is done in streaks of chocolate-brown, deep yellow-brown, or black. There is iron-red on the lips, and in a faint smear on the cheeks and other flesh-tones. On some of the figures the flowers are gathered into a more sophisticated bunch, with outlines in black, but there are transitional stages suggesting that this was the work of the same artist as he grew more experienced.

The painting as well as the modelling form important links between the 'girl-in-a-swing' figures and a large proportion of the miniature scent-bottles, patch-boxes, bonbonnières, needle-cases and seals that have hitherto passed under the title of 'Chelsea toys', as the productions of Sprimont's Chelsea factory.[3] Recent study[4] suggests that the

[1] Lane and Charleston, *E.C.C. Trans., loc. cit.*; example in the National Museum of Ireland, Dublin.

[2] Raised-anchor Chelsea birds, Lord Fisher's Colln.; Meissen figure of Winter, Boston; both illustrated by Lane and Charleston, *E.C.C. Trans., loc. cit.*

[3] See especially G. E. Bryant, *The Chelsea Porcelain Toys*, London, 1925.

[4] Lane and Charleston, *E.C.C. Trans., loc. cit.*

whole class of 'toys' was invented and developed by the 'girl-in-a-swing' modeller, whose peculiar aptitude for miniature-work was already apparent in the detail of his larger figures. Analysis confirms that the very white paste of these 'toys' and the figures is the same, with an abnormally high content of lead. No doubt this paste, with its thin, close-fitting glaze, was particularly suitable for making very small objects by the slip-casting process. There is reason to believe that the 'girl-in-a-swing' factory closed down late in 1754, and that only after that date did Sprimont's Chelsea factory embark on a programme for making 'toys'.[1] Very few of the surviving 'toys' which can confidently be attributed to Chelsea show the characteristics of the 'red anchor' period, but a large number of models are in the 'gold anchor' style which developed after about 1757.

Miniature scent-bottles and similar objects were made in many of the Continental factories, but most of the surviving examples appear to date from the second half of the eighteenth century.[2] Some are actually imitations of Chelsea 'gold anchor' models. Miniature figures were made at Meissen before the outbreak of the Seven Years War in 1756, but even Meissen, responsible for so many porcelain inventions, appears to have made relatively few 'toys' of the kind we are discussing. These were an English speciality, and they have enjoyed a deserved popularity in Continental markets ever since they were first made. They struck exactly the note of sophisticated *galanterie* that appealed to the Rococo age.

The little figures on the 'girl-in-a-swing' scent-bottles mostly pose before a tree or some architectural object, at the top of which is the mouth with its stopper—in the form of billing doves, a butterfly, a flower. In Plate 35A Venus, Cupid and a spotted Dalmatian dog stand round a clock inscribed LHEURE DU BERGER FIDELLE. The dog reappears with a standing girl (*Fidelle me guide*)(1), and another girl asleep is guarded by a large mastiff (*Fidelle me garde*)(2). On a smaller scale, this is the same girl that we have met in the larger figures, with her characteristic head and the slender limbs tapering to tiny hands and feet. Scheemakers' monument to Shakespeare is reproduced both as a scent-bottle and as a miniature seal, these antedating the earliest Derby figures of this subject. Cupids alone or in pairs appear in a

---

[1] See also p. 75.
[2] The following articles illustrate Meissen and other Continental 'toys'. E. W. Braun, 'Porzellangalanterien aus der Sammlung Dr. Paul Ostermann in Darmstadt,' *Cicerone*, II, 1910, p. 12: idem, 'Die Sammlung von Porzellanflakons der Frau Cahn-Speyer in Wien,' *Kunst und Kunsthandwerk*, XVIII, 1915, pp. 1–21.

(1) *Plate* 35F; (2) *Plate* 35E.

variety of roles—as a drummer (*Iengage les cœurs*)(1), or busied at a furnace or alchemist's still (2). Other scent-bottles show pairs of lovers, Harlequin and Columbine, or a Chinese family. There are also scent-bottles, more ineptly modelled, in the form of standing dancers or Chinese, whose removable heads form the stoppers; and of stiffly modelled animals and birds, also with detachable heads. Patch-boxes in the form of a girl's head, sometimes with masks and inset brilliants for eyes, are conspicuously less realistic in their painting and modelling than similar objects in Sprimont's Chelsea porcelain. The painting of the 'girl-in-a-swing' toys is arresting for its bright, fresh colours, especially a crimson-pink and strong pale yellow. As on the larger figures, their hair is done in streaks of chocolate-brown. A simply stylized rose with leaves is commonly painted under the concave bases of the scent-bottles;[1] less often there is a more complex bouquet (both kinds of painting appear on the larger figures). Marbling in soft black under a transparent emerald green appears on pedestals or under the bases; or the base may be washed in pale green with soft purple-brown feathering towards the edge. Jagged flecks of bright orange-red often appear on the supporting tree-trunks. The inscriptions in often mis-spelt French invariably have some amorous suggestion, and are painted in black, or more seldom in red. There is no painted gilding, but the toys often have the most sumptuous gold mounts with Rococo scrollwork.

It may now be asked when, where, and by whom the 'girl-in-a-swing' figures and toys were made. There is so little evidence that the answers must depend largely on inference and conjecture. Sprimont's Chelsea factory can be ruled out at once as their source; the paste, colouring and modelling are quite distinct from those of the contemporary Chelsea 'raised anchor' porcelain. Yet there are significant links with Chelsea of the late 'triangle' period; the glassy paste is of the same general character; it was formed in the same way, by slip-casting; and the models of *birds* and of the *rustic lovers* group were imitated from Chelsea pieces of about 1749 which could not have been easily available to the public. One might conjecture that the 'girl-in-a-swing' factory was a small concern started by workmen who had left the Chelsea factory about the time of its reorganization under Sprimont in 1749. And indeed that not always trustworthy historian of the Staffordshire potteries Simeon Shaw, writing in 1829, has a story from one Carlos Simpson, aged sixty-three, who said he was born in Chelsea,

[1] Bryant had already noted the distinct character of what he calls the 'rose pattern' group of toys, and the corresponding series of seals. Pieces so classified in his book are all 'girl-in-a-swing'.

(1) *Plate* 35c; (2) *Plate* 35d.

where his father Aaron Simpson had gone in 1747 to work at the Chelsea China Manufactory, along with six other named Staffordshire potters.[1] 'They soon ascertained that they were the principal workmen, on whose exertions all the excellence of the Porcelain must depend, they then resolved to commence business on their own account, at Chelsea, and were in some degree successful; but at length owing to disagreement among themselves, they abandoned it and returned to Burslem, intending to commence there the manufacture of China; but soon after their return Aaron Simpson died, the design was relinquished and each took the employment quickly offered in the manufacture of white stoneware. . . .' Shaw's story can be confirmed in one vital particular; the registers of St. Luke's Church, Chelsea record on December 4, 1754, the baptism of 'Careless Simpson, son of Aaron Simpson and Elizabeth his wife'. We may reasonably assume that Simpson and his colleagues had been working at a second factory located in Chelsea. They would hardly have had the capital to finance it themselves. We learn from notices in the *Daily Advertiser* between March 3, 1749 and May 15, 1750, that Mr. Sprimont and his Manufactory at Chelsea 'was not concern'd in any Shape whatsoever with the Goods exposed to Sale in St. James's Street, called the Chelsea China Warehouse'. On the other side S. Stables, writing from that Warehouse in January 1751,[2] gave notice that 'my China Warehouse is not supply'd by any other Person than Mr. *Charles Gouyn*, late Proprietor and Chief Manager of the Chelsea-House, who continues to supply me with the most curious Goods of that Manufacture, as well useful as ornamental . . .'. These goods may have been the share of the original Chelsea stock that fell to Gouyn when he parted from Sprimont in 1749. But Gouyn was evidently still interested in porcelain, and thus a likely patron for a new factory which was not explicitly mentioned in the notice of January 1751, and might therefore not yet have advanced beyond experiment to actual production. Gouyn was by profession a jeweller; and the 'toys' later made by the 'girl-in-a-swing' factory, with their rich gilt mounts, were precisely the class of porcelain that a jeweller would wish to sell.

The earliest written reference to porcelain 'toys' we have is the notice of a sale by auction inserted in the *Public Advertiser* from November 23 till December 21, 1754. 'By order of the Proprietors of the Chelsea Porcelain Manufactory' Mr. Ford would sell on December 16 and four following days 'All the entire Stock of PORCELAIN TOYS, brought from their Warehouse in Pall-Mall; consisting of Snuffboxes, Smelling Bottles, Etwees and Trinkets for Watches (mounted

---

[1] *History of the Staffordshire Potteries*, Hanley, 1829, p. 167.
[2] *General Advertiser*, Jan. 29, 1751 (new style).

in Gold, and unmounted) in various beautiful Shapes, of an elegant Design, and curiously painted in Enamel. . . . Nothing of the above kind was in their former Sale, nor will any Thing of the same Sort as this be sold from the Manufactory till after next year'. This was the second Chelsea sale in 1754; in April the same paper had advertised the sale, by the same auctioneer, of 'The large, valuable and entire stock of the CHELSEA PORCELAINE, brought from the Manufactory and the Warehouse in Pall Mall'. The April notice went on to say that the Undertaker of the Manufactory had determined 'that he will positively not open his Warehouses, nor exhibit any Article to Sale, after this, till next Year'. The December 1754 sale thus came contrary to expectation, and certain points in the notice may be specially observed. Nowhere does it state or imply that the items offered were *made* by the Chelsea factory; they were to be brought 'from the Warehouse', not from 'the Manufactory'. The tone is quite different from the notices advertising the sale of April 1754 and the sales in March 1755 and subsequent years till 1763, which all speak of 'The last Year's large and valuable Productions of the Chelsea Porcelain Manufactory'. We may therefore infer that Sprimont had unexpectedly acquired a very large stock (the sale lasted five days) of 'toys' made elsewhere, having perhaps bought up the stock of the 'girl-in-a-swing' factory on its demise in the months preceding November 1754. A second point in the sale-notice is the statement that 'nothing of the above kind (i.e. toys) was in their former sale [i.e. April 1754], nor will anything of the same Sort as this be sold from the Manufactory till after next year'. Evidently Sprimont's factory had not hitherto made toys itself, nor did it expect to be in a position to do so till 1756.

To sum up then, the 'girl-in-a-swing' factory is likely to have been set up somewhere in Chelsea about 1749, by workmen who had seceded from the original Chelsea factory with the financial support of Charles Gouyn. Experiments did not result in effective production till some time in 1751—the probable date of the group of *Britannia mourning for Frederick Prince of Wales*. The earliest productions were figures (no useful wares have so far been identified), and at first these were left unpainted. Later the factory employed its own painter, and embarked on its main speciality—the new class of miniature porcelain 'toys'. The modeller remains anonymous; Shaw did not name him, doubtless because he was not a Staffordshire man. For unknown reasons the factory closed in the late autumn of 1754, when the entire stock was acquired and put up to public auction by the proprietors of the original Chelsea factory.

7

BOW

The important factory at Bow[1] (Stratford-le-Bow, Middlesex, in East London), was probably founded about the end of 1748, after earlier experiments, and flourished especially between 1750 and 1759, with Thomas Frye as manager and Messrs. Weatherby and Crowther as proprietors. (Alderman George Arnold, the first promoter, had backed out early in 1750.) In 1763 John Crowther, sole proprietor since Weatherby's death in the preceding year, was declared bankrupt. It has been suggested, without any evidence, that William Duesbury of Derby perhaps gave him the financial help that enabled him to continue the Bow factory till 1775 or 1776, when Duesbury finally bought it and removed the moulds to Derby. In its heyday three hundred hands are said to have been employed at Bow, including ninety painters. The huge output consisted mainly of useful wares, simpler and cheaper than those of Chelsea. But figures also were made in abundance, these too being relatively unsophisticated in style.

In 1744 Edward Heylyn of Bow, merchant, and Thomas Frye, an Irish painter and engraver (b. 1710, d. 1762) took out a patent for making a kind of porcelain with kaolinic clay from 'the Chirokee nation in America'. They had contact with the potter Andrew Duché, who since 1738 had attempted to make porcelain at Savannah in the new colony of Georgia. Twenty tons of the Chirokee clay were actually imported in 1743–4, but it is highly improbable that Heylyn and Frye ever succeeded in making porcelain from it. In 1748 Frye alone took out a second patent implying the use of calcined bone-ash as an ingredient. Analysis shows a high proportion of phosphate, from

[1] A satisfactory book on the Bow factory has not yet been written. Frank Hurlbutt, *Bow Porcelain*, London, 1926, contains useful illustrations. Especially valuable is the British Museum Exhibition Catalogue, *Bow Porcelain 1744–1776* (London, 1959, by Hugh Tait); and articles by the same author in *Apollo*, LXXI, Feb., April and June, 1960, pp. 40, 93, 181. Other illustrations here referred to are in G. Savage, *18th-Century English Porcelain*, London, 1952; and Y. Hackenbroch, *Chelsea and Other English Porcelain etc. in the Irwin Untermyer Collection*, London, 1957.

bone-ash, in all the porcelain which on various grounds can be attributed to Bow.

The work at Bow does not fall into sharply-defined chronological periods, but the first series of figures and groups to be discussed was probably made between 1750 and about 1754. Their distinctive style suggests that all were the work of a single modeller, who took most of his ideas from engravings, and only in a few cases adapted his models from Meissen figures. The earliest examples of his work yet identified bear the incised date 1750—a negress standing beside a large covered basket,[1] copied from a Meissen model; and a pair of large standing portraits, 10¼ and 10¾ inches high, of the actress *Kitty Clive* and the actor *Henry Woodward* as the Fine Lady and Fine Gentleman in Garrick's farce 'Lethe' (I).[2] They were based respectively on an engraving by Charles Mosley and a mezzotint by James McArdell after a painting by Hayman, both published in 1750. The figures are found either on low rectangular bases or on high pedestals with trophies in relief, and show coarse but competent modelling, with bits of paste applied to represent embroidery and other details of dress. (Two different, smaller versions of the Kitty Clive are known, one on a star-shaped base; these were made at the Derby factory.)[3] Other closely related figures show an actor (not James Quin) as *Falstaff*,[4] and another unidentified actor, probably David Garrick.[5] These and other early Bow figures are most often left 'in the white', and the paste has a pleasant creamy tone which distinguishes it from the cooler-looking, more finely-grained Chelsea material. Some of the Kitty Clive figures are left open at the base, and the thick walls and irregular surface visible inside show that they were formed by pressing the paste into the moulds by hand. Bow seems not to have adopted the 'slip-casting' method followed at Chelsea and Derby,[6] and the Bow figures are thus relatively heavy in weight.

[1] British Museum, *Bow Exhibn.*, 1959, no. 44, Fig. 6.

[2] *Ibidem*, no. 40, Fig. 18 (dated Kitty Clive, from the Fitzwilliam Museum, Cambridge). *Untermyer Cat.*, Fig. 241 (dated Woodward, and list of other examples). Savage, Plates 52, 53 (coloured).

[3] See p. 97.

[4] Victoria and Albert Museum, *Schreiber Coll. Cat.*, I, no. 2. The source is not the mezzotint by McArdell showing James Quin in the part, but an earlier engraving of 1743 by C. Grignion after Francis Hayman. See Raymond Mander and Joe Mitchenson, 'The china statuettes of Quin as Flastaff,' *Theatre Notebook*, XII, no. 2, 1958, pp. 54–8, Plates 3, 6. Also, A. J. Toppin in *E.C.C. Trans.*, vol. II, no. 10, 1948, p. 273, Plate C1.

[5] Sotheby, Sale Cat., Aug. 25, 1939 (Wallace Elliot), Lot 203; Cecil Higgins Museum, Bedford; Brighton Museum, Willett Collection (coloured, with falsely restored head).   [6] See pp. 17, 18.

(I) *Plates* 36, 37.

Similar in style to the actors is a series of standing or seated Muses (1),[1] most of which have their names 'Polimnie', 'Clion', 'Eraton for the Love', 'Euterpe for the musical instruments', etc. incised on the side or back by the 'repairer'—perhaps in a semi-literate attempt to translate the titles of the unidentified French engravings[2] from which they must have been adapted. The mark 'T' or 'To' impressed on some of them recurs on many later Bow figures, and is subsequently found on ornamental vessels and figures made at Worcester about 1770 and at Bristol a little later. It is believed to be the mark of a 'repairer' who worked successively at these factories, and who may be identified with the 'Mr. Tebo' (perhaps anglicized from the French 'Thibaud') who in 1774–5 gravitated to Wedgwood's factory at Etruria.[3] There he tried his hand at original modelling, and he may already have done the same at Bristol, Worcester and Bow. But if Josiah Wedgwood's low opinion is any guide ('Mr. Tebo is not equal to a figure'),[4] we should expect that any porcelain figures designed by Tebo would be tame pastiches of other modellers' work. He is most unlikely to have been the original modeller of the early Bow figures which, as 'repairer', he put together, and on which he impressed his mark. These we must continue to attribute to that fertile but anonymous artist, the 'Muses modeller'.

Including the actors and Muses already named, his style is seen in about forty surviving models. Some are quite complex groups. There is a large standing woman and children as *Charity* (2); a *fortune telling* group[5] with standing figures of an old man and a girl, from an engraving after Boucher; and seated groups of *lovers with a bird-cage* (3), lovers as *fisher-folk*,[6] and as *hunters*.[7] Three seated groups of Italian Comedy subjects may have been directly suggested by French engravings after Watteau, but were more probably derived from these through the Meissen porcelain versions—*Mezzetin and Isabella*,[8]

[1] A. J. Toppin, 'Some early Bow Muses,' *Burlington Magazine*, LIV, 1929, p. 88. From the set of nine, Calliope and Thalia have not yet been recognized in surviving examples.

[2] A. J. Toppin, 'The origin of some ceramic designs,' *E.C.C. Trans.*, vol. 2, 1948, Plate C1 shows that the Clio was probably adapted from the frontispiece to the works of the *Abbé de Saint Réal*, by D. Coster, about 1700.

[3] See also pp. 121, 125–6, for his presumed work at Bristol and Worcester.

[4] Letter to Bentley, July 3, 1775.

[5] Savage, Plate 44. A white example in the Victoria and Albert Museum. Tait in *Apollo*, 1960, p. 95, Figs. IV, V.

[6] British Museum, Bow Exhibition, 1959, no. 48a, Fig. 15.

[7] Dublin, National Museum of Ireland (unpublished).

[8] *Untermyer Cat.*, Figs. 240, 243; Toppin in *E.C.C. Trans.*, vol. 2, Plate CIII (with engraving).

(1) *Plate* 39; (2) *Plate* 42; (3) *Plate* 38, *after Lancret.*

Harlequin and Columbine,[1] and *Harlequin spying on two Lovers.*[2] Two very messy groups with Chinese figures symbolizing *Fire* and *Air*[3] come from Boucher engravings, and a large triangular group of two *Chinese kneeling before a goddess*[4] from an engraving after Watteau. Of the single figures, a large striding *bagpiper*[5] goes back to an engraving by Daullé, also adapted for a Meissen figure. A more original model shows a *Thames waterman*, bearing on his sleeve the fouled anchor badge of the Admiralty barge (1).[6] There are two *Minervas* of different sizes (2), a *Mercury*, a pair of *Turks*, a *boy and girl with grapes* (3), a pair of *gardeners*, and a *sailor with his lass* (4). Two large busts on pedestals, $10\frac{3}{4}$ inches high, show a fancy dress *Chinese man and woman.*[7] Most of the figures and groups have simple square or low rustic bases. At their best they show commendable vigour of pose and movement. But they were evidently designed to make their effect without the help of painting, and the heavy-handed modeller had much ado to conjure expressive detail from the soft material with its thick coat of glaze. Hence the prominent eyelids, the open mouths, the receding brow and chin, the deeply furrowed drapery, and the accents in relief provided by the exaggerated ear-rings, ruffles and strings of beads. It is probable that many of the figures that survive in the white were once painted in unfired and therefore perishable oil colours.

This work was entrusted to independent outside decorators such as William Duesbury, whose note-books mention figures of Mrs. Clive and Woodward that passed through his hands in 1751–2.[8] Duesbury charged 1s. 3d. to 5s. for painting a figure, according to size, and in a few cases specifies 'inhamild' decoration at about three times the price. His enamelled work has not been convincingly identified, and the very distinctive painting found on many Bow figures of the

[1] Toppin, *loc. cit.*, Plate CIII (with engraving).
[2] E.C.C. Exhibition Cat., *English Pottery and Porcelain*, 1948, Plate 36, no. 166.
[3] *Untermyer Cat.*, Fig. 239 (coloured); *Apollo*, 1960, p. 96, Fig. VII (white).
[4] Toppin in *E.C.C. Trans.*, vol. 2, Plate CII (with engraving).
[5] Savage, Plate 57 (white); W. King in *Apollo*, 1925, p. 154 (with engraving by Daullé after J. Dumont le Romain, 1739); coloured example in Victoria and Albert Museum.
[6] Not the prize-winning badge for the competition instituted by Thomas Doggett in 1715; see Mrs. E. J. Marshall, 'Porcelain figures of the china factory at Stratford-le-Bow,' *Apollo Annual*, 1951, pp. 12–16.
[7] *Untermyer Cat.*, Fig. 242; Savage, Plate 42. Bowcocke's accounts for April 1756 say 'Think of the Chinese head for Mr Weatherby' (Jewitt, vol. I, p. 209).
[8] Mrs. Donald MacAlister, *William Duesbury's London Account Book*, London, 1931, pp. 12, 27.

(1) *Plate* 41A; (2) *Plate* 41B; (3) *Plate* 40; (4) *Plate* 40.

'Muses type' was certainly done in the factory. It shows sprigs of large blue and crimson flowers on the dresses, and smeary washes of chocolate-brown, strong yellow, brown-red, and lilac, with a few touches of gilding laid over the darker colours. The untidy red mouths and black eyebrows look like over-emphatic *maquillage*. A dull pale green wash with streaks of brown appears on the bases—sometimes, too, there are large and clumsy applied leaves and flowers, these painted in orange-red. Another curious feature on some of the bases are patches of 'moss' in relief covered with punctures.

It is of interest to note that certain figures in the style of the 'Muses modeller', which must have been made in the years between 1750 and about 1754, already show rudimentary Rococo bases. Even at Chelsea these were uncommon before the late 'red anchor' period, about 1756–7. Thus a curious coloured figure of a *woman in seventeenth-century dress playing a lyre*,[1] closely akin to the early *Muses*, sits on a high four-footed scroll base with applied leaves and flowers. Pairs of Bow *sphinxes*,[2] which appear in an earlier and a later simplified version, perhaps owe their well developed Rococo scroll bases to the fact that they were copied from contemporary bronze ornaments. Two very large standing *boys with flower-baskets* on their heads, in classical dress (1),[3] may well have been imitated from a pair of bronze fire-dogs of a type which goes back to the seventeenth century, and which was also imitated in Delft earthenware. But these Bow figures of boys have misunderstood Rococo bases of a kind also seen on the *shepherd* and *shepherdess* with a bird-cage, symbolizing *Liberty* and *Matrimony* (2). The latter are fumbling adaptations of a pair of almost contemporary Meissen figures. A 'waster' found on the Bow factory-site corresponds exactly with the base of the figure of *Liberty*. There are slightly later versions of this pair of figures showing a more competent handling of the Rococo scrollwork, and a further stage is reached in the *shepherd and shepherdess* of Plates 46, 47, these also imitated, and much more closely, from Meissen originals.[4] In a close study of the early Bow figures one cannot fail to observe that improvements and modifications were going on all the time, calling for new sets of moulds

[1] Tait in *Apollo*, 1960, p. 97, Fig. IX (S. J. Katz Collection).
[2] *Apollo*, 1960, pp. 183–5, Figs. III, VII–XI.
[3] Victoria and Albert Museum, *Schreiber Cat.*, I, no. 32. Compare N. M. Penzer, 'The Royal fire-dogs,' *Connoisseur*, Antique Dealers' Fair Number, June 1954, p. 10, for a somewhat similar fire-dog of 1696. See also F. W. Hudig, *Delfter Fayence*, Berlin, 1929, Fig. 198.
[4] C. H. Fischer Sale Cat., Cologne, 1906, no. 441 (shepherdess); Victoria and Albert Museum, C. 147–1931 (shepherd).

(1) *Plate* 43; (2) *Plates* 44, 45.

and presumably new clay master models of the same subject. The modellers, and the painters too, were feeling their way.

There was thus no sharp division between the first phase at Bow and the second, which should correspond roughly with the 'red anchor' period at Chelsea, running from about 1754–9. In November 1753 the factory advertised in Birmingham for enamellers and painters, and for a 'Person who can model small figures in clay neatly'.[1] It now became a regular practice to paint the figures in enamel colours, instead of leaving many of them white; and with painting to supplement detail, the modelling began to lose its previously rugged character—in fact, it became 'neater'. Draperies were smoothed out, and the faces were simplified, though in shape they still recalled those of the early Muses. Indeed the 'Muses modeller', whoever he was, seems to have played a leading part in developing a new factory-style based on close observation of the Meissen models that had now become much commoner in England. Duesbury's note-book already refers in January 1753 to 'Bogh Sesons', but most surviving examples of this charming set of seated *Seasons* in contemporary dress probably date from about 1755 and later (1). Lists of orders drawn up in 1756 by John Bowcocke, general clerk to the factory,[2] help us to recognize other models then popular; the standing *huntsman* and companion ('sporters' (2)); a pair of *cooks* carrying dishes (3); *Harlequin*, *Columbine* and *Pierrot*;[3] a *Turk* and companion;[4] a small shepherd *bagpiper* and his dancing companion, with a dog and lamb at their feet;[5] 'fluters', fiddlers and 'Paris cries'. Direct imitations from Meissen are the *gallant throwing a kiss*, the group of '*Tyrolese dancers*', and the large standing woman representing *Smelling*, which was selected for imitation from Eberlein's Meissen series of the Five Senses and may at Bow have been called 'Flora'.[6] There are some dangerous modern fakes of Kaendler's Meissen Harlequins, which pretend to be Bow and have the mark of an anchor and dagger painted in red. A figure of *Spring* was pirated from the small Chelsea series of

[1] *Aris's Birmingham Gazette*, Nov. 5, 1753.

[2] Previously in the Royal Navy, he worked at Bow from 1753 till his death in 1763. Extracts from his papers are published in Ll. Jewitt, *Ceramic Art in Great Britain*, 1877, vol. I, pp. 206–13; they are now lost, except for a few in the British Museum (*Bow Exhib. Cat.*, 1959, no. 152).

[3] *Schreiber Cat.*, I, nos. 47, 48; Savage, Plate 54.

[4] Sotheby, Sale Cat., May 25, 1938 (Wallace Elliot), Lot 204; *Schreiber Cat.*, I, no. 33.

[5] These models are also found in Derby porcelain.

[6] *Schreiber Cat.*, I, no. 53 (gallant); King, *Figures*, Fig. 8 (dancers); Savage, Plate 43b (Smelling).

(1) *Plate* 50B; (2) *Colour Plate B*; (3) *Plate* 50A.

B. *Huntsman. Bow; about 1756.*
Height, 6¾ in. Victoria and Albert Museum.
(See p. 90)

standing *Seasons* (1), and figures of *monks* and *nuns* are common to both factories (2). The *pedlar* wearing late sixteenth-century dress in Plate 49 derives from a bronze figure.[1] Whatever their source of inspiration, these small Bow figures of the mid 1750's show a delightful freshness and naïveté that is thoroughly characteristic. By the alert tilt of the heads, the flexed knees, and the exaggerated turn of the body from the hips, they attain a spontaneity of movement which makes up for the sketchiness of the modelling. The painted decoration shows much variety. For an exquisite moment it was done in pale washes of mauve-pink, pale yellow, and opaque turquoise, with slight floral sprigs on the dresses. But Bow soon developed its typical palette of opaque light blue, deep crimson, yellow, and transparent emerald green, and in the later 1750's these strong colours were applied with a cheerfully discordant, even garish, effect. The rather painstaking flower-painting on the large *shepherd bagpiper* and *shepherdess*[2] in Plates 46, 47 represents a transition from the earlier 'Muses' style; here the Rococo scrolls on the base are outlined in purplish black. A later example of the same bagpiper, with crimson-scrolled base, bears the painted date 1757 and initials 'IB', suggesting that it was made for John Bowcocke himself.[3] The bases of the smaller figures were at first left plain, or decorated with applied leaves and flowers in relief. Then come painted scrolls in purple-black or crimson, and finally scrollwork in relief with touches of crimson. A rare figure of *Frederick the Great* of Prussia,[4] $9\frac{3}{4}$ inches high, stands on a pad base and has a separate pedestal with arms and trophies at the side, and is likely to date from the years of his great popularity in England soon after the outbreak of the Seven Years War in 1756. Unlike the more sophisticated Chelsea factory, Bow made relatively few mythological or allegorical figures. But *Neptune* astride a dolphin (3) and *Jupiter* astride an eagle[5] are spirited models, perhaps derived from seventeenth-century Baroque bronzes in the manner of Bernini. In another tamer series of *Elements* the deities stand more placidly beside their attri-

[1] Bronze examples in the Victoria and Albert Museum (A. 52–1953) and Wallace Collection (J. G. Mann, Cat. of *Sculpture*, 1931, no. S. 244, suggesting a Flemish origin and date in the second quarter of the nineteenth century).

[2] Perhaps the models referred to in John Bowcocke's accounts for May 1756 as the 'new shepherd and companion'.

[3] British Museum Exhib. Cat., 1959, no. 101, Figs. 31, 32.

[4] *E.C.C. Trans.*, vol. 4, part 4, 1959, Plates 2, 3; Sotheby, Sale Cat., May 31, 1945, Lot 104; do. April 30, 1957, Lot 152.

[5] The Neptune has been tested and found phosphatic. Jupiter in *Connoisseur*, LXXIX, 1927, p. 13, no. VI, $6\frac{1}{2}$ inches high (Wallace Elliot Collection), there wrongly attributed to Derby.

(1) *Plate* 18; (2) *Plate* 51; (3) *Plate* 48.

butes.[1] The large figure after the *Flora Farnese* will be discussed on a later page, though it too probably dates from before 1760. A peculiarity of the Bow figures which helps in their identification is a small square hole low down at the back, for the insertion of metal branches supporting candle-sconces or porcelain flowers (these have seldom survived). Similar holes on the Derby figures are circular, and not square. Various 'repairers' marks are found; on the earliest figures are an incised caduceus or an arrow with a ring; then an impressed 'B', 'T', or 'To'; and an incised 'AF' or 'D'.

A third very productive period at Bow, lasting from about 1759 till 1763, corresponds more or less with the 'gold anchor' period at Chelsea, and shows in its own way a parallel striving after lavish effects. Now appeared the characteristic Bow Rococo base, with four S-shaped feet and a pierced U-shaped scroll hanging between them. The opaque light blue, crimson and yellow were copiously applied, and the gaudy effect was often heightened by 'bocages' imitated from Chelsea and painted in clear emerald green. Gilding, however, was less conspicuous, and of rather poor quality. Many earlier models reappeared on the scroll bases. Most important of the new models were the fine large standing portraits of the *Marquess of Granby*[2] and *General Wolfe* (1), commemorating victorious battles against the French at Minden and Quebec in 1759 in which the two generals were engaged. Both derive from engravings by Richard Houston, of which the Granby, after a painting by Sir Joshua Reynolds, was published in 1760. The repairer's mark 'T' or 'To' appears on these figures, and on an equally large *Minerva* in the same style (2). A smaller *Minerva* $7\frac{1}{2}$ inches high has the cypher 'GR III' on the helmet, and probably dates from George III's accession in 1760; it derives from the same seventeenth-century bronze as the Longton Minerva mentioned on page 116.[3] The gay frivolity of this over-ornate phase at Bow is well seen in a figure of *Spring* adapted from Elias Meyer's 1755 Meissen series of Seasons with vases (3), and in the figure of a dancing sailor (4). A pair of small bocage groups representing 'Price's Horsemanship'[4] and a similar pair of pugilists[5] recall the gold-anchor Chelsea groups that also represent contemporary showmen.

---

[1] Savage, Plates 65a, 66b. Victoria and Albert Museum, nos. C. 661–1925; C. 240, 241, 250–1940. They appear both on low rustic bases and in later versions on Rococo pedestals.

[2] *Schreiber Coll. Cat.*, I, no. 54.

[3] Hurlbutt, *Bow Porcelain*, Plate 56b.

[4] Sotheby, Sale Cat., May 16, 1947, Lot 81; *ibidem* Feb. 28, 1951, Lot 146.

[5] Sotheby, Sale Cat., July 3, 1957, Lot 106.

---

(1) *Plate* 53; (2) *Colour Plate C*; (3) *Plate* 54; (4) *Plate* 55.

C. *Minerva. Bow; about* 1760.
Height, $15\frac{7}{8}$ *in. Victoria and Albert Museum.*
(*See p.* 92)

In 1763 John Crowther, sole proprietor of the factory since Weatherby's death in the preceding year, was declared bankrupt. It has been conjectured that William Duesbury of Derby may have given the financial help that enabled him to continue the Bow factory in this fourth period, from 1763 till 1775. An unexplained mark of an anchor and dagger in brownish red enamel was henceforward commonly applied to the vessels and figures. The paste deteriorated in quality, with a glaze often of bluish tone, and the colours lost their previous freshness. An inky, translucent underglaze blue replaced the beautiful opaque blue enamel; the crimson on the bases gave place to a pale, watery turquoise with gilding; and the dresses were painted with floral medallions and diapers in imitation of Chelsea gold anchor, with considerable use of iron-red and gold. Actual Chelsea models were copied in a very large figure of the Muse *Clio*[1] and in the equally large gardener from a pair symbolizing *Autumn* and *Spring*,[2] these all standing on plain round plinths. A set of miniature *Continents* stand on open bases with four straight stilt-like supports,[3] and the typical four-footed Bow base was gradually abandoned for scrolled mounds in the Chelsea manner. In a pair of *boys playing fife and drum*[4] the faces resemble those of Derby figures both in modelling and in the deep salmon-pink painting of the cheeks. The factory advertised for two new modellers in 1770, but to the end showed no sign of abandoning its now seedy Rococo style for the more fashionable Louis Seize.

A very large figure of *Flora* (1), 18 inches high, on a square base, occupies a place apart in the Bow series, being a reproduction of the antique marble Flora Farnese in Naples. Surviving examples are of various dates, but to judge from the material and painting the earliest are likely to have been made before 1760.[5] Tradition ascribes the model to the sculptor John Bacon (*b.* 1740, *d.* 1799), but more recently it has been suggested that the Bow Flora derives from a terracotta version made and signed in 1759 by the famous sculptor Michael Rysbrack.[6] Rysbrack's model was a study for the marble statue

[1] Warren E. Cox, *The Book of Pottery and Porcelain*, New York, 1944, Fig. 1072.

[2] *Schreiber Cat.*, 85 (man); King, *Porcelain Figures*, Fig. 15 (woman); Boston Museum, *English Porcelain Figures*, Figs. 23, 24.

[3] Savage, Plate 67; also in Victoria and Albert Museum.

[4] *Schreiber Cat.*, no. 84; *Untermyer Cat.*, Fig. 247.

[5] Bowcocke's account-book for March 27, 1756 mentions 'white floras' (or, 'what floras?')—Jewitt, I, p. 209. But this may refer to the figure copied from the Meissen *Smelling*, in the Senses series.

[6] R. J. Charleston and Geoffrey Wills, 'The Bow Flora and Michael Rysbrack,' *Apollo*, LXIII, 1956, pp. 125–7.

(1) *Plate* 52.

delivered to Sir Richard Hoare of Stourhead in 1761; the face is fuller, and the draperies more flowing, than in the Bow version. Moreover Rysbrack, who had not himself been to Italy and seen the original, mentioned in correspondence of December 1758[1] that in preparing his model he used a plaster Flora, apparently not his own work. This might have been one of a set of five plaster casts after the antique, including a Flora, made for sale by the sculptor Scheemakers in 1747;[2] the Bow factory might also have used a Scheemakers' cast. But no doubt casts of such famous antique statues were also commercially available from sources in Italy.[3] A plaster Flora in Sir John Soane's Museum comes closer to the Bow Flora than does the Rysbrack model.[4] The Farnese Flora was later reproduced at Coade's Artificial Stone Manufactory in Lambeth, whose Catalogue of 1799 attributes the model to John Bacon. Bacon had in fact worked for Coade's after 1769, and may like Rysbrack have contributed his own version of the famous antique statue—perhaps following a plaster cast of the same edition.

There is good documentary evidence that in 1755 Bacon, then aged fifteen, was apprenticed for seven years to Nicholas Crisp, jeweller, of Bowchurch Yard, Cheapside, London (not to be confused with Bow, Middlesex, and the Bow porcelain factory).[5] Crisp and his partner Saunders also maintained in LAMBETH or VAUXHALL, London, a mysterious porcelain factory whose products have never been identified, but which apparently existed from 1755 or earlier till 1762. A notice in the *British Magazine and Review* for October 1782 stated that Bacon was first inspired to become a sculptor through seeing, on his occasional visits to Lambeth, the terracotta models which various sculptors sent for baking to a pottery in the same premises as Crisp's porcelain factory. Not until 1799 did an obituary notice of Bacon in the *Gentleman's Magazine* state that Bacon actually worked *in* Crisp's china factory, and made there 'Shepherds, Shepherdesses, and such like small ornamental pieces'—a statement much elaborated in Cecil's 'Memoir of Bacon' (1801) and Cunningham's 'Lives of the Most Eminent British Sculptors and Architects' (1830). Whether

[1] See p. 32, n. 3.   [2] See p. 32.

[3] A plaster cast of the companion Farnese Hercules, also about 2 feet high, is shown in a painting of his own studio done by the French painter Pierre Subleyras in Rome about 1748. (L. Dimier, *Les peintres français du XVIIIe siècle*, Paris, 1930, Plate 11.) A cast of the Flora herself, about the same size, is conspicuously shown in Gainsborough's portrait of his two daughters, painted about 1770, in the Worcester Art Museum, Mass. (Illustrated in the Museum publication, *Art Through Fifty Centuries*, 1948, Fig. 95.)

[4] Comparative heights: Rysbrack terracotta, $22\frac{1}{2}$ inches; Soane plaster cast, $20\frac{1}{2}$ inches; Bow porcelain figure, $16\frac{1}{2}$ inches.

[5] A. J. Toppin, 'Nicholas Crisp, jeweller and potter,' *E.C.C. Trans.*, vol. I, 1933, pp. 38–43.

porcelain figures were in fact made by Crisp at Lambeth, with or without Bacon's assistance, remains an open question. Models by Bacon were subsequently acquired by the Derby factory (1769) and by Wedgwood, but the idea that he worked for the Bow factory appears to have arisen through confusing that factory with Crisp's premises at Bowchurch Yard in Cheapside. Similarly, the attribution to him of the Farnese Flora model made in Coade's 'artificial stone' appears to have worked retrospectively, to claim as also his the Flora in Bow porcelain.

8

DERBY

Founded in or about 1750, and not finally closed till 1848, Derby outlived all the other early English factories except Worcester. The numerous figures made throughout are for the most part technically accomplished though often tediously banal and derivative in style. But some interesting 'primitives' of the first five years show great merit and originality, and the unglazed 'biscuit' figures and groups made after 1770 have no English parallels.[1]

Apart from unreliable traditions, the earliest evidence that a factory had started is given by some small white cream-jugs with the incised mark 'Derby' or 'D' and the date 1750. The London account-books of William Duesbury refer to 'Darbey' or 'Darbishire figures' that passed through his hands for decorating in 1752 and 1753. These are believed to have been made between 1750 and 1755 by Andrew Planché,[2] in a small factory just east of St. Mary's Bridge, perhaps with financial support from John Heath, who also had interests in the local Cockpit Hill earthenware factory. A draft agreement dated January 1, 1756, but never executed, apparently refers to a plan for re-

[1] Useful source-material in John Haslem, *The Old Derby China Factory*, London, 1876 and W. Bemrose, *Bow, Chelsea and Derby Porcelain*, London, 1898. F. Hurlbutt, *Old Derby Porcelain*, London, 1925; W. B. Honey, B. Rackham and H. Read, 'Early Derby porcelain,' in *Burlington Magazine*, XLIX, 1926, pp. 292–302; E. Percival Allam, 'The artist-modellers of the Old Derby Porcelain Factory,' *Connoisseur*, LXXXII, 1928, pp. 29–37. F. B. Gilhespy, *Crown Derby Porcelain*, Leigh-on-Sea, 1951. Illustrations in W. King, *English Porcelain Figures of the Eighteenth Century*, London and Boston, 1925; Victoria and Albert Museum, *Catalogue of the Schreiber Collection*, vol. 1, 1928 (by B. Rackham); Y. Hackenbroch, *Chelsea and Other English Porcelain . . . in the Irwin Untermyer Collection*, Cambridge, Mass., 1957.

[2] Born London, 1928; apprenticed to a London goldsmith 1740–7; documents for his residence in Derby 1751–6 (perhaps there earlier); *d*. Bath, 1809. See Ll. Jewitt, *Ceramic Art of Great Britain*, London, 1878, vol. 2, pp. 63–6; Mrs. D. A. MacAlister, 'The early works of Planché and Duesbury,' *E.P.C. Trans.*, II, 1929, p. 45; W. H. Tapp, 'The earliest days of the Derby china factory,' *Apollo*, XVIII, 1933, pp. 96–105 (conclusions to be treated with caution); and Franklin Barrett, 'The Derby China Factory sites on Nottingham Road,' *E.C.C. Trans.*, vol. 4, part 5, 1959, p. 26.

establishing the factory on a more spacious site further to the east, adjoining the Nottingham Road; the partners were to be Heath, Planché (described as 'china maker', of Derby), and Duesbury, 'enamellor, of Longton'. The other two evidently dropped Planché as soon as they had learnt his secrets, and he disappeared from the scene. From 1756 till his death in 1786 Duesbury ran the Derby factory with great commercial success. In 1770 he and Heath bought up the moribund Chelsea factory, which was maintained as a subsidiary of Derby till 1784, when it too was closed and the moulds removed to Derby. It is not known exactly how the work was apportioned between the two factories during this 'Chelsea-Derby' period, but the Derby styles prevailed. From 1786 till 1811, the 'Crown Derby' period as it is called, from the mark generally in use, the factory was successively managed by William Duesbury the first's son, also named William (d. 1796), and Michael Kean. In 1811 the factory was bought by Robert Bloor, who became insane in 1828; his representatives however maintained it till it finally closed at the end of the 'Bloor period' in 1848. A small independent factory was started in 1848, and the still-existing 'Royal Crown Derby Porcelain Company' in 1876.

The figures presumed to have been made by Andrew Planché between 1750 and 1755 are unmarked, and have been identified partly by process of elimination (unlike Bow porcelain, they contain no bone-ash), partly by the recurrence of certain models in later periods at Derby. So far not many vessels of this period have been identified, apart from the cream-jugs of 1750. An early white figure of the actress Kitty Clive is known in two versions, of which the smaller[1] was apparently moulded direct from an example of the Bow Kitty Clive of 1750 (I). The larger Derby version[2] has been remodelled; it differs in details of drapery from the Bow figure, and stands on a star-shaped base with a spray of flowers in relief resembling those on the dated Derby cream-jugs. Both versions are of non-phosphatic paste, and it can be seen through the open bases that they were made by the slip-casting process which was thus used at Derby from the beginning.

---

[1] One example only, in the S. J. Katz Collection.

[2] *Schreiber Cat.*, Ia; H. Tait in *Apollo*, LXXI, Feb. 1960, Figs. I, III. In view of the non-phosphatic paste, it was formerly suggested that this figure might have been made at Bow before Frye's second patent of 1748; but the engraving from which the figure is derived was only published in 1750. A Longton Hall attribution has also been unconvincingly proposed; Detroit Institute of Arts, Exhib. Cat., *English Pottery and Porcelain*, 1954, no. 234.

(I) *Plate* 37.

Pairs of charging bulls,[1] of seated or trotting *wild boars*,[2] some figures of *goats*,[3] and a naked *boy milking a goat*[4] are found either in plain white or with primitive-looking enamel-painting; the spirited modelling is partly due to their derivation from Meissen originals. These figures show a peculiarity commonly found in the Planché period at Derby—a 'dry edge' left bare of glaze round the lower sides of the bases. That this was a deliberate precaution is suggested by other examples in which the uncontrolled glaze has overrun the edge of the foot and needed to be ground smooth on the underside. A second less constant peculiarity is the funnel-shaped 'screw-hole' in the underside of the rather massive pad bases, different from the circular hole with straight sides found under the Bow figures. The figures were made by the 'casting' process (see p. 18), and are hollow inside but fairly heavy in weight. At its best, the paste has a very rich, creamy appearance, with a thick, glassy glaze. It is admirably handled, with great breadth and simplicity, in a series of five groups of *Chinese men, women and children* representing the *Senses*, seated or standing in pairs on plain bases (1).[5] These are among the most impressive and original of early English porcelain figure-models. They are sometimes painted with plain washes of pale yellow, pink, mauve, yellow-green, and a strong iron-red, giving an effect somewhat similar to that of the painted early Bow figures by the 'Muses modeller'.[6] Two other powerfully-modelled large figures, standing on circular mound bases with Rococo scrolls in relief, show a bearded, bare-headed *Roman soldier*,[7] and an *old man*, barefoot, in a ragged ermine mantle, gazing at a crucifix held in his right hand (2).[8] The first of these has been

[1] *Untermyer Cat.*, Fig. 278. The models, from engravings after Elias Ridinger, are also known in Meissen porcelain.

[2] Victoria and Albert Museum, *Cat. of the Herbert Allen Collection*, 1923, no. 1 as (Bow); *Untermyer Cat.*, Fig. 279. Fakes of these and other early Derby animals and birds were made in England in the 1950's, in a chalky material resembling white earthenware rather than porcelain; they have a dull, greasy-looking glaze, and the exposed paste under the base often appears blackish.

[3] *Schreiber Cat.*, nos. 307 and 307a.   [4] *Herbert Allen Cat.*, no. 2 (as Bow).

[5] *Seeing*, seated woman with bird and man, Dixon, Plate 34, *Untermyer Cat.*, Fig. 269. *Hearing*, standing woman with lyre, seated child, Sotheby, Sale Cat., May 26, 1938 (Wallace Elliot), Lot 317, now British Museum. *Feeling*, standing man chastising boy, Honey, *O.E.P.*, Plate 43a and *Schreiber Cat.*, I, no. 284. Children and other components of the groups are also found as separate figures.   [6] See pp. 86–9.

[7] *Schreiber Cat.*, no. 287 (white); the Victoria and Albert Museum also has a later example, painted with the 'pale' colouring of about 1756–8 (no. C.298–1940). The figure probably held a spear in wood or metal, and may represent St. Thomas.

[8] Victoria and Albert Museum, no. C.36–1944, with early colouring: no. C.299–1940, later example with colouring of about 1760. C. Earle, *The Earle Collection of Early Staffordshire Pottery*, London, 1915, nos. 133 and 136 show the figure labelled 'St. Philip'; others in the Staffordshire set show St. Peter and St. Paul.

(1) *Colour Plate D, Plate 58*; (2) *Plate 59.*

D. *Chinese group, symbolic of 'Tasting'.*
Derby; about 1750–4. Height, $8\frac{3}{4}$ in.
Victoria and Albert Museum.
(See p. 98)

called 'King Lear', without any good reason, for both must represent saints; in fact the old man is known in later Staffordshire earthenware with the label 'St. Philip' on the base. A seated group of a *hunter and companion* (1) recalls the rather messier treatment of a similar subject by the 'Muses modeller' at Bow, and is related to an admirably modelled set of five seated male and female figures in contemporary dress representing the *Senses*, best known being the ladies in pannier skirts with a parrot (*Feeling* (2)) and a basket of fruit (*Taste* (3)).[1] The last-named figure was adapted in the next period at Derby as a mandolin-player, with a low Rococo base. The *Seasons* are represented twice; first by a set of four seated putti (4); and second, by a series of eight standing or striding figures in pairs. Best known of these is *Winter* (5)—an old man and old woman who stand warming their hands over braziers[2] (sometimes miscalled 'Old Age'); *Autumn* is a pair of young peasants in large hats, the man with a basket of grapes slung over his shoulder;[3] *Summer* is a pair of harvesters, and *Spring* a pair of gardeners.[4] Closely related in style are the two figures of a male *absinthe seller* and female *vegetable-seller* in Plate 61B, C, enlarged adaptations from the contemporary Meissen set of small 'Paris Cries' made in 1753; these figures are painted in curiously mottled pale colours, and show a rather uncomprehending attempt to imitate the Meissen Rococo bases. Small groups of *Pluto and Cerberus* (6), *Jupiter and the eagle*, and *Neptune with a dolphin* apparently belong to a set of gods as *Elements*. Other figures of *Jupiter with an eagle* and *Juno with a peacock* are heavily draped standing figures, about $6\frac{1}{2}$ inches high; and there is also a *Mars* in Roman armour and a *Venus and Cupid*.[5] These small models are the prototypes of the much larger figures of gods made in the 1760's. A small and slender *shepherd bagpiper* with a dog, and his dancing companion with a lamb, made in two sizes, exactly repeat the Bow models (7). Perhaps both factories were here following common Meissen originals, such as may also be presumed for other small and delicate early Derby

[1] *Taste, Schreiber Cat.*, I, no. 286, Honey, *O.E.P.*, Plate 43b. *Sight*, seated man in cap, legs crossed, arms raised sideways, bird in left hand, *Apollo*, Dec. 1928, p. 332, no. IX. *Smell*, seated man, snuff-box in left, pinch in raised right. *Hearing*, seated woman with bird-cage.
[2] *E.P.C. Trans.*, vol. 2, p. 58, Plate XII; *E.C.C. Exhib. Cat.*, 1948, nos. 302, 303; Gilhespy, Fig. 158.
[3] A. Hayden, *The Lady Ludlow Collection*, 1932, no. 242.
[4] Gilhespy, Figs. 182, 183.
[5] E.C.C. Exhib., 1948, no. 306 (Mars); Gilhespy, Fig. 141 (Venus).

(1) *Plate* 56B; (2) *Plate* 57B; (3) *Plate* 57C; (4) *Plates* 56A, 57A; (5) *Plate* 60B; (6) *Plate* 60A; (7) *Plate* 61A.

figures of *Turks* and fancy-dress *dancers*.[1] A large *shepherdess* on a high and elaborate Rococo base is closely imitated from a near-contemporary Meissen model. But generally speaking the figures assumed to have been made by Planché between 1750 and 1755 show little Meissen influence. They could very readily be mistaken for French porcelain, by reason of the creamy quality of the paste and the broad manner of handling it. Whether Planché himself was the modeller must remain doubtful. But the anonymous modeller evidently departed with Planché when Duesbury assumed control of the new Derby factory in 1756. None of the later figures show the *élan* in movement, the three-dimensional sense of depth and mass, for which some of these early models are so remarkable.

There is a small 'transitional' class of figures, probably made at the end of the 'Planché period', about 1755, in which experiments were tried with a new paste—perhaps to facilitate more complicated modelling. It is light in weight, rather opaque, and apt to be disfigured by dirty black specks in the glaze. A curious mark of two triangles incised within a circle appears under the wide pierced Rococo base of a much-beribboned *dancing youth* (1); on one figure of a seated *boy and girl with dogs* (2); and on a fragmentary Rococo candlestick-base with a tree and animals.[2] Here also belong the scroll-based *candlesticks with birds* and attached pairs of *Chinese boys*,[3] and a *watch-stand* which has a Chinaman with flying drapery perched high on open scrollwork and a boy below.[4] A large group of *Neptune* seated aloft on the stern of a ship,[5] with a sea-horse in the waves beneath, also has its place in the 'transitional' class.

In 1756 a new era began at Derby under the energetic management of William Duesbury. Through the *Public Advertiser* for December of that year the 'Proprietors of the DERBY PORCELAIN Manufactory' offered for auction in London 'A Curious Collection of fine *Figures, Jars*' etc., 'after the finest Dresden models'. In May 1757 another advertisement offered 'the largest variety of the Derby or second Dresden',[6] remarking on 'the Perfection the Derby figures in particular are arrived to'. Again, in 1758, the Proprietors advertised

[1] *Untermyer Cat.*, Fig. 271.   [2] Victoria and Albert Museum, no. C. 162–1929.
[3] *Untermyer Cat.*, Figs. 280 (bird candlestick), and 289 (Chinese boys on candlestick).
[4] Gilhespy, Fig. 140.   [5] *E.C.C. Trans.*, vol. 1, no. 4, 1937, p. 41, Plate XIb.
[6] A small figure of a *boy with a basket of flowers* has inscribed under the base 'New D', perhaps for 'New Dresden' or 'New Derby'. (*E.P.C. Trans.*, II, 1929, p. 58; A. L. Thorpe, 'Some early Derby porcelain,' *Connoisseur*, CXLVI, 1960, pp. 260–4, Fig. 6.)

(1) *Plate* 62B; (2) *Plate* 62A.

the sale of 'great variety of Figures, the nearest the Dresden', adding that they had 'engaged double the number of hands they used to employ'. No doubt Duesbury hoped to pass off his unmarked figures as Meissen, but only the very ignorant could be so deceived. For artistically and technically the early Duesbury figures of about 1756–1758 are inferior to those made previously by Planché. The paste is chalky and light in weight, with an unpleasantly blued glaze; and the pale and sickly colour-scheme is dominated by lemon yellow, dull turquoise, and pinkish crimson, these being laid side by side on the ill-understood Rococo scrollwork of the often very wide bases. Straggling flower-sprays are painted on some of the dresses, but there is little or no gilding. At its best, the modelling of this 'pale-coloured family' has a slender delicacy, and there is fine detail in the applied ribbons and flowers; but the figures are stiff and doll-like in their attitudes compared with the Meissen originals that so often inspired them. The typical blueish glaze and sickly colours of the 'pale-coloured family' are seen in groups of *seated lovers with a clown*,[1] *of Harlequin and Columbine standing*, and of seated and standing shepherds and shepherdesses symbolizing the *Seasons*.[2] Single figures include a large *Diana*,[3] shepherds and shepherdesses (I), various small *dancers* and musicians, and a pair of *Turks*.[4] Some of the models which first appeared with the 'pale' colouring, about 1756–8, were reissued in the next period, with more sophisticated scroll bases and stronger colouring. Among these are the large so-called *'Ranelagh figures'* of a pair in fancy dress, the man proffering a letter and the woman wearing an admission-ticket for the Ranelagh Gardens;[5] the large *Minerva* and *Mars*;[6] and the ever-popular *Milton* and *Shakespeare* (2), whose derivation from models by the sculptor Scheemakers has been discussed on a previous page.[7] The large so-called *'antique Seasons'*, after the Meissen models made by Kaendler and Eberlein in 1745, first appear at Derby about 1758, on square bases;[8] later editions, with scroll bases, were made over the next fifteen years.

[1] *Schreiber Cat.*, I, no. 290; *Untermyer Cat.*, Fig. 272.
[2] *Untermyer Cat.*, Fig. 274.
[3] Dixon, *English Porcelain of the Eighteenth Century*, Plate 38.
[4] Honey, *O.E.P.*, Plate 44; *Apollo*, XVIII, 1933, p. 98, Fig. III; *E.C.C. Exhib. Cat.*, 1948, nos. 297, 298.
[5] *Schreiber Cat.*, I, no. 296. See also A. J. Toppin in *E.C.C. Trans.*, vol. 3, 1951, Plate 29 and p. 70.
[6] *Schreiber Cat.*, I, no. 303.   [7] Pp. 32–3.
[8] Gilhespy, 'The first Derby sale of 1756,' *Connoisseur*, CXXXIX, 1957, p. 10, with the Meissen originals; *Connoisseur*, LXXIII, 1925, p. 232 (with scroll bases, illustrated as Chelsea); *Schreiber Cat.*, no. 341 (Autumn, Chelsea-Derby).

(I) *Plate* 63; (2) *Plates* 64, 65.

In its third period, from about 1758 till 1770, Derby borrowed ideas from the contemporary 'gold anchor' figures of Chelsea, but failed to achieve the same nobility of style. The chalky, light-weight paste of the 'pale-coloured family' now gave place to a more substantial creamy white body with a colourless glaze. An almost constant feature of the figures is the presence under the base of three or four dark unglazed patches left by the balls of clay on which it was supported while the glaze was fired. The base, sometimes a simple pad, as in two spirited large early figures of a *Jew pedlar* and his wife,[1] is more normally a scrolled pedestal picked out with gold and with the very prevalent dull turquoise—a colour apt to take a dirty brownish tone if overfired. The figures are often given bocage settings and fitted as candlesticks. Their attitudes are usually stiff and wooden, and the long-nosed faces often have patches of deep salmon-pink on the cheeks.[2] Dresses are painted with 'oriental' flowers, reviving a Meissen manner, or with floral medallions resembling those on Chelsea 'gold anchor' figures, using a good deal of gold. Favourite models such as the *Britannia*[3] were made in three sizes, and as a consequence of mass-production figures of this so-called 'patch family' have a tediously repetitive effect. The series of large classical *gods* and *goddesses*,[4] some 15 to 19 inches high, look provincial and uncouth beside the Chelsea gold-anchor Muses. Two Derby Muses, *Clio* (1) and *Erato*, are large reclining figures adapted from engravings by Daullé after Boucher,[5] and there are important groups of *Leda and the Swan*[6] and *Europa and the Bull* (2). A mixed sale at Christies in 1768–9 advertised 'A pair of beautiful enamelled figures of Jupiter and Juno, in triumphal cars, of the Chelsea porcelain,'[7] but these were more probably

---

[1] *Schreiber Cat.*, no. 294; *Untermyer Cat.*, Fig. 276, from Meissen models also imitated at Chelsea.

[2] Somewhat similar figures were made at Longton Hall, and it has been suggested that the modeller went on to Derby when Longton closed in 1760. (B. Watney, *Longton Hall Porcelain*, Plates 73, 74 and p. 43.)

[3] *E.C.C. Exhibn. Cat.*, 1948, no. 315 (wrongly called Minerva). Jewitt, *Ceramic Art of Great Britain*, II, 1878, p. 69 quotes lists of the figures in boxes sent for sale to London in 1763. These are helpful in dating some models—e.g. '4 Shakespeares at 42s., 6 Miltons at 42s., 4 large Britannias at 36s., 4 large Quarters (i.e. Continents) at 40s., 2 Jupiters at 68s., 2 Junos, 5 Ledas at 36s., 2 bird-catchers at 10.6d., 18 second-sized boys at 1.6d.'

[4] King, *Figures*, Figs. 44–6 (Vulcan, Juno, Jupiter); *Schreiber Cat.*, no. 303 (Minerva and Mars).

[5] King, 'Derby porcelain group,' in *British Museum Quarterly*, IV, 1929, p. 83 and Plate XLIX; *idem*. VII, 1932, p. 6 and Plate VII, with the engravings.

[6] Dixon, *English Porcelain of the Eighteenth Century*, Plate 39 (Leda).

[7] Nightingale, *Contributions*, p. XXXIX.

---

(1) *Plate* 68; (2) *Plate* 66.

the Derby groups of which there are examples in the Ashmolean Museum, Oxford (Cyril Andrade Loan). The Chelsea gold-anchor series of large standing children as *Continents* (1) was exactly reproduced at Derby about 1760, but is more familiar in later Chelsea-Derby versions of various sizes.[1] A rare large group in the Schreiber Collection shows the *Virgin with St. John and Mary Magdalene*,[2] and has a slot at the back to receive a Crucifix. The portrait-figures of *Milton* and *Shakespeare* (2) remained very popular, and new portraits showed the actors David Garrick as *Tancred*[3] and James Quin as *Falstaff*[4] after a mezzotint by McArdell. The woman street-seller in Plate 69A has been given the fanciful identification of 'Mrs. Cibber in the character of a Vivandière',[5] for which there is no evidence whatever. 'Folk-types' are represented by a pair of *map-sellers*, by a lively dancing *sailor* and companion[6] and by the satirical '*tithe pig*' group, in which a farmer's wife offers the parson her baby in payment, instead of the pig held by her husband.[7] But shepherds and shepherdesses form the commonest subjects, often with some allegorical meaning. A typical seated *shepherd bagpiper*, from a set of the Senses, bears the incised mark 'WDCo' (William Duesbury & Co.),[8] and a standing *shepherd in fancy dress* has an inscription incised by the repairer 'George Holmes did this figer 1765'.[9] The banality of the Derby style is well seen in a pair of large groups, after compositions of Carle Van Loo, with a youth and girl teaching a dog to dance or sing (3).[10] In 1769 the sculptor John Bacon R.A. was paid £75 7s. 2d. for models supplied to Duesbury, but these have not been identified in Derby or 'Chelsea-Derby' porcelain. The models in question may well have been large figures from Coade's Artificial Stone Manufactory at

[1] *Schreiber Cat.*, I, no. 298; King, *Figures*, Fig. 47; Gilhespy, Fig. 159.

[2] *Schreiber Cat.*, I, no. 295; Dixon, Plate 37.

[3] *Schreiber Cat.*, I, no. 301.

[4] *Schreiber Cat.*, I, no. 305; for other versions after the McArdell mezzotint, see Raymond Mander and Joe Mitchenson, 'The china statuettes of Quin as Falstaff,' in *Theatre Notebook*, XII, no. 2, 1958, p. 54, plates 8–10.

[5] Apparently Mrs Willoughby Hodgson, *Old English China*, London, 1913, p. 36, Plate 10, was responsible for the suggestion. Messrs. Mander and Mitchenson inform me that it is quite impossible.

[6] King, 'Early Derby porcelain figures,' *Old Furniture*, I, 1927, p. 25, Figs. 7, 9, 10.

[7] *Schreiber Cat.*, no. 304; Savage, *18th-Century English Porcelain*, Plate 82a. Also found with the figures made separately.

[8] *Burlington Magazine*, XLIX, 1926, p. 292, Plate I (now in the British Museum).

[9] Tapp, 'The earliest days of the Derby China factory,' *Apollo*, XVIII, 1933, p. 100, Fig. XII (formerly Leverhulme Collection).

[10] *Schreiber Cat.*, no. 299; *Untermyer Cat.*, Fig. 275.

---

(1) *Plates* 22B, 23B; (2) *Plates* 64, 65; (3) *Plate* 67.

Lambeth, of which Bacon had just become manager; they would be used for the academic instruction of the Derby modellers.

In the Chelsea-Derby period (1770–84) the technical quality of the colouring improved, no doubt thanks to the experience of the Chelsea painters. The turquoise became clearer and bluer in tone, and was much used with gilding on the Rococo bases of earlier models that still continued in production. Flesh-tones were rendered in a mawkish pale pink, and the now slighter and often very delicate flower patterns allowed far more of the white ground to show. A deep salmon-pink with streaks of watery yellow-green appeared on the new rockwork bases, and in the generally pale colour-schemes only a rich brownish-red struck a stronger note. In 1771 the 'Chelsea and Derby Porcelain Manufactories' held their 'first public sale of the last year's produce',[1] and from the Catalogue we can recognize significant new trends of taste. Many figures and groups offered were in unglazed 'biscuit', now for the first time adopted in England. The same models were also made in glazed and painted porcelain, this being cheaper than the biscuit, which needed special care in firing to avoid defects that could not be covered up. Among the new models offered in 1771 is a group *'with Minerva crowning Constancy and Hercules killing the Hydra'*, the figures being represented as children.[2] This and another 'all round' group with a tree and *cupids robbing a bird's nest* have almost exact counterparts in biscuit-porcelain made at Tournay.[3] A list of hands working at Chelsea in 1773 includes as a new arrival a highly-paid modeller or 'repairer' named Gauron;[4] he is believed to be Nicholas-Francois Gauron, who had worked as chief-modeller at Tournay between 1758 and 1764.[5] But it is unlikely that he brought Tournay models with him to England, as he had left that factory long before; nor do the scanty records and traditions ascribe to him any of the Chelsea-Derby models. It is more likely that the factory

---

[1] Catalogue published by Nightingale, *Contributions Towards the History of Early English Porcelain*, Salisbury, 1881, together with extracts from successive sales till 1783. Jewitt, *Ceramic Art of Great Britain*, II, pp. 78–83 prints entire the Derby sale-catalogue of 1785.

[2] *Schreiber Cat.*, no. 422; Gilhespy, Figs. 156, 157.

[3] H. Nicaise, 'Porcelaines de Tournay et de Chelsea-Derby,' *Revue Belge d'archéologie et d'histoire de l'art*, V, 1935, pp. 5–16, Figs. 7–12.

[4] Jewitt, vol. I, p. 186.

[5] B. Paris, 1736; came to London ca. 1750 as apprentice to his uncle Jacob, a silversmith; porcelain-modeller at Mennecy (1753), and perhaps Vincennes (1754); chief-modeller at Tournay (1758–64); made unsuccessful attempts at faience-manufacture in Brussels and Liège (1764–1770); traces then lost till 1773. See H. Soil de Moriamé, *La manufacture impériale et royale de Tournay*, Tournai-Paris, 1937, pp. 46, 47; W. H. Tapp, 'The Gaurons, father and son,' *Apollo*, XXXV, 1942, pp. 62, 89; C. Deroubaix, *Les porcelaines de Tournai au Musée de Mariemont*, Mariemont, 1958, p. 67.

deliberately imitated various continental figures in the new Louis XVI style. Thus a series of Cupids grouped in pairs as the *Liberal Arts* were copied in 1773 or earlier from the almost contemporary models made by Acier at Meissen.[1] Among adaptations from Sèvres biscuit models by Falconet are two coloured groups, the *Bergère des Alpes* and *L'Oracle* or *Le nœud de cravate*;[2] these, like a third pastoral group entitled '*Pensent-ils au raisin?*'[3] have the new rockwork bases streaked with salmon-pink and pale green. Similar bases are found in other small groups of *shepherds* (1),[4] of a *monk and nun* (2), and in the fine pair of figures known as the *Vauxhall singers*.[5] The chief modeller in the first years of the combined Chelsea-Derby concern appears to have been Pierre Stephan, who in 1770 contracted to work at the factory for three years and subsequently, as an independent artist, continued as late as 1795 to supply models both to the Derby factory and to Wedgwood.[6] He was probably the unnamed modeller at Derby with whom Richard Champion corresponded in 1772 about models to be made for the Bristol factory;[7] Champion praised this modeller's Derby *Seasons* and *Elements*. The '*French Seasons*' listed in the 1771 sale-catalogue, and attributed to Stephan in a later price-list, are large-headed, smirking children in contemporary dress (3);[8] the standing *Elements* (4),[9] which are closely related in style to a set of seated *Senses*,[10] show limp young shepherds and shepherdesses with simpering faces and an arch but awkward tilt of the heads and hips, the pelvis being almost dislocated sideways. Children as *Prudence* and *Discretion* standing beside large urns[11] are similar models from the 1771 sale-catalogue. The same sentimental mood extended to figures and groups in the early neo-classical manner. Here some subjects are taken from engravings by C. Monnet in the Paris 1767–71 edition of the Abbé

[1] *Schreiber Cat.*, no. 345, etc., on openwork pedestals (one dated 1773).

[2] *Schreiber Cat.*, nos. 352, 353.

[3] *Schreiber Cat.*, no. 355, from an engraving by J. P. Le Bas after Boucher's painting of 1747.

[4] Honey, *Old English Porcelain*, Plate 47B.

[5] Victoria and Albert Museum, *Cat. of the Herbert Allen Collection*, no. 95.

[6] Contract, Jewitt, II, p. 97. His earlier history is unknown. His name does not occur in the index of the Huguenot Society's publications, nor in the published records of the Tournay Factory.

[7] See p. 126.

[8] *Herbert Allen Cat.*, no. 95 (later coloured examples of these popular models). Nicaise (see p. 104, note 3) illustrates similar Tournay models and mentions others made at Copenhagen.

[9] *Herbert Allen Cat.*, no. 119, biscuit. Probably an edition later than that of 1771, with neo-classical base substituted.

[10] King, *Figures*, Figs. 48, 49, coloured.

[11] *Schreiber Cat.*, no. 344, coloured.

(1) *Plate* 70A; (2) *Plate* 70B; (3) *Plate* 69B; (4) *Plate* 74A.

Banier's *Les Métamorphoses d'Ovide*; for example the groups of *Jason and Medea* at the Altar of Diana, and of *Cephalus and Procris*.[1] A group of *Time clipping the wings of Love* was taken from Charles Phillips' mezzotint dated 1772, after Vandyck,[2] and engravings of 1776 by Bartolozzi and Ryland after Angelica Kauffmann inspired a series of three all-round groups—*Two Bacchantes adoring Pan*, *Two virgins awaking Cupid* (1), and *Three Graces distressing Cupid*.[3] These can be recognized in the sale-catalogues of 1778 and 1782, and occur both in biscuit and in coloured porcelain. The later price-list of the factory is certainly incorrect in attributing them to Spengler, who cannot yet have reached England; the modeller was doubtless Pierre Stephan. Notable additions were made to the Derby gallery of portraits. Four of these were inspired by the popularity of John Wilkes, M.P., and those who had supported him in his spirited and scurrilous attacks on the illiberal policies of King George III. Wilkes was first arrested for his libel on the King, published in the *North Briton*, no. 45, in 1763, and his turbulent career reached its climax when he was elected Lord Mayor of London in 1774. To judge by their colouring, the Derby portraits should date from after 1770. *John Wilkes* himself is shown standing on a Rococo base with scrolls inscribed 'Magna Charta' and 'Bill of Rights';[4] he forms a pair with *General Henry Seymour Conway*,[5] who had spoken in his favour in 1764, and had been temporarily dismissed from his posts in consequence. Charles Pratt, as Chief Justice of the Court of Common Pleas, had in 1763 decided that Wilkes' arrest was illegal; in 1765 he was created first *Baron Camden*, and in 1766 he became Lord Chancellor in Chatham's administration. The Chelsea-Derby figure (2) shows him as Lord Chancellor, and was adapted from Ravenet's engraving after Sir Joshua Reynolds, published in 1766.[6] *William Pitt* was created Earl of Chatham and became Lord Keeper of the Privy Seal in 1766, in which year he declared himself in favour of a conciliatory policy

[1] Gilhespy, Fig. 155.

[2] *Schreiber Cat.*, no. 343. An example in biscuit mounted with a clock by B. Vulliamy in Buckingham Palace; L. G. G. Ramsey, 'A masterpiece of clockmaking,' *Connoisseur*, CXXXVIII, 1956, p. 230, Fig. 1. There is a very large coloured version in the Fitzwilliam Museum, Cambridge.

[3] *Herbert Allen Cat.*, nos. 114–16; Honey, *Old English Porcelain*, Plate 51; Dixon, Plate 96.

[4] *Schreiber Cat.*, I, no. 362a.

[5] *Schreiber Cat.*, I, no. 362.

[6] The figure has previously been published as Chelsea; King, *Chelsea Porcelain*, Plate 61; Boston, Museum of Fine Arts, *English Porcelain Figures*, Fig. 36. Both examples are unmarked, and have the typical Derby patches under the base.

(1) *Plate 71*; (2) *Plate 72*.

towards the American colonies; this is commemorated in the Chelsea-Derby figure,[1] which shows him leaning against an inscribed pedestal with an American-Indian woman kneeling at his feet. *George III and the Royal Family* were represented in three biscuit groups after an engraving by Earlom of Zoffany's painting of 1770 at Windsor Castle (I); the models are mentioned in a list of new productions published by the factory in 1773.[2] That obscure historian, *Mrs. Catherine Macaulay*, was reproduced after a statue of 1777 by J. F. Moore,[3] and there followed a series of Generals and Admirals (Howe, Drinkwater, Rodney, etc.), some of which are incised under the base with the name of the modeller Stephan.[4] A large and somewhat ponderous figure of David Garrick in the character of Richard III[5] was modelled from an engraving by J. Dixon after the painting by Nathaniel Dance exhibited at the Royal Academy in 1771. It appears (in biscuit) in the Chelsea-Derby sale-catalogue of 1773, and as no. 21 in the list of Derby moulds published by Haslem it is attributed, most improbably, to 'Bacon'—presumably the sculptor John Bacon, R.A. During its long subsequent popularity the figure was issued with the face painted in such a way as to alter entirely the original portrait, and it has been suggested that a likeness was sought to the actors John Philip Kemble and Edmund Kean, later famous in the role. But the differences were confined to the painting, the original moulds remaining unchanged. These apparently passed into the possession of Messrs. Copeland of Stoke-on-Trent in 1849, and were used by them for an edition in 'Parian ware'.

We should not forget that alongside these new models the factory continued to reproduce earlier ones still popular among its provincial customers. Such were the *'Welch Taylor'* and his wife riding on goats,[6] derived from the Meissen models by Kaendler and Eberlein, and the pair of Callot *dwarfs*,[7] called 'grotesque Punches' in the sale-catalogue of 1784. One of these reproduces a Chelsea raised-anchor

[1] *Schreiber Cat.*, I, no. 306; King, *Figures*, Fig. 36 (as Chelsea).

[2] *E.C.C. Trans.*, vol. I, no. 4, 1937, p. 26, Plate IX (complete set at Windsor, with painting); Jewitt, II, p. 73 (Derby list).

[3] King, *Figures*, Fig. 54; Gilhespy, Fig. 158.

[4] Stephan may have supplied identical models of Admiral Rodney both to Derby and to Wedgwood, who reproduced it in black basalt ware; M. H. Grant, *The Makers of Black Basaltes*, Edinburgh and London, 1910, Plate XLVIII. In the same work another Stephan model, the Bristol *Winter* (our Plate 93), appears in a black basalt version by Turner (Plate LXIV, I).

[5] *Schreiber Cat.*, I, 342. For discussion see a series of articles in *Theatre Notebook*, vol. XI, 1957, by Martin Holmes (pp. 53–5), and Raymond Mander and Joe Mitchenson (pp. 129–30) and vol. XIII, 1958, p. 36.

[6] Gilhespy, Fig. 151.   [7] Gilhespy, Fig. 142.

(I) *Plate 73.*

model. Various advertisements on the large hats of the Derby pair recall the practice of attaching public advertisements to the figures of dwarfs that formerly stood outside the Mansion House in London.

The 'Chelsea Derby' mark of a gold anchor intersecting a 'D' is hardly ever seen on the figures, but from 1775 these normally have a numeral, 'No. 3' etc., incised under the base, this corresponding to the factory price-list of numbered models. After 1784 they also usually have the incised mark of a 'D' with crossed batons under a crown, and various 'repairers' ' marks—a star for Isaac Farnsworth, a triangle for Joseph Hill. A numbered list of over 397 models drawn up in 1819, and purporting to represent the stock at the time of William Duesbury II's death in 1795, has been published by Bemrose;[1] it does not exactly correspond with the list given by Haslem. The items are not numbered in chronological order, and the traditional ascription of certain models to particular artists is not always trustworthy.

We have already considered some of the models supplied by Pierre Stephan. On the expiry in 1774 of his three years' agreement to work at Derby, Stephan went for a short while to the small porcelain factory at Wirksworth. From here, on May 9, he wrote to Josiah Wedgwood, asking for employment and saying that he thought of going to London to improve his ideas in the art of modelling.[2] In August of the same year he was paid £2 10s. for two wax models of 'Hope' and 'The Conquered Province', supplied to Wedgwood from London.[3] It is amusing to read Wedgwood's comments in a letter to his partner Bentley:

'I have received & examined Mr. Steven's moulds of Hope & the Conquer'd Province, & am glad to find the drawing and proportions so well preserved, but in everything else they are infinitely short of the exquisite originals. The Drapery is hard and unfinish'd, & the characters of the Faces are those of common mortals *of the Lower Class*. The armour in the Conquer'd Province comes out too much a great deal. The face of the figure is crooked, greatly so, and there is a total want of finishing in both the pieces. They are in my opinion far from being equal to our figures of the same class. . . . Mr. Stevens can do it better than us, if he would bestow a little more *attention* and *labour* upon them.'

On September 1, 1774, Stephan further received from Wedgwood 10s. 6d. each for three models of animals for teapots (presumably the

---

[1] W. Bemrose, *Bow, Chelsea and Derby Porcelain*, pp. 67–85; compare the list in Haslem, *The Old Derby China Factory*, pp. 170–81.

[2] Letter in the Wedgwood archives, quoted by R. Gunnis, *Dictionary of English Sculptors*, London, 1952.

[3] Eliza Meteyard, *The Life of Josiah Wedgwood*, London, 1866, vol. II, pp. 326, 327.

ornamental knobs for the covers) and 10s. 6d. for '3 Moulds of the above'. We may infer that over the next twenty years Stephan continued, as an outside modeller, to supply the Derby factory with models and moulds; for a letter from him written at Shelton in 1795 to William Duesbury II asks whether the moulds have arrived safely.[1] Other models were procured from various artists in London through the Swiss clock-maker Benjamin Vulliamy, who between 1780 and 1793 was a regular and exacting client and collaborator of the two Duesburys, father and son.[2] The clocks and barometers in which Vulliamy specialized were elaborate confections on high painted satinwood pedestals, with allegorical biscuit-porcelain figures mounted in marble and gilt-bronze settings. Of a pair in the Victoria and Albert Museum (nos. W. 15, 16–1958), the clock is inscribed 'Vulliamy LONDON 1787'; similar clocks are in Buckingham Palace, Syon House, and the Bank of England.[3] A most interesting letter of November 1790 from Vulliamy to William Duesbury II refers to two figures, with their moulds, which had been sent to Derby for reproduction in porcelain.[4] The modeller is not named; but we hear in other letters of models made in London by young artists who later achieved distinction as sculptors; John Deare (mentioned in 1784); Charles Peart (1787); and John Charles Rossi (1788–9).[5] Rossi's models for Derby porcelain, made under the watchful eye of Vulliamy, included *Aesculapius* and *Hygieia*; a female 'sacrificing figure' and her companion; and some very popular draped figures of boys. Other clock-figures made in biscuit for Vulliamy—androgynous Angels with or without wings, and draped classical females 'leaning on the right hand' or the left—are conventional and lacking in interest.[6] But in May 1790 Duesbury's London agent, Joseph Lygo, conducted to Vulliamy's house a new

[1] Jewitt, II, p. 97; Gilhespy, p. 62.

[2] Extracts from the Vulliamy-Lygo-Duesbury correspondence are quoted by Jewitt and Bemrose; and by Gilhespy, 'Joseph Lygo's letters to Derby,' *E.C.C. Trans.*, vol. III, part 5, 1955, pp. 203 ff. Some additional letters, not previously quoted, are in the Victoria and Albert Museum Library, MSS. English, *Duesbury and the Derby Porcelain Factory*; one of these is here reproduced as Appendix II for its technical interest.

[3] L. G. G. Ramsey, 'A masterpiece of clock-making,' *Connoisseur*, CXXXVIII, 1956, p. 230.

[4] Quoted in full as Appendix II, p. 139, from the unpublished original in the Victoria and Albert Museum Library.

[5] For other work by these sculptors, see R. Gunnis, *Dictionary of English Sculptors*, London, 1952.

[6] Such figures appear on the Victoria and Albert clock and barometer dated 1787; they cannot therefore have been modelled by Rossi, who was away in Italy and only began working for Derby biscuit in 1788. Bemrose, pp. 117, 118 quotes orders from Vulliamy in 1791 for female leaning figures and Angels without wings, at £6 6s. 0d. each.

modeller who had just arrived from abroad.[1] This was Jean Jacques
Spengler (*b.* Berne 1755), who may between 1772 and 1777 have
worked as modeller for his father, the director of the Zürich porcelain
factory.[2] It was arranged that Spengler should prove his skill by
modelling, in London, a figure of *Astronomy* from a drawing supplied
by Vulliamy;[3] and in July 1790 Spengler signed with Lygo and
Vulliamy a provisional agreement, later confirmed by Duesbury, to
go and work at the Derby factory, where he first arrived in August
1790. His erratic behaviour caused his employers much trouble during
the next five years, during part of which he lived in London; but in
January 1795 he signed a fresh agreement and returned to Derby,
before disappearing from the scene altogether. He was highly, and
rightly, valued as a modeller. The 1795 agreement refers to three important groups previously made by him—the *Russian Shepherds* (1),
consisting of four separate interlocking sections, *Palemon and Lavinia*,[4]
and the *Blind Beggar and Daughter*, this last imitated from a French
terre de Lorraine group of the Blind Belisarius by Paul Louis Cyfflé.
A pair of figures with bases, representing *Morning* and *Noon*, were
modelled by him soon after arriving at Derby; also a group of the
Three Graces.[5] Particularly charming are Spengler's slender, sentimental pastoral figures in contemporary dress, such as the *pair
burying a dead bird* (2) and the *shepherdess leaning over a gate* (3).[6] A
large mythological group, perhaps representing the *infant Bacchus*

[1] Victoria and Albert Museum MS., unpublished letter from Lygo dated May
27, 1790. (See Appendix II.) It is clear from this and subsequent letters that
Spengler was hitherto unknown either to Vulliamy or to the Derby factory.

[2] S. Ducret, *Die Zürcher Porzellanmanufaktur*, etc., Band II, *Die Plastik*,
Zürich, 1959, attributes to him 40 Zürich models, but these show no close stylistic
connection with the figures and groups which he made for Derby after 1790.
In the Derby factory-lists the groups of *Virgins awaking Cupid*, etc., already sold
in 1778, are attributed to Spengler. This is certainly an error of tradition (the list
quoted by Haslem was not compiled until 1819). But the mistake has given rise to
a belief, contradicted by the documentary evidence, that Spengler spent an earlier
sojourn in England before 1790.

[3] The *Astronomy* was finished at Derby; Duesbury paid Spengler £2 10s. for
it (Jewitt, II, p. 95).

[4] W. Bemrose, *A descriptive Catalogue . . . of the Collection of W.B.*, Derby (privately printed), 1898, Plate facing p. 26. From an engraving of 1788 by C. Knight
after Angelica Kauffmann, illustrating a subject from James Thomson's *Seasons*.

[5] Jewitt, II, p. 95. Biscuit figures from these three models have apparently not
been identified.

[6] Perhaps the figure of 'Rosina' modelled in London by Spengler in 1793 (letter
from Lygo, quoted by Gilhespy, *E.C.C. Trans.*, vol. 3, p. 205; a male figure to
match was then still to be made). The figure was incorrectly attributed by Haslem
and Allam to Pierre Stephan.

(1) *Plate 75*; (2) *Plate 74*B; (3) *Plate 77*.

with the Nymphs of Mount Ida,[1] may be attributed to him on grounds
of style; also 'a pair shepherd and shepherdess playing on fluit'
(no. 369).[2] The companion *shepherd* (1) for Spengler's *shepherdess*
was eventually modelled, according to Bemrose, by William Coffee,
who had previously been employed as a fireman at Coade's Artificial
Stone factory in London, and apparently worked at the Derby factory
as a modeller between 1794 and 1810.[3] The model was adapted, by
the addition of clothing, from a cast of an antique figure of Antinous
in the collection of the painter Joseph Wright of Derby. Lygo wrote
disparagingly of Coffee's work in 1794: 'The figure No. 359 is one of
the most stupid looking things I ever saw, and the figure of Apollo
in group No. 379 is very vulgar about the bosom, for sure never such
bubbys was seen and so much exposed—the design is pretty enough.'[4]
Coffee later worked on his own in Derby, making terracotta figures.
The late biscuit figures of the period 1790–1810, including those
modelled by Spengler and Coffee, are among the most attractive of
those made at the Derby factory. The material was deliberately given
a waxy sheen, due to the presence of volatilized glaze in the kiln.

Between 1810 and 1830, in the 'Bloor period', the modellers
Edward and Samuel Keys made small figures of actors on round bases,
and also caricatures—some after Thomas Rowlandson's illustrations of
the Tour of *Dr Syntax* (published 1810), others of characters from
Pierce Egan's *Life in London* (1820).[5] Inferior versions of many
eighteenth-century models, with the same incised numbers, were
still issued in the period between 1811 and the closing of the factory
in 1848. These late productions have conspicuous brassy gilding and
tasteless decoration in strong, heavy colours, especially a deep maroon
and dark blue. Some insignificant small human and animal figures in

[1] E. Percival Allam, 'Artist modellers of the old Derby porcelain factory,'
Connoisseur, LXXXII, 1928, p. 36, no. IX; marked 'No. 376'.

[2] Shepherdess in Victoria and Albert Museum, no. 3014–1901.

[3] See p. 37 above.

[4] Jewitt, II, p. 97. Contemporary English prudery about rendering the nude
received interesting comment from Josiah Wedgwood, writing to Flaxman in
Rome on February 11, 1790: 'The history of Orestes is an excellent classic subject
likewise, . . . but there is one objection which I am afraid is insurmountable and
that is the nakedness of the figures. . . . The same objection applies to the *Judgment
of Paris* and the other pieces, and indeed the nude is so general in the works of the
ancients, that it will be very difficult to avoid the introduction of naked figures. On
the other hand, it is absolutely necessary to do so, or to keep the pieces for our
own use, for none either male or female, of the present generation, will take or
apply them as furniture, if the figures are naked.' (Quoted, W. G. Constable, *John
Flaxman*, London, 1927, pp. 12–13.)

[5] Lists in Haslem, pp. 180–1; Gilhespy, Figs. 169, 170.

(1) *Plate* 76.

a chalky biscuit-porcelain were made at Derby between 1825 and 1840 by George Cocker (*b.* 1794, *d.* 1868),[1] who had been trained at the Derby factory before setting up on his own. In 1840 he moved to London, and in 1853 to Staffordshire, where he worked for a time at Minton's factory. His figures are usually marked with an incised cross, less often with his name.

[1] Gilhespy, Figs. 164, 171, 172.

9

LONGTON HALL (STAFFORDSHIRE)

The factory adjoining the then remote country house at Longton, on the southern outskirts of 'the Potteries' (Stoke-on-Trent), made figures throughout its existence between about 1749 and 1760. In advertisements these were evidently considered of secondary importance to the useful and ornamental vessels, whose rough and somewhat 'primitive' character they share.[1]

William Jenkinson (*d.* London, 1771), an inventive speculator chiefly interested in mining, obtained the 'secret' of making porcelain, perhaps from the factory at Limehouse, London, which had failed after three years (1745–8). At least one ex-Limehouse hand was working for him in 1750.[2] In October 1751 he took into partnership William Nicklin and William Littler (*b.* Burslem 1724, *d.* Burslem 1782). Littler was a practical potter who had already perfected a deep blue glaze for the local Staffordshire salt-glazed stoneware. He became the manager and active spirit of the Longton undertaking, henceforward styled 'William Littler & Co.', but failed to make it pay, in spite of extensive production. In 1753 Jenkinson withdrew, and in May 1760 the then chief shareholder, the Rev. Robert Charlesworth, dissolved the partnership. Littler carried on for a few months, but in September 1760 the entire stock of some 90,000 pieces was advertised as for sale by auction at Salisbury. Littler is said by Simeon Shaw to have subsequently managed a short-lived porcelain factory at Shelton belonging to Messrs. Baddeley and Fletcher, about which nothing is known. From 1764 till about 1770 he set up as a 'china maker' at West Pans near Musselburgh (Fife) in Scotland, but

[1] W. Bemrose, *Longton Hall Porcelain*, London, 1906, was a valuable pioneer work, still fairly reliable in its attribution of figures. But all previous writings have been superseded by Dr. Bernard Watney's excellent *Longton Hall Porcelain*, London, 1957.

[2] Dr. Richard Pococke, *Travels Through England during 1750, 1751 and Later Years*, London, Camden Soc. Publications, N.S., XLII, 1889–9, vol. I, pp. 7, 8. Pococke visited the factory in July 1750, but his memory of its location (given as Newcastle-under-Lyme, the nearest market town), as also of its productions, had become very confused when he described it in a letter written some weeks later.

apparently confined his activities there to re-decorating and selling old Longton stock.[1]

A few early vessels have a blue-painted mark resembling crossed L's or JL ('Littler, Longton', or 'Jenkinson-Littler', or perhaps merely an imitation of the Vincennes mark). The difficult task of distinguishing the normally unmarked Longton vessels and figures from those of other factories (especially Bow and Derby) had till recently proceeded by stylistic and technical analogies. The vessel-shapes often resemble those found in Staffordshire earthenware and salt-glazed stoneware, as do some of the earliest figures. The strong, deep underglaze blue associated with William Littler appears alike on salt-glazed ware and on porcelain which might therefore presumably have been made by him. Dr. Bernard Watney's discovery and excavation of the Longton kiln-site in 1956 have at last confirmed and clarified the nature of the productions, which included salt-glazed ware as well as porcelain.

The always variable Longton material is a glassy 'frit' porcelain akin to that made in the 'triangle' period at Chelsea, but much coarser in grain. Highly translucent and pale greenish by transmitted light, it is shown by chemical analysis to contain up to ten per cent of lead-oxide, due to the use of quantities of broken flint-glass as an ingredient. Chemical analysis of a few late Longton pieces suggests that after 1758 a certain amount of soapstone (steatite) was also incorporated, perhaps from local Staffordshire deposits. The thick uneven glaze is usually cold, even bluish, in tone, and sometimes has a dry, waxen quality perhaps caused by over-firing. The plastic properties of the material are poor, and the Rococo bases of the figures especially appear heavy and clumsy in potting, with blunted and ill-defined detail. The figures were made by the 'slip-casting' technique already used by the local Staffordshire potters for salt-glazed ware.[2]

Watney divides the production into three periods—'early' (about 1749–53), 'middle' (about 1753–7), and 'late'. First comes the aptly nicknamed 'snowman' family of some forty primitive white figures, in which the artless modelling is almost obliterated under a very thick glaze full of minute bubbles (1).[3] They often have very large

[1] A. Lane, 'William Littler, "china maker" of West Pans,' *E.C.C. Trans.*, vol. 5, part 1, 1960.

[2] See p. 18.

[3] B. Watney, 'Porcelain figures of the "snowman" technique,' *Connoisseur*, CXXXIX, 1957, pp. 149–53. The class had already been recognized and attributed to Staffordshire by Mrs. D. MacAlister, 'The early work of Planché and Duesbury,' *E.P.C. Trans.*, II, 1929, pp. 45–62, and 'Early Staffordshire china,' *E.C.C. Trans.*, vol. 1, 1933, pp. 44–53. Watney's discovery of kiln-wasters now proves them to be early productions of Longton Hall.

(1) *Plate* 78A.

flat rosette-like flowers and leaves applied to their simple pad bases, and the tone of paste and glaze is warmer than in later Longton figures. (The workman with whom Dr. Pococke conversed in 1750 said that the use of coal instead of wood for firing turned the porcelain yellow.) There are fairly large pheasants and other birds, and reclining horses, cows, and sheep. Four Chinese deities were imitated from *blanc-de-chine*, and other models from Meissen. Among these last are two versions of Cupid at a forge; small figures of Harlequin and Columbine from the Italian Comedy; and a group in which *Ceres* (or *Summer*) stands holding a sheaf of corn, with a child (1). This model appears in three sizes, and derives from a small Meissen group which in turn recalls Balthasar Permoser's treatment of the subject in ivory. As Mrs. MacAlister has shown, several 'snowman' types are also found in Staffordshire earthenware and salt-glazed ware. A figure of a *pug-dog* bears the incised date 1750. Very few 'snowmen' have enamel-painted decoration. Nevertheless their production may have lasted over two or three years, for a small standing woman as *Summer* and an old man as *Winter*[1] were apparently imitated from those in the well-known set of Seasons made at Chelsea early in the red-anchor period (2)—unless, as remains to be proved, there exists an earlier Meissen set from which all the English versions take their common origin.

Advertisements of sales in Birmingham, Manchester and London from 1752 onwards make no mention of figures till June 1757.[2] There is little sign of continuous development between the early 'snowman' class and the later Longton figures; a fresh start had to be made, and the preponderance of Rococo bases, rare even at Chelsea before 1756, suggests that most of the 'middle period' Longton figures were made after that date. It is possible that the emphasis then given to figure production by William Duesbury at the Derby factory encouraged similar efforts at Longton. A very curious experimental white *candlestick group* of a young man and woman sitting in an arbour, with two flanking candlesticks,[3] is eloquent of the difficulty encountered with the Longton paste; the example of the group in the Victoria and Albert Museum (3) is actually made of a hard buff-coloured material resembling the body of the salt-glazed ware, and

---

[1] Watney, *Longton Hall Porcelain*, Plate 4B, C. The *Winter* also appears in painted Longton porcelain of the 'middle period', with the brazier on the ground.

[2] *Aris's Birmingham Gazette*, June 20, 1757, quoted by Watney, p. 66.

[3] Watney, Plate 26 (S. Katz Collection); the example of the arbour-group in the Victoria and Albert Museum, no. C. 268–1940, has unfired oil-painting on the leaves. A pair of white standing figures perhaps by the same modeller, on flat octagonal bases, is in the collection of Mr. Thomas Burn at Rous Lench.

---

(1) *Plate* 78A; (2) *Plate* 18; (3) *Plate* 78B.

has a streaky white glaze evidently containing tin-oxide as an opacifier. Much careful but unsophisticated handwork has gone into the ribbons, buttonholes and other details. The same modeller probably produced a naive but charming *seated boy and girl* on low Rococo bases, in enamel-painted porcelain,[1] and another seated pair mounted as candlesticks.[2] Imitations of Meissen figures with pad bases include pairs of seated *musicians*, standing *Turks*, and *horses with Turkish and negro grooms*.[3]

It seems that Longton, more than other English factories, was led to seek figure-models from sculptural sources. Thus a pair of cupids mounted on galloping horses (I)[4] were copied, one in reverse, from a bronze by the Florentine sculptor Francesco Fanelli, who worked in England for Charles I before 1642.[5] Standing groups of *Hercules* wrestling with the *Nemean lion* and the *Keryneian stag*[6] also appear to have been copied from earlier Italian bronzes, and a standing *Minerva* reproduces a bronze used as a finial on a famous clock made by Thomas Tompion for the Bedchamber of William III at Hampton Court.[7] A clothed figure trampling a prostrate lion and tearing its jaws apart, on a Rococo base, appears to represent *Samson*[8] rather than Hercules; and a seated *nurse*[9] was evidently moulded from the well-

[1] Watney, Plate 34B and C. The models are imitated in Derby porcelain of the 1760's (examples in the Victoria and Albert Museum).

[2] Watney, Plate 18A, B; surely not so early as he suggests. There are affinities in style and colouring with Derby figures of the 'pale-coloured family' made by Duesbury after 1756.

[3] All illustrated by Watney.   [4] Watney, Plate 31B and *Schreiber Cat.*, no. 440.

[5] See John Pope-Hennessy, 'Some bronzes by Francesco Fanelli,' *Burlington Magazine*, XCV, 1953, p. 157. Dr. Watney was the first to recognize a Longton prototype in the galloping Cupid, no. A. 37–1952, in the good collection of Fanelli's work at the Victoria and Albert Museum.

[6] Savage, *18th-Century English Porcelain*, Plate 18b (with lion). The *Hercules and stag*, also in the Katz Collection, somewhat resembles the bronze by Vittore dei Gambelli (called Camelio); see L. Planiscig, *Piccoli bronzi italiani del Rinascimento*, Milan, 1930, Fig. 231.

[7] Watney, Plate 78 (porcelain); R. W. Symonds, *Thomas Tompion, His Life and Work*, London, 1951, Fig. 33. First observed by Dr. Watney. The same model also appears in Bow; Hurlbutt, *Bow Porcelain*, Plate 56B, with cypher of George III.

[8] Watney, Plate 59A.

[9] F. Tilley, *Teapots and Tea*, Newport 1957, Plate LXV illustrates the Chelsea model ($7\frac{1}{2}$ inches); a coloured example of the copy here attributed to Longton ($6\frac{1}{2}$ inches); and the smaller white Worcester copy ($5\frac{7}{8}$ inches). Tilley and Watney hesitate to accept the intermediate-sized *nurse* as a Longton piece; the paste, on analysis, shows some 6 per cent magnesia due to the incorporation of soapstone (steatite); but steatite is present in other late Longton pieces that have been analysed. A second coloured Longton *nurse* is illustrated (as Worcester, about 1753) in Detroit Institute Ex. Cat. *English Pottery and Porcelain*, 1954, no. 258 (Katz Collection).

(I) *Plate* 81B.

known Chelsea raised-anchor model. A very large white figure in the Statham Collection (1) represents a *river-god*, perhaps Father Thames, with a crown formed from the prows of ships; water with fish pours from an urn to his left, and there are bales of merchandise at his feet. The source (unidentified) is obviously a sculptor's model or cast in the contemporary classical manner followed by Rysbrack and Scheemakers, and no attempt has been made to adapt it to the Rococo idiom of porcelain. Another white figure, also in the Statham Collection, represents a dramatic poet, almost certainly *Dryden* (2). Here too the treatment is sculptural, resembling that of Scheemakers' monument to Shakespeare in Westminster Abbey, and it is tempting to suppose that Scheemakers may himself have circulated a set of plaster-casts of the English poets.[1] A smaller Longton figure in the same style represents an actor, perhaps *David Garrick*, holding a scroll inscribed with the epilogue of *The Tempest*.[2] Besides using bronze and plaster figures in the round, the Longton factory made at least three plaques cast from bronze reliefs.[3]

But despite these various borrowings, Longton had at least one modeller who developed a distinct and original style.[4] He made several pairs of seated figures, turned and leaning sideways towards each other—a *boy and girl with grapes* (3), the same as *flower-sellers* and *fruit-sellers*; a woman *butter-seller*, a pair of *cooks, boys with a barrel*, and so on. There are also a standing *flower-seller* and a woman *cabbage-seller*, and a fine striding *goatherd* with a goat over his shoulders. Groups of *putti feeding a goat* (4) were made in pairs. These and other similar figures, mostly small, have clumsy Rococo scroll bases or high pedestals picked out in crimson-pink and a characteristic pale yellow-green. Other typical Longton colours are the patches of deep underglaze 'Littler's blue', and a thick opaque orange-red which strikes a discordant note wherever it appears on dresses or on the bases, and which is also smeared on to the cheeks and often used to outline the eyes. The faces have a distinct, almost naturalistic liveliness of expression not found in the work of other factories. Dresses are seldom painted with flowers, more often with large formal star-patterns. The cabbage-like flowers and leaves applied to the bases are sometimes

[1] See p. 33.
[2] *Schreiber Cat.*, I, no. 431.
[3] See A. Lane, 'William Littler, China-Maker of Longton Hall and West Pans,' *E.C.C. Trans.*, vol. 6, 1960, pp. 82–92.
[4] The same hand, in successive stages of skill and experience, can perhaps be traced from the 'arbour-group' (Watney Plate 26) through his Plates 34B, C; 30, and 31A to the accomplished seated figures such as Plate 37A.

(1) *Plate* 85; (2) *Plate* 79; (3) *Plate* 81A; (4) *Plate* 80A.

very large, and often have stems rising in loops detached from the surface—like the Meissen flowers. Gilding of rather poor quality is sparingly used on dresses during the 'middle period' (about 1756 to 1758).

In its last two years (1759–60) the Longton Hall factory, evidently inspired by the example of the Chelsea 'gold anchor' figures, itself produced some exceptionally large and massive figures of the four *Continents*[1] standing on scrolled bases, in which an improved shiny gilding is lavishly used (1). These fine models are better known in the later versions made at the Plymouth factory. Another very large figure of *Britannia*, seated in profile to our right, supports a medallion relief portrait of George II in her left hand and has a shield and French trophies below on her right (2). This figure is sometimes found with a separate three-cornered stand,[2] and with two- or three-colour outline transfer-printed decoration and added enamels of a kind believed to have been done at Liverpool. Another very fine late Longton model shows the Duke of Brunswick on a prancing horse, with French trophies below and a green-painted rustic base (3); he wears the Order of the Garter, with which he was invested on August 16, 1759, after the Battle of Minden. Some late figures of naked putti as *Seasons* sit on high scroll pedestals.[3] There is a group of two *dancers* (4), and a pair of standing *musicians* with tambourine and lyre,[4] which stand on four-footed scroll bases and in their tall, slender stature and facial features bear a strong resemblance to the typical Derby figures of the 1760's. Watney indeed suggests that this particular modeller went on to Derby after the Longton factory closed in 1760, but against this it may be said that the characteristic Derby style already appears there in figures of the so-called 'pale family', made about 1758.[5] Here, as so often, we are baffled by our ignorance of the identity of the modeller or modellers who worked at Longton. In the turning attitudes and faces of the figures the work shows much vitality and a command of

[1] Watney, Plate 78. They can immediately be distinguished by their finer modelling and the flat underside of the bases from the Plymouth versions, which are hollow underneath. (See p. 124.)

[2] Watney, Plate 77; *Schreiber Cat.*, no. 436, with a scene from the Seven Years War crudely printed on the separate stand.

[3] Watney, Plate 75 (Winter); two more in the Royal Scottish Museum, Edinburgh.

[4] Watney, Plates 73, 74.

[5] E.g. the so-called 'Ranelagh figures' (*Schreiber Cat.*, no. 296) and the *Milton* and *Shakespeare*, Plates 64, 65. It seems likely that the Longton modeller deliberately imitated the style of the Derby figures, including their scroll bases.

(1) *Plate* 83; (2) *Plate* 84; (3) *Plate* 80B; (4) *Plate* 82.

style, but to the end its effect was marred by the unresponsive paste and the harshness of the enamel colours. In a pioneer attempt to introduce the London fashion for porcelain into the Staffordshire stronghold of the English earthenware industry, the Longton factory never quite threw off its provincial accent.

It is a curious fact that many Longton models reappear in the hard-paste porcelain made after 1768 by William Cookworthy at Plymouth and Bristol. Among them are the large late *Continents*, the *putti with a goat*, and some of the standing and seated figures with scroll bases. It has been suggested that the moulds were included in the Salisbury sale of Longton stock in September 1760, though the advertisements made no mention of factory-equipment. Watney has made the alternative suggestion that the original models were retained by an independent artist, and that new moulds were later cast from them at Plymouth. This seems far less probable than the supposition that the moulds themselves somehow reached Plymouth.

10

WORCESTER

The highly successful and still surviving Worcester factory was established by a company in 1751, and in the next year took over the equipment and technical 'secrets' of the small factory started at Bristol in 1749 by William Miller and Benjamin Lund. The slightly greyish paste made first at Bristol and thereafter at Worcester, incorporating as it did some thirty to forty per cent of Cornish 'soap-rock' (steatite), was harder and could be more thinly shaped than that of other English factories. Very few figures were made, these dating from about 1770.[1]

A rare white figure of a standing *Chinaman*, moulded from a blanc-de-chine original, has the name 'Bristoll' embossed on the back of the base, sometimes with the date 1750 added.[2] But the prevailing attitude at Worcester as regards figures is indicated in a letter from a visitor to the factory in 1766; 'The great improvements made in the Worcester manufactory of china would have afforded you great pleasure as it did me. It is hardly surpassed by the Vincennes, and much cheaper. They have not yet debased it by making vile attempts at human figures, but stick to the usefull.'[3] Nevertheless a sale advertisement of 1769 mentioned figures, and though none were included in the actual sale-catalogue (December 13, 1769), they were reliably reported as being made in 1771, by two independent visitors.[4] But probably not

[1] The most accessible of many books on Worcester is Franklin A. Barrett, *Worcester Porcelain*, London, 1953, with a chapter on the figures. Examples of all known figure models are illustrated and discussed by H. Rissik Marshall, *Coloured Worcester Porcelain of the First Period*, Newport, Mon., 1954, pp. 60–7. Mr. Marshall munificently presented his entire collection to the Ashmolean Museum, Oxford.

[2] Barrett, Plate 2A.

[3] Letter from T. Falconer to C. Gray, Aug. 1766, Chester. Quoted by Wallace Elliot, 'Worcester porcelain figures,' *E.C.C. Trans.*, vol. 1, no. 2, 1934, pp. 29–40. See also W. King, 'Worcester porcelain figures,' *Connoisseur*, LXVI, 1923, pp. 67–9.

[4] Mrs. Philip Lybbe Powys, Aug. 28, 1771; and Captain Joseph Roche, R.N., Oct. 21, 1771. Both quoted by Wallace Elliot, *E.C.C. Trans.*, *loc. cit.* See p. 19 above for Captain Roche's remarks about Worcester technique; instead of being slip-cast, the figures were made by pressing the paste into the moulds—a practice also followed at the Bow factory.

for long; only eight Worcester figure-models have been identified, and examples are so rare that they command fantastic prices among collectors, in spite of their artistic insignificance. An awkward, long-necked *sportsman* and his companion, on low scrolled and gilt bases, were sold at Sotheby's in 1949 for £1800 (1).[1] The *gardener* holding a flower-pot and spade, with his companion, may stand on pad bases with prickly applied leaves and flowers; alternatively they have bocage settings and four-footed scroll pedestals like those of earlier Bow figures (2).[2] Of the pair of *Turks* (3) one example bears the incised mark 'To'.[3] This mark, found on many Bow figures made from about 1752–63, and again on ornamental vessels and figures made by Cookworthy and Champion at Bristol about 1772–4, is believed to be that used by 'Mr. Tebo', who in 1774–5 was earning disapproval as a modeller for Wedgwood at Etruria.[4] At Bow, where there were others more competent to supply models, Tebo seems only to have worked as a 'repairer'. But the stiff, prim style of the Worcester *gardeners* resembles that of certain Bristol figures,[5] and it seems likely that at both these factories Tebo made some original models himself. He may even have suggested the brief Worcester experiment with figures that began in 1769 and ended with his own departure for Bristol about 1772. Besides the three pairs already mentioned, two other Worcester figure-models are at present known, both in white examples; a *king-fisher* perched on a tree-stump, and a seated *nurse*.[6] The latter may well have been moulded from a similar but slightly larger figure made at Longton Hall, this in turn being derived from the well-known Chelsea 'raised anchor' model.[7]

The attribution of the rare Worcester figures depends primarily on chemical analysis of the paste, which should show a content of eleven per cent or more of magnesia (due to the use of three times that

[1] Sotheby, Sale Cat., Oct. 21, 1949, Lot 65. A white *sportsman's companion*, *ibid.*, Sale Cat., Oct. 27, 1953, Lot 36.

[2] A pair with scroll pedestals, but no bocage, in the Albany Institute; D. Rosenfeld, *Porcelain Figures*, London and New York, 1949, Plate 113. The head of the woman is also known as a pipe-stopper; Savage, Plate 70B.

[3] Former Trapnell Collection, *Catalogue*, no. 145, Plate XIII (as Bristol).

[4] See pp. 87 (Bow), and 125–6 (Bristol and Etruria).

[5] P. 125.   [6] Marshall, *op. cit.*, nos. 384, 392A.

[7] See p. 116. F. Tilley, *Teapots and Tea*, Newport, Mon., 1957, Plate LXV, illustrates a Chelsea example ($7\frac{1}{2}$ inches high); the coloured example ($6\frac{1}{2}$ inches) in the Rous Lench Collection considered by the present writer to be Longton; and the unique white Worcester example in the Marshall Collection ($5\frac{7}{8}$ inches). A second coloured example of the intermediate Longton figure illustrated as 'Worcester, about 1753' in Detroit Institute Exhib. Cat., *English Pottery and Porcelain 1300–1850*, 1954, no. 258.

---

(1) *Plate* 86B; (2) *Plates* 87, 88B, (3) *Plate* 86A.

amount of soapstone). But the colours of the painting and shapes of the applied leaves have their own character, and the slightly concave closed bases are pierced on the underside by a small circular hole. The mark of a crescent in underglaze blue occasionally appears on figures made at Bow, but not on those made at Worcester.

11

PLYMOUTH AND BRISTOL

The factory founded at Plymouth in 1768, transferred to Bristol in 1770, and there carried on till 1781, was the first in England to make hard-paste porcelain, the productions including some ambitious but artistically mediocre figures.[1]

William Cookworthy (b. Kingsbridge, Devon, 1705; d. Plymouth, 1780), a Quaker chemist of Plymouth, was already familiar with writings on the Chinese manufacture of porcelain before 1745. In that year he met Andrew Duché, the potter who since 1737 had conducted an experimental manufacture of hard-paste porcelain in the American colony of Georgia.[2] Cookworthy discovered kaolin deposits in Cornwall about 1748, and the so-called 'growan stone', corresponding to the Chinese *petuntse*, at some unascertained later date. In 1768 he took out a patent for using these materials and founded the factory at Coxside, Plymouth, with the help of Thomas Pitt, later Lord Camelford, and a company of Quakers. Among the latter was Richard Champion of Bristol (b. 1743, d. 1791), who since 1765 had himself experimented with clays brought from Cornwall and Georgia. Three years after the transfer of the factory to Bristol in 1770 Cookworthy retired, having sold the patent to Champion. The latter's application for renewal of the patent in 1775 was granted, but only as regards porcelain; Wedgwood and the Staffordshire potters secured the right to use the Cornish material in earthenware. This was a severe economic setback, and in 1781 Champion disposed of the porcelain-patent to a company which later made useful wares only, at the New Hall factory at Shelton, Staffordshire.

Containing less fusible matter than Chinese or German hard-

---

[1] Hugh Owen, *Two Centuries of Ceramic Art in Bristol*, London, 1873; Lady Radford, 'Plymouth china', in *Devonian Year-Book*, 1920, p. 31. (Both valuable for source-material.) F. Hurlbutt, *Bristol Porcelain*, London, 1928; F. Severne Mackenna, *Cookworthy's Plymouth and Bristol Porcelain*, Leigh-on-Sea, 1946; and *idem.*, *Champion's Bristol Porcelain*, Leigh-on-Sea, 1947. (Text of the last three books to be regarded with caution.)

[2] For Duché's connection with the Bow factory, see p. 85.

paste porcelain, the Plymouth-Bristol material had to be fired at an even higher temperature. In the early Plymouth phase the glaze was often stained brown by smoke, and the figures throughout were apt to sag and develop fire-cracks. The paste did not lend itself to finely detailed modelling, and the close-fitting hard glaze refused to absorb the enamel colours, which stand out as a superficial incrustation and are apt to flake off. At its best, the Bristol porcelain has a cold, glittering and unsympathetic brilliance, which never allows us to forget its extreme hardness and intractability.

Factory-marks are not found on the figures, but an impressed mark 'T' or 'To' is seen on some of the best figures made at Bristol. It is believed to be that of the repairer 'Mr. Tebo', who worked at Bow (about 1750–65), then at Worcester, Bristol, and in 1774–5 at Wedgwood's factory.[1]

It is impossible to draw local distinctions between pieces made at Plymouth or Bristol, and more appropriate to speak of porcelain made by Cookworthy (1768–73) and Champion (1773–81). Apart from a large white *sphinx*[2] and some birds and animals, Cookworthy's figures number barely a score. Almost all are reproductions or adaptations of models made previously at the Longton Hall factory, and we must assume that Cookworthy, with an eye to the future, had acquired the Longton moulds—perhaps at the time when the remaining stock was sold at Salisbury in 1760.[3] The large standing *Continents*,[4] the standing *rose-seller* and *cabbage-seller*,[5] the group of *two putti with a goat*, the seated putti as *Seasons*, and other small seated figures (I) all re-appear in the Plymouth hard paste, sometimes with added bocages. The Plymouth versions are less distinctly moulded and 'repaired', and can immediately be distinguished from the Longton ones by their material and by the fact that they have open hollow bases and are glazed inside. The Rococo scrollwork is usually picked out in a dull brownish crimson, less often in gold and dull turquoise. Other typical colours also used later under Champion are a dull mauve ground on the dresses, with openings left for the insertion of elaborate gold floral sprays, and light orange-brown or dirty greyish yellow on the hair. Flesh tones are left white, with a faint suspicion of red on the cheeks.

[1] See pp. 16, 87, 121.
[2] Mackenna, *Cookworthy*, Fig. 73, 12 inches long.   [3] See p. 119.
[4] *Schreiber Cat.*, no. 696; Honey, *Old English Porcelain*, Plate 104; Mackenna, *Cookworthy*, Figs. 91–4; complete set in Victoria and Albert Museum, nos. C. 553 to 556–1920. Compare B. Watney, *Longton Hall Porcelain*, Plate 80.
[5] *Schreiber Cat.*, no. 704; compare Watney, Plate 61c and Colour Plate C.

(I) *Plate* 88A.

A ponderous large group of *Venus and Adonis*,[1] probably made after the transfer to Bristol, might derive from a lost Longton Hall model in the same manner as the large *Continents*. On the other hand, a stiff but dignified large *shepherd bagpiper* and *shepherdess* (1), standing on Rococo bases, appear to be original late Cookworthy models.[2] Smaller *shepherd* and *gardener* pairs on the rock bases of the Champion period are evidently by the same modeller, and in style recall the rare pair of *gardeners* made at the Worcester factory (2).[3] It has been suggested elsewhere that the models for the latter were made by the repairer 'Mr. Tebo', whose incised or impressed mark 'T⁰' is found on Worcester figures and ornamental vases of about 1770.[4] As this mark also appears on shell-shaped salts and ornamental vases in the Cookworthy-Champion porcelain, and on many of the best Champion figures, circumstantial evidence suggests that 'Mr. Tebo' left Worcester about 1772 and worked at Bristol till some time before November 1774, when we find him employed as a modeller by Wedgwood. In letters from Wedgwood to his partner Bentley we read:

'Mr. Tebo is modeling the two lamps from St. Non—but goes on very slowly. . . .' (Nov. 16, 1774.)

'I wish you could send me some Prints of Greek or Roman Heads to make your suits a little more complete. I think we can manage to model them and Mr. Tebo has nothing else to do. He is not equal to a Figure, but I can make him bost out and others finish these Heads. . . .' (July 3, 1775.)

'Mr. Tebo has had a cast of a Hare's Head before him some time, *but it is not a likeness*. The wet plaister in casting presses down the hair upon the face, and makes it look more like the head of a drown'd Puppy; and Mr. Tebo cannot model anything like the face of a Hare, —he has made many attempts at sundry times, but they generally turn out to be full as like Pigs as Hares. . . .' (July 11, 1775.)

'Mr. Tebo leaves the 11th of this month and not before he has done

---

[1] *Schreiber Cat.*, no. 731; another example in the Walters Art Gallery, Baltimore.
[2] *Schreiber Cat.*, no. 732; King, *Figures*, Fig. 68; Honey, *Old English Porcelain*, Plate 105A; Mackenna, *Cookworthy*, Fig. 90.
[3] *Schreiber Cat.*, no. 746, and Mackenna, *Champion*, Fig. 95 (shepherd bagpiper, 6¾ inches, and shepherdess, holding flowers in apron); Mackenna, *Champion*, Fig. 4, gardener and companion, 4½ inches, like the Worcester pair but with attitudes reversed.
[4] See p. 121. If 'Mr. Tebo' was at Worcester between 1769 and 1771, the period when figures were being made there, he can hardly have worked for Cookworthy at Plymouth (1768–70), as has been suggested by most writers on English porcelain. The shell-shaped salts attributed to Plymouth, on which his mark occurs, must have been made at Bristol towards the end of the Cookworthy period.

---

(1) *Plate* 89; (2) *Plate* 88c.

us very considerable mischief, for our Modelers do less by one half than they did before, charging double prices for their work, and when talk'd to about it have their reply ready "that it is cheaper than Mr. Tebo's and is finished, which his work never is".' (Oct. 28, 1775.)[1]

Tebo was evidently a difficult character, and Wedgwood was prejudiced against him, as he was against Champion, Tebo's former employer—and indeed against anything to do with porcelain and the Rococo style. Tebo was first and foremost a 'repairer', who put together figures moulded from other artists' models. His mark 'To' appears on many Bristol models designed, as we shall see, by a Derby modeller; it does *not* appear, to the knowledge of the present writer, on any of the Bristol shepherd and gardener figures mentioned in the last paragraph. Yet there seems to be a strong case that he created the actual models for these. Correct in detail, the figures are curiously rigid and lifeless, with their up-and-down draperies and awkwardly held hands. They confirm our opinion that Tebo was not the designer of the lively Bow figures on which, at an earlier stage in his career, he so often impressed his 'repairer's' mark.[2]

Cookworthy's figures, made at Plymouth and Bristol, represent the fag-end of the English Rococo style; Champion introduced an even more lumpish Louis Seize. He was not content with the modest offerings of Tebo as a modeller. In a letter dated February 17, 1772, he gives detailed iconographic instructions for the modelling of a set of *Elements*, and another of *Seasons*, to be about 10 inches high; he also refers to a set of *Elements* which the unnamed modeller he was addressing had already made at Derby.[3] The modeller in question was almost certainly Pierre Stephan, who was then working for Duesbury;[4] he evidently made at least three sets of models and sent them to Champion, without necessarily going to work at Bristol himself. A set of large standing Bristol *Elements* (1),[5] and another of adult *Seasons* in classical dress (2),[6] exactly correspond with the specifications laid down in Champion's letter. A second set of *Seasons* as large-headed children wearing contemporary dress, in the manner of Boucher, resembles in

---

[1] *Letters of Josiah Wedgwood 1772–1780*, London (privately printed), 1903, pp. 92 (Nov. 16, 1774), 119, 121, 130.

[2] See p. 87.

[3] Facsimile of letter in Owen, *Two Centuries of Ceramic Art in Bristol*; quoted in *Schreiber Cat.*, under nos. 742, 743; Jewitt, I, pp. 390–1.

[4] See p. 105.

[5] *Schreiber Cat.*, nos. 743, 744; Mackenna, *Champion*, Figs. 100–3.

[6] *Schreiber Cat.*, no. 742; Honey, *Old English Porcelain*, Plate 105c; Mackenna, *Champion*, Fig. 98.

---

(1) *Plate* 91; (2) *Plate* 90.

style the Derby 'French Seasons', and like these were presumably from Stephan's models (1).[1] The smirking archness of their expressions is at Bristol even more objectionable than at Derby, owing to the large scale and coarsening of detail. A *boy playing a salt-box* and *girl with a triangle*,[2] and a pair of *children with dogs*,[3] are unmistakably by the same hand; perhaps also two large and massive figures of a *goatherd* and a *milkmaid* (2),[4] and a *boy frightened by a dog*.[5] In fact Champion's Bristol figure-style is in the main a coarsened derivative from the Louis Seize of Derby, apparently with the modeller Stephan as the intervening link. Most of the models are known in examples with the repairer's mark 'T°', and must therefore have been created before Tebo left to work for Wedgwood towards the end of 1774. But one model can be dated as late as 1779—a white *mourning female figure* beside an urn, with a gilt inscription commemorating the death of Champion's daughter Eliza, who died in that year.[6] In contrast to the Rococo scroll bases of Cookworthy's figures, Champion's stand on irregular rockwork or rectangular bases, streaked with brown and pale yellow round the sides and with dull turquoise on top. On many of them the hair, lips and eyes were painted in colour, the slight floral or net-patterns on the dresses in gold alone. Emphasis was thus given to the whiteness of the ground, but (perhaps fortunately) Champion did not embark on figures in unglazed biscuit.[7] This was, however, subsequently used for a series of armorial plaques or medallions with incredibly laborious settings of applied leaves and flowers—the work, according to an old label pasted on the back of one example, of 'Thomas Briand of Derby'.[8]

Cookworthy's and Champion's porcelain will always command attention for the rare eccentricity of its material. This communicates

[1] *Schreiber Cat.*, no. 745 (compare Derby models, *Herbert Allen Cat.*, no. 123); Mackenna, *Champion*, Fig. 99; and our *Plate* 69B.
[2] *Schreiber Cat.*, no. 749.   [3] *Schreiber Cat.*, no. 748.
[4] *Schreiber Cat.*, no. 747 (goatherd); King, *Figures*, Figs. 66, 67; Mackenna, Fig. 104 (pair); both figures at Fenton House.
[5] King, *Figures*, Fig. 71; Mackenna, Fig. 93 (Fitzwilliam Museum, Cambridge, formerly Lord Fisher's Collection).
[6] Owen, Plate VIII; see also R. J. Charleston, 'The end of Bristol the beginning of New Hall: some fresh evidence,' *Connoisseur*, CXXXVI, 1956, p. 185 and Fig. 1. (Coloured and uninscribed example at Cambridge.) In general character the figure resembles the Derby 'Andromache mourning over the ashes of Hector', and Champion no doubt ordered the model from Pierre Stephan.
[7] Mackenna, *Cookworthy*, Fig. 95 illustrates a biscuit shepherd-boy signed 'W.C.' and marked with a cross; this is certainly not Cookworthy's or Champion's porcelain, and may have been made by William Coffee at Derby after 1800.
[8] Owen, p. 87.

(1) *Plates* 92, 93; (2) *Plates* 94, 95.

to the larger figures, raw-boned and uncouth as they are, something of its own elemental strength.

As a postscript it may be added that a tall standing figure of *Omphale* with the club of Hercules has been mistakenly published as of Bristol porcelain;[1] it was in fact made at Kloster Veilsdorf in Thuringia.

[1] W. King, *English Porcelain Figures of the Eighteenth-Century*, Plate VII. (Victoria and Albert Museum, C. 404–1919.)

12

MINOR FACTORIES: LOWESTOFT AND STAFFORDSHIRE

Lowestoft

The small factory at Lowestoft (Suffolk) was founded in 1757, expanded and opened a London showroom about 1770, and closed in 1802. It concentrated on the production of unpretentious useful wares and souvenirs ('A trifle from Lowestoft'), but also made a very few figures. The paste contains bone-ash and is highly phosphatic, this secret of composition having apparently been learnt from the Bow factory. A series of figures attributed to Lowestoft by Spelman[1] were actually made in Staffordshire towards the end of the eighteenth century. But the unglazed arm of a figure and a mould found on the factory-site confirm the Lowestoft origin of a pair of dancing putti, some 6 inches high, standing on pad bases with applied leaves and flowers.[2] Similar leaves and flowers are on the scrolled pad bases of a *dancing youth* playing a triangle and the companion *girl playing a mandolin*.[3] These last models are also known later on circular pedestals of neo-classical character, and earlier on four-footed pedestal bases.[4] But a coloured example of the youth standing on a four-footed base, in the Victoria and Albert Museum,[5] has been tested and found non-phosphatic, so that its previous attribution to Longton Hall is still a possibility. The moulds may have passed to Lowestoft on the closing of the Longton factory. Small figures of cats, sheep and swans were made, and further human figures perhaps await identification. But they are hardly likely to be of any importance.

[1] W. W. R. Spelman, *Lowestoft China*, Norwich, 1905, Plates XCII–XCVI.

[2] Geoffrey Godden, 'Lowestoft figures,' *Connoisseur Year Book*, 1957, p. 73, no. 3.

[3] Godden, l.c., nos. 1, 2, 4; youth in the Victoria and Albert Museum, C. 245–1940.

[4] A white pair, analysed and found highly phosphatic, illustrated in *Exhibition of English and Continental Porcelain of the 18th-Century*, Antique Porcelain Co. Ltd., London, 1951, p. 23.

[5] C. 931–1919, 7¼ inches high.

ENGLISH PORCELAIN FIGURES

Staffordshire

After the failure of the Longton Hall factory in 1760, no one in Staffordshire attempted to make porcelain again for over twenty years. It was an alien plant, too feeble to establish itself alongside a deeply-rooted local industry with other technical and artistic traditions. The Staffordshire men were 'earth potters' with an inventive, practical bent; since the end of the seventeenth century they had developed the fine unglazed red ware then introduced by John Philip Elers; the various lead-glazed earthenwares associated with the names of the master-potters Astbury and Thomas Whieldon; and the fine white salt-glazed stoneware. The international Rococo style appeared only as a thin veneer over a strong local idiom, having many of the characteristics of popular art. The young Josiah Wedgwood started business as Whieldon's partner (1754–8), making the normal Staffordshire types. On his own after 1759, he improved one of these, the cream-coloured earthenware, with such success that it captured the European markets and eventually became, with certain modifications, the standard useful ware of modern times. Wedgwood was a whole-hearted pioneer of the new neo-classical fashion, and the 'black basalt' and 'jasper' wares which he perfected during the 1770's were appropriately used for ornamental vases and plaques in the 'Grecian' or 'Etruscan' taste. Their matt, unglazed surfaces showed a deliberate reaction against the glitter of glazed porcelain which had appealed to an earlier generation. This aim they shared with the contemporary Derby figures of unglazed biscuit-porcelain.

It would thus seem that the future prospects for porcelain in Staffordshire were bleak. Nevertheless, in 1781 a company of six Staffordshire potters bought the patent held by Richard Champion of Bristol for making hard-paste porcelain, and in the next year set up a factory, in Shelton which they called 'New Hall'. Here they made unpretentious hard-paste table-wares painted in the same 'cottage china' style as late Bristol, but no figures. Meanwhile, thanks to political pressure stirred up by Josiah Wedgwood, Champion's patent had lost much of its point. When the patent was renewed in 1775, it covered only the manufacture of translucent porcelain; thereafter the essential materials, china clay and china stone, could be, and were, used by any manufacturers as ingredients in opaque earthenware. There is a small class of Staffordshire wares, dating from the last twenty years of the eighteenth century, in which, either by design or accident, the ingredients have been so combined as to produce a kind of hard porcelain. This class includes some figures.

The Staffordshire potters of the eighteenth century had already made many figures in other materials.[1] There were the salt-glazed 'pew-groups', in each of which two or three figures, modelled free-hand, were shown seated on a bench; these probably date from about 1735–40. There were also the amusing equestrian figures and musicians of 'Astbury' type, made in clays of contrasting colour, with coloured glazes, and the 'Whieldon' figures of colour-glazed earthenware, dating from the 1750's and 1760's. But the most considerable class of figures, in white or cream-coloured earthenware with transparent coloured glazes, was that made by the Ralph Woods, father and son, between about 1765 and 1790. Enoch Wood (*b.* 1759, *d.* 1840) had been in partnership with his cousin, the younger Ralph Wood, before joining James Caldwell in 1790; his numerous figures, some of considerable size, are usually of white earthenware painted in opaque overglaze enamel colours.

The sources of inspiration that lie behind the Staffordshire earthenware figures have not yet been systematically studied. Some early models are clearly derived from *blanc de chine*, and others from Meissen porcelain. It may be possible to demonstrate other borrowings from Bow porcelain and from Derby. But it would be a mistake to regard the whole genus as derivative. It seems rather to be a phenomenon of parallel growth with the porcelain figures, called into existence by the same spirit of the times, but on a lower social level. The series begins well before the foundation of the first English porcelain factories, and continues without a break into the middle of the nineteenth century. In spite of their crude technique, the later examples show more vitality than the contemporary figures in Derby and Rockingham porcelain. The figures and groups made by John Walton and others about 1820 revive the taste for spreading *bocages* found in porcelain of the 1760's.

We are here concerned only with the relatively small number of Staffordshire figures that were made in porcelain. They may be dated roughly between 1780 and 1800. Most of them are so like the contemporary Staffordshire earthenware figures that it seems almost an accident that they were made in the harder material. A large porcelain group in the Victoria and Albert Museum[2] shows a shepherd boy and girl seated aloft on rocks, holding a bird and bird-cage, with a tree behind and a fountain between them. The same model is known in earthenware, with an impressed serial 'No. 90' of the kind used by

---

[1] See especially C. Earle, *The Earle Collection of Early Staffordshire Pottery*, London, 1915; F. Falkner, *The Wood family of Burslem*, London, 1912; Bernard Rackham, *Catalogue of the Glaisher Collection of Pottery and Porcelain in the Fitzwilliam Museum*, Cambridge, 1934.

[2] No. C. 25–1928.

Ralph Wood.[1] Another porcelain group, also with an earthenware counterpart, shows a boy and girl perched on a high rock base, each holding a basket;[2] here the heavy faces resemble those so characteristic of the Ralph Wood figures. A curious opaque pale turquoise enamel appears on the base of this group, and also on a number of single porcelain figures which stand on low rock pads set over square plinths. Such figures include classical gods and *Virtues* (1), often with inscriptions, and children as gardeners or representing the Seasons.[3] Large reclining figures of *Mark Antony* in Roman armour and *Cleopatra* in classical dress[4] are known in this hardish porcelain, and also in white earthenware or black basalt ware, bearing the impressed marks of various factories. The circumstantial evidence suggests that most of these Staffordshire porcelain figures were made by Ralph or Enoch Wood. But some of the children bear a close resemblance to earthenware figures bearing the mark 'NEALE & CO', of this very competent factory working at Hanley between 1778 and 1786.

[1] Compare the earthenware version, illustrated in *Earle Collection*, no. 169. The Victoria and Albert Museum has an earthenware example, no. 101–1874, unmarked.

[2] Honey, *O.E.P.*, Plate 109. Earthenware version, B. Rackham, *Catalogue of the Glaisher Collection*, no. 897.

[3] Honey, *O.E.P.*, Plate 109; Spelman, *Lowestoft China*, Plates XCII, XCIII.

[4] Spelman, *op. cit.*, Plates XCIV, XCV, and Victoria and Albert Museum C. 1–1932 (porcelain); *Glaisher Collection*, no. 908 (earthenware, probably by Enoch Wood). A Mark Antony in black basalt bears the mark 'SWANSEA' impressed (Victoria and Albert Museum, no. 3501–1901). The companion Cleopatra is known with the mark 'G. BENTLEY, SWANSEA, May 22, 1791' (M. H. Grant, *The Makers of Black Basaltes*, Edinburgh and London, 1910, Plate XCV).

---

(1) *Plate* 96.

APPENDIX I

DOCUMENTS RELATING TO JOSEPH WILLEMS, MODELLER AT THE CHELSEA FACTORY

References are to E. J. Soil de Moriamé, *Les porcelaines de Tournay*, Tournai, 1910, pp. 94–6 (drawn from the Tournay archives, which were destroyed in the war of 1939–45, and from parish registers); and to W. H. Tapp, 'Joseph Willems, china modeller, died 1766,' *Connoisseur*, CI, 1938, pp. 176–82.

1715.   Willems born at Brussels (retrospective date given in register-entry of his burial at Tournay, March 19, 1767; see below. His Contract of 1766 with Peterinck named him as a native of Brussels).

1739, November 16. Marriage of Pierre-Joseph Willems and Marie-Josephe Lahaize (Tournay parish registers).

1749.   Pair of terracotta models signed WILLEMS 1749 (Oxford, Ashmolean Museum; illustrated by Lane, *Connoisseur*, CXLV, 1960, p. 249, Figs. 12–14).
Willems probably joined the Chelsea factory in this year, when figure-production first effectively began.

1755–8. 'Mr Williams or Mr Sprimont—Church Lane, East, Rent £14—taxes 11/-' (Chelsea Rate-Books, quoted by Tapp).

1760–6. Exhibition Catalogues of the Society of Artists of Great Britain (Algernon Graves, *The Society of Artists of Great Britain 1760–1791, The Free Society of Artists 1761–1783, a Complete Dictionary*, London, 1907, mistakenly lists the contributions for 1760–63 as by 'S. Williams').

1760	'Mr Williams	100	A Charity.'
1761	'Mr Williams	166	A bust of Mr. Martinelli.'
1762	'Mr Williams	152	A figure representing Generosity
		153	Ditto Heroic Virtue
		154	Ditto Seneca
		155	A boy after nature.'
1763	'Mr Williams	147	A model of Leda
		148	Emblematic figure of Honour
		149	Figure of Cleo.'

1764 'Mr Williams, at the Brussels Coffee House, Chelsea

    160 A young student and a country girl sleeping, a model

    161 Bust of a gentleman.'

1765 'Mr Williams at Chelsea

    184 Charity a model.'

1766 'Mr Williams at Chelsea

    219 Sincerity a model.'

Some of these models appear to correspond with those listed as in Willems' possession at the time of his death in 1766 (see below); they might also include replicas of models made previously for the Chelsea porcelain factory (Leda, the red-anchor group; 'Cleo', the gold-anchor Muse Clio, *Colour Plate A*; Sincerity, the red-anchor Venus. One of the 'Charities' could be the gold-anchor Roman Charity, *Plate 28*. 'Generosity' and 'Heroic Virtue' are doubtless the two figures combined in the gold-anchor group of Liberality and Modesty).

1763. 'Willems, Joseph, Modeller, At the Brussels Coffee House, Chelsea; this artist teaches Drawing, Modelling, and has modelled for the Chelsea China Manufactory for many years.' (*Mortimer's Universal Director*, part 1, p. 19.)

1764, July 24–6. 'Yesterday died at Chelsea, Mrs. Mary Williams, wife of Mr. Williams, Modeller at the Chelsea Manufactory.' (Notice in *The London Chronicle or Universal Evening Post*, vol. XVI, no. 1185.)

1766, February 25. François-Joseph Peterinck, proprietor of the Tournay porcelain factory, addressed a suggestion to the City Councillors, 'qu'étant intentionné, pour l'avantage de sa fabrique, de demander un *certain Willems*, très entendu dans la partie de la sculpture et du modelage, dans la croy-ance qu'il pourrait concourir par son talent au bien-être de l'academie, il offrit de lui en écrire et de lui mander qu'il en serait professeur.'

A minute written on the margin and dated March 1, 1766, reads: 'on a été d'avis d'accepter l'offre reprise et que la ville fournirait la somme de florins 200.0.0 pour trois leçons la semaine.' (Tournay Archives, quoted by Soil.) The con-tract with Peterinck was mentioned in the inventory of Willems' effects after his death.

In 1763 Peterinck had similarly obtained permission to invite to Tournay the painter Henri-Joseph Duvivier, who

till then had been employed at the Chelsea factory. Duvivier
was made professor of drawing at the Tournay Academy, at
a salary of 200 florins a year, in addition to his work at the
porcelain factory. On Willems' death in 1766 he became
also professor of modelling. Duvivier appears to have
been a native of Tournay, as was Willems' first wife. (Soil,
pp. 72–4.)

1766, November 1. Joseph Willems died at Tournay, after signing his
will, in which he appointed three executors and trustees on
behalf of his wife Marie. He especially requested that
Peterinck should send information of his death to his brother,
who was still working in England—probably the 'Mr
Wollams' mentioned as a 'motto and seal painter' in the
Chelsea factory accounts between 1771 and 1773. (Tournay
Archives, quoted by Tapp.)

A preliminary inventory of his effects made on November
6, 1766 included '27 groupes de différentes grandeurs'
(quoted by Soil).

1767, March 5. The second Inventory of effects of Joseph Willems
included:

'. . . plusieurs grouppes de ronde bosse de terre cuite et
colorées en blanc de sa composition, et par lui modelés, un
paquet de desseins concernant histoires et études, un
paquet de desseins antiques et histoires modernes tant en
rouge qu'en noir, un paquet de desseins en rouge et noir
lavées à l'encre de la chine, et en bistre, un paquet
d'estampes de différents maitres, en paysages et en figures,
un recueil des proportions et contours du corps humain
avec toutes ses mesures et une partie d'études d'architecture, douze desseins de paysages dessinés après nature,
dont quelques-uns se trouvent lavés á l'encre de la chine
très bien dessinés, douze estampes de différents maîtres,
treize estampes françoises représentant des sujets poétiques
et grotesques de différends maîtres, cinq livres de desseins
en rouge et en noir, douze estampes de différends maîtres,
représentant des sujets poétiques, grotesques et saints, cinq
estampes représentant des sujets poetiques, neuf estampes
représentans des badinages, cinq estampes des sujets pas-
torals, vingt quatre dessins à la plume représentans les cris
de paris, vingt quatre dessins idem, six estampes représentans des pièces d'architecture, et deux représentans des
sujets saints, une estampe, une estampe représentant
Diane au bain, deux autres estampes, quatre autres

135

estampes représentant des sujets poétiques, une autre estampe représentant un crucifix, et un grand nombre d'adorateurs, quatre autres estampes, une tête peinte sur toile, un grouppe représentant la Vierge et le Sauveur descendu de la croix, avec un adorateur, un grouppe de ronde bosse, representant la charité romaine, un grouppe représentant un sujet poetique, un grouppe représentant le chaste Joseph et la femme de Putiphar, un arracheur de dents à une femme, et deux enfans, un grouppe représentant Euleda (Leda?), un grouppe représentant charité, une vierge avec l'enfant Jésus qui dort, un grouppe représentant Flore et Zéphir et un petit amour, deux enfants faisant un grouppe, une vierge avec l'enfant Jésus, un grouppe représentant deux enfants jouans avec des fleurs, un saint Jérôme, une figure, appuyée suz un globe et une couronne d'étoiles sur la tête, représentant l'astronomie, une figure avec un bouclier, une figure debout, et un coeur dans la main, une figure droite tenant un sceptre dans la main, deux médaillons représentant les portraits du roy et reine d'Angleterre, quatorze petits plâtres représentans différends sujets, une figure tenant une lance dans la main, un enffant de plattre, un livre de dix figures d'académie dessignées d'après le naturel, et plusieurs têtes dessignées en rouge et noir.' (Soil, quoting from the trustee accounts, 1769, of 'Joseph Willems, modeleur à la fabrique de porcelaines, directeur et professeur a l'académie, décédé le Ier novembre 1766'. Tapp, quoting the same inventory, adds several 'silk frock coats, embroidered with lace, English', and English coin to the value of £44 17s. The material effects were sold on May 5, 1767 in 21 lots, and realized 714 livres—approximately £36.)

The inventory is of particular interest, since it appears to describe the equipment accumulated by Willems as chief-modeller at Chelsea and brought by him to Tournay when he came there to work in a similar capacity. Of the drawings, some at least might have been by his own hand, though hardly the landscapes. The forty-eight pen-drawings of 'cris de paris' might conceivably have been copied from the famous set of engravings by the Comte de Caylus after Bouchardon. On the other hand, some Chelsea red-anchor figures in the same vein appear to be original inventions.

The engravings, some French, cover landscape, religious

subjects, 'histoires' and 'poétiques' (perhaps classical mythology), pastoral, 'grotesques' and 'badinages' (perhaps Italian Comedy and Teniers subjects), and thus appear comprehensive.

The 'groups in the round, of terracotta and painted white, of his own composition and modelled by him' no doubt include replicas of models previously made for Chelsea porcelain, as well as exhibits shown at the Society of Artists of Great Britain between 1760 and 1766. The following correspondences may be suggested:

> 'Group representing the Saviour taken down from the Cross, with a worshipper'; Chelsea red-anchor group, and similar group in Tournay porcelain.

> 'Roman Charity'; Chelsea gold-anchor group (1), and perhaps one of the two 'Charity' groups exhibited in 1760 and 1765.

> 'Group representing Euleda'; Chelsea red-anchor group of Leda, and 'Leda' exhibited in 1763.

> 'Virgin with the infant Jesus asleep'; perhaps the Chelsea raised-anchor Nurse, after the school-of-Palissy model.

> 'Two children forming a group', and 'group representing two children playing with flowers'; perhaps the two Chelsea red-anchor groups of 'Spring and Summer' and 'Autumn and Winter' (Savage, Plate 30).

> 'A Virgin with the infant Jesus'; perhaps the Chelsea red-anchor group (2).

> 'A figure leaning on a globe, with a crown of stars on its head, representing Astronomy'; the Chelsea gold-anchor Muse Urania.

> 'A figure with a shield'; perhaps the Chelsea red-anchor Mars (Savage, Plate 24A).

> 'A standing figure, with a heart in one hand'; the Chelsea red-anchor Venus (Savage, Plate 22A), and the 'Sincerity' exhibited in 1766.

1767, March 19. Burial of Pierre-Joseph Willems, aged fifty-two (Tournay parish registers, quoted by Christiane Deroubaix, *Les porcelaines de Tournai du Musée de Mariemont*, Mariemont, 1958, p. 77, n. 110). This date disagrees with that of death quoted by Soil; Mlle. Deroubaix can offer no explanation for the discrepancy.

---

(1) *Plate* 28; (2) *Plate* 13.

1767, June 8. Letter from P. C. Canot, recommending Mrs. Marie Williams, Widow of Mr. Williams, Sculptor, to the Charity of the Incorporated Society of Artists (Letter among the papers of the Incorporated Society, quoted by Tapp).

1769, July 25. Recent death of 'Mrs Mary Williams, wife of Mr Williams, for a long time Modeller at the Chelsea Manufactory'. (Notice in the *Chiswick Times*, quoted by Tapp; apparently Willems' second wife, also named Mary.)

APPENDIX II

LETTERS FROM BENJAMIN VULLIAMY AND JOSEPH
LYGO, LONDON, TO WILLIAM DUESBURY THE
YOUNGER, CHINA MANUFACTORY, DERBY
from the originals in the Victoria and Albert Museum Library, MSS.
English, *Duesbury and the Derby Porcelain Factory* 1755–95

London, November 23, 1790 (Vulliamy to Duesbury)
'Dear Sir—
    You will have received the Figure & Mould before this letter. . . .
I was in hopes of hearing from you to know how you liked the first
Figure in every respect it is impossible for me to tell you how much
trouble has been taken in hopes of making these two figures as perfect
as possible. I forgot in my former letter to beg that you would have a
box made for each Figure to be kept in separate that they may be
preserved clean for your modeller to repair the figures from. I saw
some French figures this morning at Ld. Holderness's which are
really admirably well repaired. I have not the least doubt that if your
modeller attends to my former letter & directions, the Subject will be
according to our Wishes, for it is absolutely necessary that the original
models should be looked at to repair the China Figures or else by
degrees the original would be lost. . . .   Bn Vulliamy.'

London, May 27, 1790 (Lygo to Duesbury)
. . . 'I yesterday went with the Modeler to Mr Vulliamy agreeable to
his own appointment, and Mr V took a great deal of pains with him,
he thinks from his conversation he may be a clever person in his way,
but that he cannot answer for till he has first see some of his work—
and as the man did not seem quite agreeable to come to Derby till Mr
V was satisfied with his abilities it is agreed on for him to Model a
figure here from a Drawing of Mr V's which he says will sell. The
man thinks he shall be about three weeks of Modeling the figure and
it will be done under the instructions of Mr V. . . .'
    In a further letter of January 7, 1791 Lygo discusses the project of
getting a 'Layman' (lay figure) made, 3 feet high, and refers to one
used 'when Mr. Spengler was here'. Spengler was evidently the artist
referred to in the letter of May 27, 1790.

BIBLIOGRAPHY

References to scattered articles and more general books have been given in the footnotes, and are here omitted. The following is a selective list of the works most useful for discussion or illustrations of the porcelain figures.

GENERAL WORKS

Llewellyn Jewitt, *The Ceramic Art of Great Britain*, 2 vols., London, 1878.

J. E. Nightingale, *Contributions Towards the History of Early English Porcelain from Contemporary Sources*, Privately printed, Salisbury, 1881.

William King, *English Porcelain Figures of the Eighteenth Century*, London, 1925.

Bernard Rackham, *Catalogue of the Schreiber Collection of English Porcelain, Earthenware, Enamels, etc.*, vol. I., *Porcelain* (2nd edition), Victoria and Albert Museum, London, 1928.

Mrs. Donald MacAlister (ed.), *William Duesbury's London Account Book: 1751–53*, London (English Porcelain Circle Monograph), 1931.

W. B. Honey, *Old English Porcelain* (2nd edition), London, 1948.

J. L. Dixon, *English Porcelain of the Eighteenth Century*. London, 1952.

G. Savage, *Eighteenth-Century English Porcelain*, London, 1952.

Yvonne Hackenbroch, *Chelsea and other English Porcelain, Pottery and Enamel in the Irwin Untermyer Collection*, Cambridge, Mass., 1957.

Kathryn C. Buhler, *English Porcelain Figures*, Picture Book, Museum of Fine Arts, Boston, Boston, n.d.

English Porcelain Circle Transactions, Nos. I to IV. London, 1928–34; later *English Ceramic Circle Transactions*, vols. I and following, London, 1933.

English Ceramic Circle, *English pottery and porcelain, Commemorative Catalogue of an Exhibition held at the Victoria and Albert Museum May 5–June 20, 1948*, London, 1949.

BIBLIOGRAPHY

CHELSEA

William King, *Chelsea Porcelain*, London, 1922.

The Cheyne Book of Chelsea China (ed. Reginald Blunt), London, 1924.

G. E. Bryant, *Chelsea Porcelain Toys*, London, 1925.

F. Severne MacKenna, *Chelsea Porcelain. The Triangle and Raised Anchor Wares*, Leigh-on-Sea, 1948.

F. Severne MacKenna, *Chelsea Porcelain. The Red Anchor Wares*, Leigh-on-Sea, 1951.

F. Severne MacKenna, *Chelsea Porcelain. The Gold Anchor Wares*, Leigh-on-Sea, 1952.

BOW

Frank Hurlbutt, *Bow Porcelain*, London, 1927.

Hugh Tait, *Bow Porcelain 1744–1776, A special Exhibition of documentary material to commemorate the bi-centenary of the retirement of Thomas Frye*, British Museum, London, 1959.

DERBY

John Haslem, *The Old Derby China Factory*, London, 1876.

F. Brayshaw Gilhespy, *Crown Derby Porcelain*, Leigh-on-Sea, 1951.

LONGTON HALL

W. Bemrose, *Longton Hall Porcelain*, London, 1906.

Bernard Watney, *Longton Hall Porcelain*, London, 1957.

WORCESTER

F. A. Barrett, *Worcester Porcelain*, London, 1953.

H. Rissik Marshall, *Coloured Worcester Porcelain of the First Period, 1751–1783*, Newport, Monmouthshire, 1954.

PLYMOUTH AND BRISTOL

Hugh Owen, *Two Centuries of Ceramic Art in Bristol*, London, 1873.

F. Hurlbutt, *Bristol Porcelain*, London, 1928.

F. Severne MacKenna, *Cookworthy's Plymouth and Bristol Porcelain*, Leigh-on-Sea, 1946.

F. Severne MacKenna, *Champion's Bristol Porcelain*, Leigh-on-Sea, 1947.

INDEX

INDEX

Chinese porcelain, 11

Chinese porcelain figures, *see* blanc-de-chine

chinoiserie and *Chinese* subjects, 2, 51; Chelsea, 58, 59, 60, 62, 65, 69, 70, 72; 'girl-in-a-swing', 82; Bow, 88; Derby, 98, 100; Longton Hall, 115; Worcester, 120

Chippendale, Thomas, 5

Chirokee clay ('unaker'), 11, 12, 85

Cibber, Caius Gabriel, sculptor, 34

Cibber, Mrs., Derby, 53, 103

Clarke, T. H., 31

Clay, Charles, 40

Cleopatra, Staffordshire, 132

Clive, Kitty; Bow, 86, 88, Derby, 97

Coade, Mrs. Eleanor, 36

Coade's artificial stone, 36, 37, 94, 103, 111

Coan, John, Chelsea, 73

Cochin, C. N., 62

Cocker, George, modeller, 112

Coffee, William, modeller, 37, 111

Continents, Four, 47; Chelsea, 66, 71; Bow, 93; Derby, 103; Longton Hall, 118, 119; Plymouth, 124

Conway, General, Derby, 106

Cookworthy, William, 11, 123, 124

Cooks, Bow, 90; Longton Hall, 117

Copeland, Messrs., 19, 68, 107

Cox, James, 56, 70

crescent mark, 122

Crespin, Paul, 58

Cries of London, 49

Cris de Paris, 44, 45, 49, 136; Chelsea, 73; Bow, 90; Derby, 99

Crisp, Nicholas, 36, 94, 95

Crowther, John, 85, 93

Cumberland, Duke of, Chelsea bust, 60

Cupid, 48; Chelsea, 67; 'girl-in-a-swing', 82; Derby, 104, 106; Longton Hall, 115, 116

Cyfflé, Paul Louis, modeller, 110

'D' mark, 92

Dance, Nathaniel, 107

dancing-lesson, Chelsea, 72

Daullé, Jean, 88, 102

Deare, John, sculptor, 37, 109

Deposition from the Cross, Chelsea, 73; Tournay, 74

Derby porcelain, 19, 20, 37, 96–112, 118, 126

De Vaere, John, sculptor, 36, 37

Diana, Derby, 101

Dietz, Ferdinand, sculptor, 26

Dirmstein earthenware, 33

Dixon, J., 107

dogs; Chelsea, 59; 'girl-in-a-swing', 79, 81; Longton Hall, 31, 115

Dossie, Robert, 70

Drinkwater, General, Derby, 107

Dryden, John, portrait, 33; Longton Hall, 117

Duché, André, 11, 85, 123

Duesbury, William, the elder, 22, 36, 37, 56, 62, 88, 90, 93, 96, 97, 100, 101, 103

Duesbury, William, the younger, 37, 97, 109, 110, 139

Du Halde, 11

Duquesnoy, François (il Fiammingo), sculptor, 27, 31, 34, 59

Dutch dancers, 49; Chelsea, 68

Duvivier, Henri-Joseph, 134, 135

dwarfs, 52; Chelsea, 62, 73; Derby, 107

Dwight, John, 10

Earlom, Richard, 107

Eberlein, J. F., modeller, 67, 68, 107

Edwards, George, 61

Egan, Pierce, 111

Elements, 46; 'girl-in-a-swing', 78, 79; Bow, 88, 91; Derby, 99, 105; Bristol, 126

Elhafen, Ignaz, sculptor, 39

engravings as sources of design, 43, 44, 135, 136, and *passim*

d'Entrecolles, Père, 11

Esdaile, Mrs. K., 30–3

Etruria, Staffordshire, 15; *see* Wedgwood

Europa and the bull, 'girl-in-a-swing', 79; Derby, 102

Evelyn, John, 38

fables, see Aesop

fakes, 62 n.4, 74, 98 n.2

Falconet, Etienne-Maurice, sculptor and modeller, 26, 105

Falconer, T., 120

Falstaff; Bow, 86; Derby, 103

Fame, Chelsea, 66

Fanelli, Francesco, sculptor, 38, 116

Farnsworth, Isaac, repairer, 107

Fawkener, Sir Everard, 45, 56, 60, 66

de Ferriol, 51, 52

'Fiammingo, Il', *see* Duquesnoy

INDEX

fiddler, Chelsea, 68
fisherman, Chelsea, 68; Bow, 87
fisherman, Chinese, Chelsea, 59
firing, 21, 22
Flörsheim earthenware, 33
Flora, Chelsea, 67; Bow, 90
Flora Farnese, 32; Bow, 93
fortune-teller, Chelsea, 72
Frederick the Great, Bow, 91
Frederick, Prince of Wales, 30, 57, 60, 77
French porcelain, 3, 6, 10, 11, 12
Frye, Thomas, 3, 11, 12, 85
Fukien porcelain figures, *see* blanc-de-chine

Gabarisco, David, Chelsea, 73
Galathea, Chelsea, 71
Ganymede and the eagle, 'girl-in-a swing', 78
gardener, Chelsea, 68; Bow, 88; Worcester, 121; Bristol, 125, 126
Garrick, David; Bow, 86; Derby, 103, 107; Longton Hall, 117
Gauron, Nicholas-François, 104
George II, bust, Chelsea, 30, 61
George III, bust, Chelsea, 30, 61; group, Chelsea, 55, 73; Derby, 107
German porcelain, 4, 7, 23, 26 (*see also* Meissen)
gilding, 23, 24, 70, 71, 74, 92, 117
Giles, James, 22, 79
'girl-in-a-swing' factory (Chelsea?), 18, 77–84
goatherd, Longton Hall, 117; Bristol, 127
gods and *goddesses*, classical, 46; Chelsea, 66, 67; Bow, 91; Derby, 99, 100, 101; Staffordshire, 131
Gouyn, Charles, 56, 83
Graces, Derby, 106, 110
Granby, Marquess of, Bow, 54, 92
greyhound, Chelsea, 59
'growan stone', 123
Guelfi, Giovanni Battista, sculptor, 28

Harlequin, 52; 'girl-in-a-swing', 82; Bow, 88, 90; Derby, 101
harvester, Chelsea, 72
Haslem, John, 36, 107, 108
Hayman, Francis, 86
Heath, John, 96, 97
Hercules and Omphale, Chelsea, 72; 'girl-in-a-swing', 78; and *the*

Hydra, Chelsea, 72; Derby, 104; and *the Keryneian stag*, Longton Hall, 116; and the *Nemean Lion*, Longton Hall, 116
Heylyn, Edward, 3, 11, 85
Hill, Joseph, 'repairer', 108
Hogarth, William, 2
Holt, Richard, 35, 36
Honey, W. B., 9
Houston, Richard, 92
Howe, General, Derby, 107
huntsmen or sportsmen, 49; Chelsea, 68; Bow, 87, 90; Derby, 99; Worcester, 121
Hygieia, Derby, 109

Isabella, Chelsea, 53, 62
Italian Comedy, 52, 53, 137; Chelsea, 60, 62, 69, 72; Bow, 87, 88, 90; Derby, 101
ivory figures, 39

Jason and Medea, Derby, 106
Jefferys, Thomas, 52
Jenkinson, William, 113
June, Derby, 99, 102
Jupiter, Chelsea, 66; Bow, 91; Derby, 99, 102

Kaendler, Johann Joachim, modeller, 4, 25, 29, 42, 43, 48, 52
Kandler, Frederick, 40
kaolin, 11, 85, 123
Kauffmann, Angelica, 48, 106
Kean, Edmund, Derby, 107
Kean, Michael, 97
Kemble, John Philip, Derby, 107
Keys, Edward and Samuel, modellers, 111
King, William, 8
kingfisher, Worcester, 121
Kloster-Veilsdorf porcelain, 128
Kuan-yin, Chelsea, 60

lace-work on figures, 19, 20
Lambeth, Crisp's factory, 36, 94, 95
Laroon, Marcellus, 49
lead 'master' models, 19
'*Lear, King*', Derby, 99
Leda, Chelsea, 67, 72, 134, 137; Derby, 102
Le Marchand, David, sculptor, 39
Lemoyne, Charles, 78
Liberal Arts, 47; Chelsea, 66; Derby, 105

145

1. *Ceres. Modeller, Joseph Willems. Chelsea; 1749–50. Ht. 12¼ in. The Antique Porcelain Company. (See pages 42, 59)*

2. *Chelsea.* A. *Incense-burner. 1745–9. Ht. 5½ in.*
Mr. P. E. Scarisbrick. B. *Boy piper. About 1749. Ht. 6 in.*
Victoria and Albert Museum. C. *Sleeping boy. Dated 1746.*
Length 6⅛ in. British Museum. (See pages 27, 58, 59)

3. *Chinese fisherman. Unmarked. Chelsea; about* 1749. *Ht.* 8$\frac{1}{4}$ *in.*
Mr. P. E. Scarisbrick. (*See page* 59)

4. *Rustic lovers. Modeller, Joseph Willems.*
Mark, crown and trident in underglaze blue. Chelsea; 1749–50.
Ht. 9 in. British Museum. (See pages 59, 80)

5. 'Femme du Levant', after Boucher. Modeller, Joseph Willems.
Mark, raised anchor outlined in violet. Chelsea; about 1750.
Ht. 10½ in. Lady Ludlow Collection, Luton Hoo. (See pages 52, 62)

6. *Isabella, after Cesare Vecellio. Modeller, Joseph Willems.*
Mark, raised anchor. Chelsea; 1750. Ht. 9½ in.
Glasgow, Art Gallery and Museum. (See pages 53, 62)

7. *Chinese group, after Boucher. Modeller, Joseph Willems.*
Mark, raised anchor. Chelsea; about 1751–2. Ht. 9¼ in.
Mrs. S. J. Katz. (See pages 51, 63)

8. *Britannia mourning for Frederick Prince of Wales.
Modeller, Joseph Willems. Unmarked. Chelsea; 1751. Ht. 10 in.
British Museum. (See page 61)*

9. *George III as Prince of Wales. Unmarked. Chelsea; 1751.*
Ht. 11 in.
Former Radford Collection. (See pages 50, 61)

10. *Apollo. Modeller, Joseph Willems. Mark, red anchor.*
Chelsea; about 1755. Ht. 11 in. Lord Fisher. (See page 66)

11. *Ceres. Mark, red anchor. Modeller, Joseph Willems. Chelsea; about 1755. Ht. 12¾ in. Lord Fisher. (See page 67)*

12. *Smelling, from the Five Senses. Modeller, Joseph Willems.*
Mark, red anchor. Chelsea; about 1755. Ht. 11 in.
Boston, Museum of Fine Arts. (See pages 47, 66)

13. *Madonna and Child. Modeller, Joseph Willems.*
Mark, red anchor. Chelsea; about 1755. Ht. 8½ in.
Boston, Museum of Fine Arts. (See pages 51, 69)

14. *Fruit-seller. Modeller, Joseph Willems.*
Mark, red anchor. Chelsea; about 1755. Ht. 9 in. Lord Fisher.
(See page 68)

15. *Fruit-seller. Modeller, Joseph Willems. Mark, red anchor.*
Chelsea; about 1755. Ht. 9½ in. Lord Fisher.
(See page 68)

16. *Beggar. Modeller, Joseph Willems. Mark, red anchor.*
Chelsea; about 1755. Ht. 7¾ in.
Victoria and Albert Museum. (See page 68)

17. *Fisherman's wife. Modeller, Joseph Willems.*
Mark, red anchor. Chelsea; about 1755. Ht. 7⅞ in.
Former Giddings Collection. (See page 68)

18. *Spring, Autumn, Summer and Winter.*
Modeller, Joseph Willems. Marks, red anchor.
Chelsea; about 1753–5. Ht. 5 to 5½ in
Victoria and Albert Museum. (See pages 66, 91, 115)

19. A. *The Captain, from the Italian Comedy. Ht. 6 in.*
B. *Monk and Nun. Ht. 5½, 5⅜ in. Modeller, Joseph Willems.*
Marks, red anchor. Chelsea; about 1755.
Boston, Museum of Fine Arts. (See pages 51, 69)

20. *Maypole group. Modeller, Joseph Willems. Mark, red anchor. Chelsea; about 1755. Ht. 14 in. Lord Fisher. (See pages 49, 68)*

21. *Chinese musicians group. Modeller, Joseph Willems.*
Mark, red anchor. Chelsea; about 1756. Ht. 14½ in.
R. C. H. Sloane-Stanley Trustees. (See pages 51, 69, 70)

22. *Chelsea.* A. *Monkey musicians. Marks, red anchor. About* 1756.
Ht. 5⅜, 6, 5⅜ *in. Victoria and Albert Museum.*
B. *Asia and Africa. Marks, gold anchor. About* 1759.
Ht. about 11 *in. Antique Porcelain Co. (See pages* 69, 103)

23. *Chelsea.* A. *Cupids, 'in disguise'. Marks, red anchor.*
About 1756. Ht. 4½, 4⅜, 5 in. Ex Knoblock Colln.
B. *Europe and America. Marks, gold anchor. Ht. about 11 in.*
Antique Porcelain Co. (See pages 67, 69, 103)

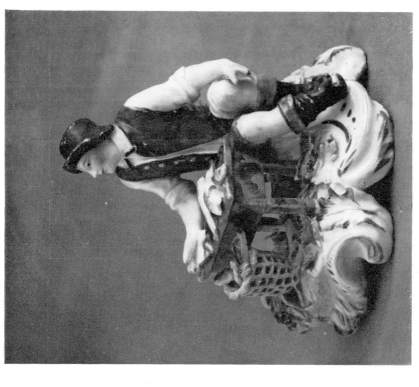

24. *Chelsea. Modeller, Joseph Willems.*
A. *Fruit-gatherers. Marks, red and gold anchors. About 1757–9.*
Ht. $6\frac{1}{4}$ in. *Ex McEuen Collection.*
B. *Fish-seller. Mark, red anchor. About 1756–7. Ht. $4\frac{1}{2}$ in.*
Boston, Museum of Fine Arts. (See page 69)

25. The 'Ranelagh Dancers' (four from a set of eight).
Modeller, Joseph Willems. Marks, gold anchor.
Chelsea; about 1759–60. Ht. 8 to 8½ in. Sir B. Eckstein Collection.
(See pages 55, 75)

26. *Shepherdess. Modeller, Joseph Willems. Mark, gold anchor.*
Chelsea; about 1759–63. Ht. 11$\frac{3}{4}$ *in. Victoria and Albert Museum.*
(See page 72)

27. *Shepherd, companion to Plate 26. Ht. 11 in.*
Victoria and Albert Museum. (See page 72)

28. *The Roman Charity, after Rubens. Modeller, Joseph Willems.*
Mark, gold anchor, Chelsea; about 1762–3. Ht. 21½ in.
Former Sir B. Eckstein Collection. (See pages 48, 74)

29. *The dancing lesson, after Boucher. Modeller, Joseph Willems.*
Mark, gold anchor. Chelsea; about 1762–3. Ht. 16 in.
London Museum. (See page 72)

30. A. *Ganymede and the Eagle. Ht,* $6\frac{1}{8}$ *in, Former Glendenning Collection*
B. *Girl in a swing. Ht.* $6\frac{1}{4}$ *in. Victoria and Albert Museum.*
'Girl-in-a-swing' factory (Chelsea?); 1751–4. (See pages 77, 79)

31. A. *Mater Dolorosa. Ht. 7¾ in.*
B. *Dancer and hurdy-gurdy player. Ht. 5⅝, 5¾ in.*
'Girl-in-a-swing' factory (Chelsea?); 1751 4. British Museum.
(See page 79)

32. *Britannia mourning for Frederick, Prince of Wales* (d. 1751).
'*Girl-in-a-swing*' *factory* (*Chelsea?*); 1751. *British Museum. Ht. 7 in.*
(*See page 77*)

33. *Gentleman presenting a bird's nest to a lady.*
'*Girl-in-a-swing*' *factory* (*Chelsea?*); 1751–4. *Ht. about* $7\frac{1}{2}$ *in.*
Dr. and Mrs. H. Statham. (*See page* 79)

34. *Hercules and Omphale.*
'*Girl-in-a-swing*' *factory (Chelsea?); about 1751–4. Ht.* $8\frac{3}{8}$ *in.*
Victoria and Albert Museum. (See page 78)

35. *Scent-bottles.* A–F, *'Girl-in-a-swing' factory;* 1753–4.
Ht. 2½ *to* 3¾ *in.* G. *Chelsea; about* 1756.
H, I. *Chelsea; about* 1758–60. *Ht.* 3 *to* 3¼ *in.*
Victoria and Albert Museum, A–D, H, I. *Untermyer Collection,*
E, F, G. (*See pages* 51, 75, 81, 82)

36. *Henry Woodward as 'The Fine Gentleman',*
after Francis Hayman. By the 'Muses modeller'.
Bow; 1750. Ht. 10¾ in. (See pages 55, 86)

57. *Kitty Clive as 'The Fine Lady', after Charles Mosley.
By the 'Muses modeller'. Bow; 1750. Ht.* $9\frac{3}{4}$ *in.*
(See pages 53, 86)

38. *Lovers with a bird-cage, after Lancret. By the 'Muses modeller'.*
Bow; about 1752–4. Ht. 7½ in. Victoria and Albert Museum.
(See page 87)

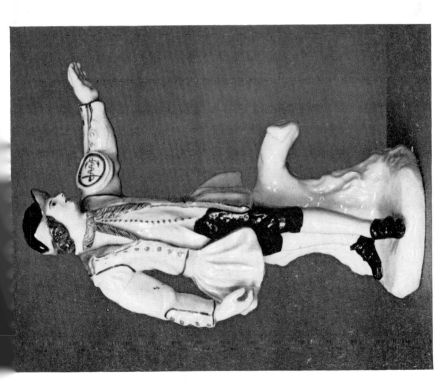

41. Bow, by the 'Muses modeller'. A. Thames waterman. About 1754.
Ht. 7¾ in.
B. Minerva. About 1750–4. Ht. 6¾ in. Victoria and Albert Museum.
(See page 88)

42. *Charity. By the 'Muses modeller'. Mark, 'T' impressed.
Bow; about 1752–4. Ht. 9¾ in. Victoria and Albert Museum.
(See pages 48, 87)*

39. *Muse, inscribed 'Euterpe for the musical instruments'.*
Bow; about 1750–2. Ht. 6⅛ in. Victoria and Albert Museum.
(*See page* 87)

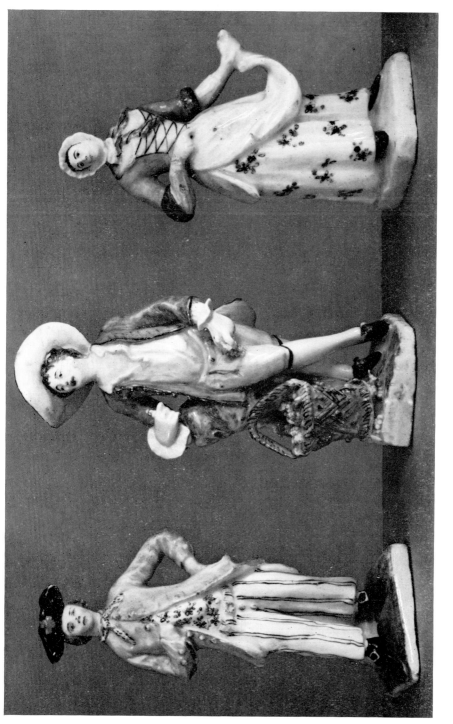

40. *Sailor and companion, and vintner. By the 'Muses modeller'. Bow; about 1750–4. Ht. 5¾, 6¼, 5½ in. Ex Knoblock Collection. (See page 88)*

43. *Boy with flower-vase. By the 'Muses modeller'.*
Bow; about 1752–4. Ht. 14⅞ in. Victoria and Albert Museum.
(See page 89)

44. 'Matrimony', pair with Plate 45. By the 'Muses modeller'.
Bow; about 1754. Ht. 9¾ in. Mrs. S. J. Katz. (See page 89)

45. 'Liberty', pair with Plate 44. By the 'Muses modeller'.
Bow; about 1754. Ht. 9¾ in. Mrs. S. J. Katz. (See page 89)

46. *Shepherdess. Bow; about 1755–6. Ht. 10$\frac{3}{8}$ in.*
Victoria and Albert Museum. (See pages 89, 91)

47. *Shepherd bagpiper, pair with Plate 46. Ht. 10¼ in.*
Victoria and Albert Museum. (See pages 89, 91)

48. *Neptune, or Water. Bow; about* 1755–6. *Ht.* $6\frac{1}{4}$ *in.*
Victoria and Albert Museum. (See pages 41, 91)

49. *Pedlar. Bow; about 1755–6. Ht.* $6\frac{3}{8}$ *in.*
Victoria and Albert Museum. (See pages 41, 91)

50. *Bow.* A. *Cooks. Mark, 'B' impressed on man.*
About 1755–6. Ht. 7, 6½ in.
B. *Spring and Autumn. About 1755–6.*
Ht. 4⅞, 5 in. Victoria and Albert Museum. (See page 90)

51. *Bow.* A. *Monk and nun. About 1757–9. Ht.* 5½, 5⅜ *in.*
B. *Nun and monk. About 1755–6. Ht.* 4⅜, 4¼ *in.*
Victoria and Albert Museum. (*See pages* 51, 91)

52. *Flora, after the Flora Farnese. Bow; about 1756–9. Ht. 18¼ in.*
Victoria and Albert Museum. (See pages 32, 93)

53. *General Wolfe, after Richard Houston. Mark, 'To' impressed.
Bow; 1760. Ht. 13⅞ in. Victoria and Albert Museum. (See page 92)*

54. *Spring. Bow; about 1759–60. Ht. 9¼ in. British Museum.*
(See page 92)

55. *Dancing sailor. Bow; about 1760. Ht. 8½ in. Lord Fisher.*
(See page 92)

56. A. *Spring, Summer. Ht.* $4\frac{7}{8}$, $4\frac{3}{4}$ *in.*
Victoria and Albert Museum.
B. *Huntsman playing flute, and girl. Ht.* $6\frac{1}{4}$ *in.*
Dr. and Mrs. H. Statham. Derby; 1750–4. (See page 99)

57. A. *Autumn, Winter. Ht.* 5¼, 4¼ *in. Victoria and Albert Museum.*
B. *'Feeling'.* 6½ *in.*
C. *'Tasting'. Ht.* 6 *in. Lord Fisher Collection (Fitzwilliam Museum).*
Derby; 1750–4. *(See page 99)*

58. *Chinese group, 'Smelling.' Derby; 1750–4. Ht.* $8\frac{1}{2}$ *in.
New York, Metropolitan Museum. (See pages* 51, 98)

59. *St. Philip, holding a Crucifix. Derby; about* 1754. *Ht.* 9½ *in.*
Victoria and Albert Museum. (*See page* 98)

60A. *Pluto and Cerberus. Ht.* $6\frac{5}{8}$ *in.*
Victoria and Albert Museum.
B. *Pair, old man and woman as 'Autumn'. Ht.* $6\frac{1}{2}$, 6 *in.*
Mrs. W. D. Dickson Collection. Derby; about 1752–4.
(*See pages 41, 99*)

61. *Derby; about 1753–4.* A. *Dancing shepherdess. Ht.* $6\frac{7}{8}$ *in.*
B, C. *Street-sellers. Ht.* $7\frac{1}{8}$, $6\frac{3}{4}$ *in. Victoria and Albert Museum.*
(See page 99)

62. A. *Youth and girl with dogs and parrot. Ht. 6, 5½ in.*
British Museum.
B. *Dancing youth. Ht. 7¼ in. Victoria and Albert Museum.*
Incised marks, two triangles in a circle.
Derby, 'transitional'; about 1755. (See page 100)

63. *Shepherd offering apple. Derby, 'pale family'; about 1756–8.
Ht. 10⅞ in. Victoria and Albert Museum. (See page 101)*

64. *The poet Milton. Derby; about 1758. Ht. 11½ in.*
Former Knoblock Collection. (See pages 33, 101, 103)

65. *The poet Shakespeare. Derby; about 1758. Ht. 11½ in.*
Former Knoblock Collection. (See pages 29, 32, 101, 103)

68. *The Muse Clio. Derby; about 1760–5. Length 9 in. British Museum (See page 102)*

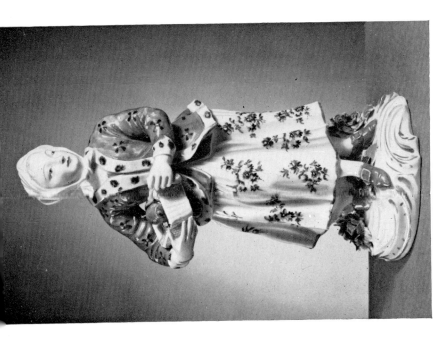

69. A. *Woman street-crier. Derby; about 1760–5. Ht. 8⅝ in. Victoria and Albert Museum.*
B. *Child as 'Autumn'. Modeller, Pierre Stephan. Chelsea-Derby;
about 1771–2. Ht. 8⅛ in. Cambridge, Fitzwilliam Museum.*
(See pages 55, 103, 105)

70. A. *Shepherd and shepherdess. Ht. 6 in.*
B. *Monk and nun. Ht. 5 in. Chelsea-Derby; 1770–84.*
Victoria and Albert Museum. (See pages 51, 105)

71. *Virgins awaking Cupid, after Angelica Kauffmann.*
Modeller, Pierre Stephan. Mark, 'No. 195', incised. Chelsea-Derby;
1778–80. Ht. 11½ in. British Museum. (See pages 48, 106)

72. *Charles Pratt, Baron Camden, as Lord Chancellor* (1766).
After Sir J. Reynolds. Chelsea-Derby; about 1770. Ht. 12¾ *in.*
Museum of Fine Arts, Boston. (See pages 55, 106)

73. *George III, after Zoffany. Biscuit figure, pedestal glazed,*
blue and gold. Ht. 14 in. British Museum. (See page 107)

74. *Derby 'biscuit'.* A. *'Earth' and 'Water'. Modeller, P. Stephan.*
Incised marks, 'No. 3', '3', and a star. About 1770 or later.
Ht. 7¾, 7⅞ in. Victoria and Albert Museum.
B. *'The Dead Bird'. Modeller, J. J. Spengler.*
Incised marks, crowned 'D' and 'N 363'. About 1790–5.
Ht. 7½ in. British Museum. (See pages 105, 110)

75. *The Russian Shepherds. Modeller, J. J. Spengler.*
Incised marks, crowned 'D' and a star. Unglazed biscuit.
Derby; 1790–5. Ht. 13 in. British Museum. (See page 110)

76. *Shepherd.* (*Pair with Plate* 77.) *Modeller, William Coffee.*
Marks, crowned 'D' and 'No. 396', *incised. Derby; about* 1795.
Ht 13¾ *in. Victoria and Albert Museum.* (*See page* 111)

77. *Shepherdess. Modeller, Jean Jacques Spengler.*
Mark, 'No. 395' incised. Derby; about 1793. Ht. 14 in.
Lady Lever Art Gallery, Port Sunlight. (See page 110)

78. *Longton Hall.* A. *Ceres. About 1750–1. Ht.* 6⅝ *in.*
Dr. B. Watney.
B. *Arbour-group. About 1755–5. Ht.* 8¼ *in.*
Victoria and Albert Museum. (See pages 42, 114, 115)

79. *A poet (Dryden?). Longton Hall; about 1758–60. Ht. 11 in.*
Dr. and Mrs. H. Statham. (See pages 33, 117)

80. *Longton Hall.* A. *Boy with grapes. About 1756–7. Ht.* $4\frac{7}{8}$ *in.*
Victoria and Albert Museum.
B. *The Duke of Brunswick. About 1759–60. Ht.* $8\frac{3}{4}$ *in.*
British Museum. (See pages 54, 117)

81. *Longton Hall, about 1756–7.* A. *Cupids and goat. Ht.* 5¼ *in.*
B. *Cupid on galloping horse, after Fanelli. Ht.* 5⅞ *in.*
Victoria and Albert Museum. (See pages 38, 116, 117)

82. *Group of dancers. Longton Hall; about 1758–60. Ht.* 10¾ *in.*
Cambridge, Fitzwilliam Museum. (See page 118)

83. *Asia. Longton Hall; 1759–60. Ht.* 12¼ *in.*
Temple Newsam, Leeds. (See page 118)

84. *Britannia, holding a medallion of George II. On the separate pedestal, transfer-prints with scenes from the Seven Years War. Longton Hall; 1759–60. Ht. 16¼ in. Victoria and Albert Museum. (See page 118)*

85. *River-god, with emblems of Commerce. Longton Hall; 1759–60. Ht. 16½ in. Dr. and Mrs. H. Statham. (See pages 33, 117)*

86. *Worcester, about 1769–71. Modeller, Tebo.* A. *Turks. Ht.* $5\frac{1}{4}$ *in.*
B. *Hunters. Ht.* $7\frac{1}{8}$ *in. Oxford, Ashmolean Museum.*
(*See page* 121)

87. *Gardener. Modeller, Tebo. Worcester; 1769–71. Ht. 10½ in.*
Oxford, Ashmolean Museum. (See page 121)

88. A. *Child with flower-vase. Plymouth; 1768–70. Ht. 7¼ in.*
B. *Gardener's companion. Modeller, Tebo. Worcester; 1769–71. Ht. 6¼ in.*
C. *Gardener's companion. Modeller, Tebo. Bristol; about 1772–4. Ht. 7 in.*
A, C. *Victoria and Albert Museum;* B. *Oxford, Ashmolean Museum.*
(*See pages 121, 124, 125*)

89. *Shepherdess. Modeller, Tebo. Bristol; 1772–4. Ht. 12¼ in. Victoria and Albert Museum. (See page 125)*

90. *Autumn. Modeller, Pierre Stephan. Bristol; about 1773–4. Ht. 10 in. National Trust, Fenton House, Hampstead. (See page 126)*

91. *Water. Modeller, Pierre Stephan. Bristol; about 1773–4.*
Ht. 10$\frac{1}{16}$ in. Boston, Museum of Fine Arts. (See page 126)

92. *Spring. Modeller, Pierre Stephan. Bristol; about 1773–4.*
Ht. 11 in. National Trust, Fenton House, Hampstead.
(*See pages* 126, 127)

93. *Winter. Modeller, Pierre Stephan. Bristol; about 1773–4.*
Ht. 10¾ *in. National Trust, Fenton House, Hampstead.*
(*See pages* 126, 127)

94. *Milkmaid. Modeller, Pierre Stephan. Bristol; about 1775.*
Ht. 10 in. National Trust, Fenton House, Hampstead.
(*See pages* 50, 127)

95. *Goatherd, pair with Plate 94. Modeller, Tebo.*
Bristol; about 1775. Ht. 10½ in.
National Trust, Fenton House, Hampstead. (See pages 50, 127)

Charity

96. *Charity. Probably made by Ralph Wood.
Staffordshire; about 1790. Ht. 8½ in.
Victoria and Albert Museum. (See page 132)*